WONDERFUL FLYING MACHINES

WONDERFUL FLYING MACHINES

A History of U.S. Coast Guard Helicopters

Barrett Thomas Beard

Naval Institute Press ◦ Annapolis, Maryland

© 1996 by Barrett Thomas Beard

Library of Congress Cataloging-in-Publication Data
Beard, Barrett Thomas, 1933–
    Wonderful flying machines : a history of U.S. Coast Guard helicopters /
Barrett Thomas Beard.
       p. cm.
    Includes bibliographical references and index.
    ISBN 1-55750-086-X (alk. paper)
    1. United States. Coast Guard Aviation—History. 2. Erickson,
Frank A. (Frank Arthur), d. 1978. 3. Military helicopters—United
States—History. I. Title.
VG93.B38   1996
363.2'86'0973—dc20   96-25922

Printed in the United States of America on acid-free paper ∞

03 02 01 00 99 98 97 96   9 8 7 6 5 4 3 2
First printing

*Dedicated to all Coast Guard helicopter aircrew members
who gave their lives "that others may live."*

The dream of vertical flight is older than history. Today, for the first time, it is a practical reality, admittedly crude. . . . You can trace this path of development in every great invention. There is first the dream, then much experimenting and failure and, perhaps, long periods of inactivity, then renewed interest and so on, until finally, due to general increase in knowledge and skills, the idea becomes practical. There is then rapid technical improvement and adaptations to many uses that sometimes lead to vast changes in our way of living. The dream of vertical and hovering flight is in that final stage. How much it may affect our civilization is anybody's guess. There have always been skeptics and always skeptics have been confounded.

Capt. William J. Kossler,
  *from a lecture delivered to officers at Coast Guard head-
  quarters in November 1942*

CONTENTS

FOREWORD

To those in peril on the sea, the sight and sound of a helicopter approaching—surely the answer to a fervent prayer—is often the first sign of help. As the helo team of pilots, hoist operator, and, ever more frequently, the rescue swimmer proceed with their well-practiced routines for survivor recovery, the frightened, cold, sometimes injured person is engulfed in a maelstrom of deafening sound and hurricane-force rotor wash whipping the water, seeming to literally take the breath away. What follows is a quick lift by cable to the welcome sanctuary of the helo cabin, the ministrations of the crew, and the usually short journey to land and safety. The ordeal may conclude rather quickly, sometimes in a flurry of activity that leaves little or no time for even a "thank you" to the aircrew who made the difference between life or disappearance forever in a watery grave.

While millions of people readily associate the trilogy of Helicopter-Rescue-Coast Guard, few are aware of the symbiotic relationship between the smallest of the armed services, the genial genius Igor Sikorsky, and the then-emerging helicopter struggling for development in the midst of World War II. Incredible as it now seems, great resistance to developing and utilizing rotary-wing aircraft was entrenched within each of the armed forces, and only the relentless, dogged determination of less than a handful of Coast Guard officers turned the tide and launched a new chapter in aviation history.

This book is an important addition to aviation lore because it chronicles the bureaucratic hurdles and internecine feud between fixed-wing-only hard-liners and a very few who had a visionary's zeal.

But it is much more than that; it also takes the reader on an actual rescue mission and describes the experience from both inside the helo and from the cold, dark waters of the North Atlantic. This mental journey, I submit, will leave no reader unmoved.

Any competent writer can tell a story. Tom Beard is an excellent one, to be sure, but he is much more than that. Tom knows aviation: he wore his wings of gold first in the Navy before transferring to the Coast Guard and serving a decade as a search-and-rescue pilot. Tom knows sailing: he is a designer and builder of boats who has circumnavigated the globe with his wife in their thirty-seven-foot cutter *Moonshadow*. Tom knows history: he has a passion for capturing the facts of eventful episodes and melding them within coherent and, above all, interesting and educational prose.

Tom is a friend. We first met and became acquainted in the most telling and unforgiving atmosphere—an airplane cockpit. Long before he became an accomplished writer he was a truly professional officer and aviator.

As a Coast Guard aviator who has experienced the "thrill" of flying a single-engine helicopter, sans copilot, along with a hoist operator—likewise alone in the cabin—offshore, at night, with no moon or stars to cast even a modicum of light, and our sole link to shore an HF radio, I am proud to be included in the special category of search-and-rescue aviator. For all the hours of unfruitful search, those moments of "uncertainty" which, later, at Happy Hour, became the seeds for tales of aeronautical prowess—when all was said and done—the indescribable feeling which flooded the senses a few hours after completing a real rescue under challenging conditions was more than sufficient reward.

When Tom asked me to write a foreword to his new book, I was flattered. After reading his words, I am greatly honored.

SEMPER PARATUS!

Vice Adm. Howard B. Thorsen,
U.S. Coast Guard (Retired)
Coast Guard Aviator Number 776
Coast Guard Helicopter Pilot Number 422

PREFACE

This is Capt. Frank A. Erickson's story. He lived much of it and laboriously typed up records of the events from his experience. Nothing was published. Between 1969 and 1978 Erickson wrote several versions of the story of helicopter development and of Coast Guard aviation history. He corresponded with friends and associates, pioneers, involved in this story. They shared with him their reflections and documents; in return he sent them chapter copies to verify. One manuscript, *Fishers of Men,* was actually microfilmed by the Naval Historical Center's Naval History Branch, Washington, D.C.

It was these isolated chapters written by Erickson, mixed with the papers of former associates, that first attracted my attention. I stumbled across these quite by accident while researching other stories and immediately recognized their value. I actively sought more. Finally, in 1994, after nearly a five-year effort, Erickson's daughters, Kay Erickson McGoff and Betty Erickson Bohs, located his unpublished works and research materials. They permitted me to use them, along with an extensive collection of Erickson's personal correspondence. Without their help and this material, this book would not have been possible.

Erickson was an aviation pioneer and is still largely unrecognized for his achievements. His attainments in a new branch of aviation—helicopters—and struggles with authority and contemporaries alike nearly paralleled those of Brig. Gen. Billy Mitchell. Erickson recognized the folly of his pioneering efforts after he read Howard E. Bloomfield's *Compact History of the U.S. Coast Guard* and saw in its pages a strong parallel between his career and that of Capt. Alexander V. Fraser of the

Revenue Marine Service. In private correspondence Erickson made several references to Fraser's career being analogous to his own, especially regarding the way his creative foresight for the armed services was rejected by those very forces. "Since starting this project," Erickson wrote, "I have read up a little on Coast Guard History, going back to the great sail vs steam controversy." He noted that while seven hundred steamers plied the waters of America, the Navy employed only two, both laid up as useless, and the Revenue Marine Service had none.[1]

Fraser persisted in his attempts to acquire two steamships but was overruled by higher civilian authority. For his single-minded effort, Fraser was relieved and ordered back to sea. "*In 1856 Fraser was still trying to get a steam cutter built* (emphasis Erickson's)."[2] Erickson quoted Bloomfield in several personal letters. One sentence that he probably felt applied particularly to him was: "In the bitter argument that resulted, a Treasury official revoked Fraser's commission out of hand. A cruel end it was for the man who had done the most for the Cutter Service. A sudden discharge, no thanks no pension."[3]

Erickson concluded one letter with, "Doesn't that remind you a little of the seaplane vs helicopter controversy? As in the case of steam, the helicopter is winning after a long fight." Then he confessed, "I might even make this comparison in my book."[4]

An early revelation of Erickson's remarkable vision of the future is revealed in a letter written to Igor Sikorsky thanking him for writing the foreword to his *Fishers of Men* (see appendix A). "Your 'Introduction' brings to mind a visit that Mr. Roy Grumman made to Floyd Bennett Field in December, 1943. I had explained with pride how the helicopters would someday replace fixed wing aircraft as the Coast Guard's primary rescue aircraft." Even at this early date Erickson was so positive about his conviction he predicted, "[I]t was inevitable from the day that the Coast Guard took delivery on its first Sikorsky R-4, that helicopters would replace fixed wing aircraft as its primary rescue aircraft."[5]

Events of the past two decades are still too close in time to totally determine their impact and ultimate voice in the history of Coast Guard aviation, specifically that of the helicopter. Some episodes are recorded in this book more to show the result of Erickson's concepts and earlier developmental work and not as historical foundations in themselves. Enough is provided, however, to see patterns developing. A professor once chided me, "You cannot write history of events less than fifty years old." My apologies to my esteemed professor, but the entire history of the Coast Guard helicopter only now spans a half century, and it is time some of this most remarkable story is told.

Forty-two percent of the U.S. Navy's crews today operate helicopters, and the Navy is unmatched in global sea power, partly because of the dreams and schemes of Coast Guard pioneers Erickson and Capt. William J. Kossler. Graham once noted: "The early development of the helicopter-dipping sonar program . . . was beset by very stiff opposition. However, there has always been a premium and a penalty on pioneering, but both must and always will be accepted by men of vision."[6]

Erickson admitted he "acquired a reputation as a nonconformist,"[7] but in a privately expressed sentiment, Capt. William Wisher, U.S. Coast Guard (Ret.), Coast Guard aviator number five, revealed:

The Coast Guard was fortunate indeed to have had you among its officers and early aviators. You proved out as having the rare qualities of vision and creative ability. Also "stick-to-it-iveness". You foresaw potentialities of the helicopter. Being a "doer," believing that the helicopter could be developed into a major life-saving instrument, you learned everything you could about [it and] became a helicopter pilot; you encountered indifference, disbelief, and opposition from those at Headquarters who determined CG policies and types of flying craft the Service would use. Finally you proved your contentions. History has proved the helicopter as the CG's most useful instrument for saving life. All honor to you![8]

ACKNOWLEDGMENTS

My research was significantly boosted with the help of Comdr. Stewart R. Graham, U.S. Coast Guard (Ret.), Erickson's first helicopter student. Together, they pioneered the helicopter. A wealth of information, no longer available from official sources, sprang from Stew's three sea chests and magnificent memory.

Comdr. John Redfield, U.S. Coast Guard (Ret.), Coast Guard helicopter pilot number fifteen, has a collection dating back to the 1940s at Floyd Bennett Field. It is a researcher's Eden. Memorabilia composed of letters, documents, books, a fifty-three-year-old broken rotor blade, and, above all, photographs, used to fill his home. During the writing of this book, though, he began donating his acquisitions to the National Museum of Naval Aviation, thus making this valuable collection available to all researchers. Without these two sources, which complemented the *Erickson Papers,* little of the story could be revealed.

Dr. Robert Browning, Coast Guard historian, graciously provided needed research assistance far beyond what a writer might expect despite his obviously heavy work load and surprisingly small staff.

Then there were the hundreds of others who contributed everything from partial manuscripts and letters written by Erickson to photos and, most important, their memories. Each person I talked to left vital clues or substantiated "unbelievable tales" I heard from others or found briefly noted.

Anecdotes in this book may be familiar to some. They are retold here to bring back elements of history lost over time when the telling of tales becomes just entertainment. Where I could determine, they were brought in line with facts in evidence. Some episodes demonstrate the abilities of equipment and the skill and bravery of the flight crews. Again, these are examples used to establish or create a message. They may not represent the most harrowing or heroic but are noteworthy in a historical sense because of their special circumstances. I was privy to thousands of stories that, unfortunately, cannot reach these pages because of their shear volume. My most sincere thanks go to each one of you who contributed to this story with the hope that I faithfully fulfilled your vision of the events leading to the story of the rescue helicopter.

PROLOGUE

Pearl Harbor, 7 December 1941

The tropical Sunday morning was peaceful. A few sailors and Marines, in addition to those preparing to raise American flags, stirred about the island and among the moored ships. Lt. Frank A. Erickson, U.S. Coast Guard, watched through the window as the Marine color guard marched to the flagpole in front of the Ford Island administration building. In a few moments the record player would start to sound colors. Erickson was the off-going naval air station duty officer and soon would be home with his wife and two infant daughters in their tiny Waikiki apartment, sharing a rare quiet day together. He watched the Marines at the ready with the flag—Frank Dudovick, James D. Young, and Paul O. Zeller—then glanced at the clock.[1]

Waiting.

The sounds of the first bombs exploding came about 0753. Erickson looked up to see a plane passing over the Ten-Ten dock in the navy yard release a torpedo. The deadly fish struck the bow of the battleship *California* (BB-44), the ship closest to the administration building moored along battleship row.

The Marines didn't wait for the traditional bugle call. The flag went up and a quickly substituted General Quarters blared from speakers across the island. The commanding officer phoned demanding, "What the hell kind of drills are you pulling down there?"[2]

Pearl Harbor was under attack. Ten days would pass before Erickson returned to his family.

1

Moments after he was relieved as duty officer, Erickson ran through showers of shrapnel to the airplane control tower, his General Quarters station. Ships' guns returned fire. From his aerie in the tower at the epicenter of attack, Erickson "had a grand view of the battle." Beneath him lay all of Ford Island, surrounded by the ships of the Pacific Fleet moored in Pearl Harbor. He saw nearby Hickam Field to the south erupt in billowing smoke and flames. On the horizon, he saw plumes of black smoke climbing from the Army base at Wheeler, up the hill to the north, and from the Marine air base at Eva, across the sugarcane fields to the west.

An attacking Japanese plane, ablaze, flashed across his view. Erickson saw it crash into the seaplane tender USS *Curtiss* less than half a mile away—just to the north, off the entrance to Middle Loch—setting the ship afire. Looking at the eastern edge of Pearl Harbor toward Aiea, he watched in helpless wonder as a "huge flaming oil slick" began drifting along battleship row. Paint on the behemoths flashed as the fiery oil reached the ships rafted alongside Ford Island. Men swarmed overboard from the blazing cauldrons into the oil-coated burning waters of the harbor.

In August 1941 Coast Guard units in the Hawaii area were absorbed from the Treasury Department into the U.S. Navy. At the time of the Navy's takeover, Erickson was an aviator assigned to the Coast Guard cutter *Taney*, then in port in Honolulu. With the new assignment in the Navy, he moved to Ford Island as assistant operations officer. At that same time, Erickson read in the magazine *Aero Digest* an article describing a small helicopter developed by Dr. Igor Sikorsky.[3] It was this helicopter, in Erickson's mind, that was unquestionably the ideal tool for Coast Guard aviators.

As Erickson witnessed the deaths of more than two thousand men within a radius of a mile and a half, and watched thousands more oil-covered and wounded men straggling onto the shoreline of Ford Island, he was greatly frustrated, swelled with emotions beyond the ignominy of the assault. He thought of the helicopter he had read about months earlier and realized that, at present, he had no methods to rapidly recover those hundreds of sailors; he could only watch.

During the ten days following the Japanese attack, Erickson flew patrols searching for the enemy carrier task force with the only planes that survived the raid. Ironically, among those few flyable aircraft were "Grumman J2F and Sikorsky JRS amphibians," armed merely with rifles and shotguns.[4] But Erickson's greatest fear was not the war itself; it was that its duration would keep him in the Pacific unable to pursue his dream to effect a way to rescue victims at sea, using the Sikorsky helicopter.

The feeling of total ineffectiveness that Erickson experienced in the few hours following the attack on Pearl Harbor constantly reignited the fuel of his dedication throughout the following decade. He was not to relinquish this dream nor the quest to fulfill it despite many obstacles to his career and life. Erickson's memory of that morning—that day of infamy—and of all its terrors became the catalyst that eventually forced the rescue helicopter into actuality.

ONE

NO PROVEN VALUE

U.S. Army Starts Helicopter Development

In the late 1930s Capt. H. Franklin Gregory, U.S. Army Air Corps, directed the program to develop rotorcraft for all U.S. military services. Part of that job was to investigate claims by inventors and builders of craft supposedly capable of vertical flight. This led him to the Vought-Sikorsky plant in Stratford, Connecticut, in 1939 to examine the helicopter simulator built the previous year based on the design by Dr. Igor Sikorsky. Sikorsky engineers Michael Gluhareff and Boris P. Labensky demonstrated the crude rig with which they evaluated different rotor systems.[1] Gregory later described the device as having three, two-blade controllable pitch propellers. Two were mounted horizontally on each side of the test unit and were lifting devices that controlled roll in the way ailerons do on an airplane. The third propeller was set vertically on the rear and operated like a rudder.

What Gregory did not see was the device for testing the single main rotor system with its anti-torque mechanism. This unlikely apparatus proved to be the genesis of the modern helicopter. The contraption consisted of a truck rear axle and differential gearbox set vertically, with a counterbalanced blade attached where the truck wheel and tire once were. An engine was connected to the axle by belts, and the whole welded-steel framework rested on the ground on three large parallel steel beams securely sunk into the turf. It was not meant to fly, even by accident.

The results of these experiments convinced Sikorsky to dedicate his efforts to advancing the single-rotor concept, whereas other aircraft manufacturers developing the helicopter during this period relied on multiple lift rotors to balance the torque. Sikorsky was convinced the single rotor theory afforded more efficient arrangement of major components and would give the "best compromise between hovering capability, horizontal speed, and precise control."[2]

Gregory returned to Bridgeport a year later and became the first military aviator to fly a helicopter when he lifted off in the VS-300 on 24 July 1940. Gregory was impressed enough with the progress of the development through the succeeding few months that, in January 1941, he approved a contract to produce a two-placed helicopter, the XR-4. But it was not until the day following the attack on Pearl Harbor, eleven months later, that Sikorsky's experimental VS-300 flew with its single main rotor and tail-rotor-on-a-boom configuration, proving it workable. This final form was adopted, and the new XR-4 was redesigned forthwith to this common arrangement that now characterizes most modern helicopters.[3]

The first flights of the early helicopters were probationary. The phenomenon of controllable vertical flight was still speculative, so the first craft were restrained by rope tethers to keep the aircraft within a few feet of the takeoff spot in the event of unexpected uncontrollable flight. Helicopter control was still highly experimental. Despite the apparent almost instant success of vertical flight, Sikorsky's VS-300 went through several configurations, with up to four rotors on a single variant spread across a skeletal tubular framework. One early version had difficulty attempting forward flight. It would go backwards and sideways satisfactorily, but as it started forward, it would lose control upon reaching twenty-five miles per hour. The VS-300 was subject to constant modifications, including complete redesigns. It underwent eighteen major revisions before its final flight in October 1943.[4]

The First Helicopter

Then a chain of events occurred—some openly manipulated and others serendipitous—that propelled Erickson toward his dream. Comdr. William J. Kossler, U.S. Coast Guard, as the aviation engineering officer in headquarters, had acquired a collateral assignment as the Coast Guard's representative on the Inter-Agency Board administering the Dorsey Act of 30 June 1938. In 1940 this board, chaired by the U.S. Army Air Corps, had secured $300,000 from the $2 million appropriated by Congress in 1938 to purchase an experimental helicopter.[5]

Platt-LePage Aircraft Company's proposal won the bid for the first experimental helicopter, but before funds were distributed, Sikorsky flew his experimental VS-300 in a public demonstration on 13 May 1940. Sikorsky's startling feat roused the committee eventually to split the prize money between Platt-LePage and Vought-Sikorsky. Furthermore, LePage's entry did not make its first tethered flight until a year later, 12 May 1941, six days after Sikorsky established an international helicopter endurance record.[6]

Kossler Witnesses First Public Flight

The first official American helicopter demonstration occurred on 20 April 1942 at the Vought-Sikorsky plant. Kossler, as a board member, was there to witness the flight of this new Sikorsky XR-4, the first production helicopter intended for military use to fly successfully.[7] It had flown a total of merely nine and a half hours when it appeared for the demonstration.[8] The XR-4 had room for an instructor and one student, with dual flight controls sufficient for flight instruction.

The helicopter performed admirably on that crisp day in April with its gray overcast sky. Winds were moderate, but gusty. The witnesses closed around the wingless craft as it sat in a meadow a hundred yards from the Sikorsky factory. Only a few members of the Inter-Agency Board had been curious enough to appear.[9] They examined the helicopter's peculiar details before it flew. Charles L. "Les" Morris, Sikorsky's test pilot, wrote: "[They] didn't get excited about it. There was a conspicuous Missouri-ness in their attitude."[10] He began his address to the dignitaries, "You, gentlemen, are about to witness a demonstration of the first successful basically single-rotor helicopter in the world."[11] Later, he reflected: "On the whole the group that assembled could not be called enthusiastic. Interested, yes. Skeptical perhaps; courteous and open minded, definitely. But not enthusiastic."[12]

How mistaken he was. Though Kossler may not have shown his enthusiasm, he later wrote vigorously about what he saw and would spend the rest of his life boldly promoting the helicopter.

Morris demonstrated maneuvers considered preposterous for flying aircraft: hovering, and flying sideways and backward. The helicopter lifted straight up about seven feet, then settled back to earth gently in the depressions made by its tires in the moist turf. A factory employee held aloft a pole that had a ring about ten inches in diameter lightly attached to its end. The helicopter's pitot/static tubular structure extended out in front of the craft. Morris flew the probe into the ring, eased it off the pole, and flew the XR-4 over to Sikorsky, who reached up and plucked the ring from the probe while Morris held the helicopter steady. The craft likewise lifted a bag of eggs from a young woman's hands, flew around for a moment, then lowered the bag gently to the ground. None of the eggs was broken. Still later, the XR-4's wheels were removed and large inflated tubular bags were installed. The helicopter proceeded to land on both the ground and the nearby Housatonic River.[13]

Following these "extraordinary maneuvers" with intense interest, Kossler noted that the craft "remained almost motionless" at an altitude of about twenty-five feet, trailing a ladder to the ground. Ralph Alex, a Sikorsky engineer, climbed the rope ladder and entered the flying aircraft. Then it flew away. "What a magnificent demonstration!! This had to be the answer to the Coast Guard rescue problem!"[14]

A disaster was averted on one maneuver a short time later during the show. Morris buckled on a parachute, planning to fly higher than any helicopter had before, but he accidentally flew into the cloud layer at five thousand feet, losing visual contact. The helicopter slowed, then began the dangerous condition of settling with power. This phenomenon occurs at a low forward speed with an established descent.[15] The XR-4 was thus partially out of control and vibrating heavily.[16] Morris recovered successfully by forcing the nose down. The climax of the show came when he, still falling toward the earth but once more in control at two thousand feet, intentionally cut the power and autorotated to a perfect landing.[17]

Kossler was so impressed that he dedicated the rest of his life to achieving a Coast Guard aviation organization built around the helicopter.

Another witness Morris misjudged that day was Wing Comdr. Reggie Brie of the Royal Air Force. Brie, an autogiro pilot, was in the United States seeking a suitable rotary-winged aircraft for Great Britain. He was encouraged to witness the demonstration flown by Morris. During the display, Brie commented to Gregory: "That chap has flown your rotor machine and what he's done, I say, beats anything I've ever observed. We've really seen something this day. I shall send a signal to my country stating the full import of this great event."[18]

It was Brie's recommendation that later provided Kossler and Erickson with an opportunity to introduce a helicopter program into the U.S. Navy.

Kossler Takes Action

Immediately following the helicopter flight demonstration, Kossler executed plans in earnest. He invited Lt. Comdr. W. A. Burton, commanding officer of the Coast Guard Air Station (CGAS) New York, to a Sikorsky demonstration.[19] Burton was openly enthusiastic. He wrote a report to the commandant listing the many advantages of using the helicopter over the blimp that was also being considered for rescues at sea. In the same letter, however, Burton conceded the open opposition already forming against the helicopter. "Both the Coast Guard's Engineer-in-Chief, Rear Admiral Harvey Johnson, and Assistant Commandant, Rear Admiral Lloyd Chalker, were convinced that the acquisition of helicopters at this time too costly, at a quarter million dollars for three aircraft, and its limited performance capabilities could not support missions essential to the war effort."[20]

Chalker already had experience with helicopter development. In 1939, on behalf of the Coast Guard, he attended a conference that set performance criteria for rotary-winged aircraft. The meeting was held in the office of Gen. Henry H. Arnold, chief of the Army Air Corps, but Col. C. L. Tinker conducted it in the general's absence. Present at the meeting were representatives from the Air Military Service; Civil Aeronautics Authority; Navy's Bureau of Aeronautics; Interior Department; Agriculture Department; U.S. Biological Survey; National Advisory Committee for Aeronautics; and Army.

Since no aircraft yet existed, real data were unavailable. Therefore, the committee established parameters that mirrored general requirements for fixed-winged airplanes of the period. But their recommendations were extreme. For instance, they agreed that an effective machine would have a useful load of fifteen hundred pounds, would take off and land vertically, would hover, and would fly at speeds of up to 250 miles per hour, with a minimum cruise speed of 120. However, since only $300,000 was available to build such a helicopter, the committee compromised and conceded that the Army Air Corps could develop a machine incorporating the novel helicopter features—not necessarily meeting their required standards—until the vertical flight concepts were proven.[21]

Seaplane Hazards

Erickson could vividly recall the hazards to Coast Guard aviators from his own experience flying seaplanes during the 1930s. He felt the change to a more practical, safer, and more useful aircraft was essential. He also remembered his experiences flying Grumman JF-2 amphibians from Coast Guard cutters in Alaskan waters in 1938. Launching and recovering the bi-winged floatplane required the efforts of nearly the entire ship's company. Flying the single-engine amphibians off the cutters was brutal to the airplanes because, as Erickson recounted, "[W]e were invariably dropped overboard and picked up from open roadsteads in fairly rough seas."[22]

From the beginning of its aviation experience, the Coast Guard chose what would often be referred to as "flying life boats" for rescue work. These aircraft were lightweight. Landing and takeoff speeds were slow, and the distances required across the water's surface were short.[23] Successful open-sea landings were common.

Disasters were too. Erickson felt the PJ-1 "was by far the best rough water plane that the Coast Guard ever had."[24] By about 1937, however, these planes were over age, obsolete, and worn out, and replacements were no longer being manufactured. At that time the Coast Guard also had a shortage of pilots: it couldn't fill both the pilots' and copilots' seats in its aircraft, so the Coast Guard qualified new pilots as "full fledged aircraft commanders after only one or two flights in a new type aircraft."[25] This practice soon led to tragedy and set some, like Erickson, to thinking about alternative methods for rescues at sea.

Five newly manufactured Hall PH-2s and seven PH-3s replaced the aging PJ-1s in the late 1930s, but these seaplanes did not solve the problems of safety and well-trained pilots. Ultimately, they saw only about five years of service.[26] The design selected for this craft, moreover, proved to be a poor choice. The biplane—with its fabric-covered wings that were designed in the 1920s—was already obsolete in a period where modern aircraft were configured with a single wing and all metal construction. Alarmingly, for some, a dangerous design deficiency allegedly existed in the Hall aircraft. The twin engines were mounted in nacelles on struts between the wings, just above and behind the cockpit. Some pilots asserted that sudden deceleration or slamming caused by waves on water landings or takeoffs could tear the mounting struts loose, thus permitting the unrestrained engines' pods, with their spinning propellers, to lurch forward into the cockpit.

What these pilots feared finally happened on a rescue 150 miles offshore from the Brooklyn air station on 15 July 1939 during takeoff. The aircraft crew recovered an ill seaman from a freighter and began a takeoff run. Close to lift-off speed, the seaplane slammed into a wave. The engines ripped loose from their mountings, still running at full power, and the propellers gnawed into the cockpit, killing both the pilot and the copilot.[27]

The frequency of such crashes at sea was troubling Coast Guard Headquarters. Shortly after the Hall seaplane accident, the Coast Guard Commandant, Adm. R. R. Waesche, requested in a 1939 bulletin that each aviator submit suggestions for developing safe procedures for open-sea rescues by airplane. Controversy over the execution of off-shore landings soon became an issue that divided aviators, and it would lead to a major split that did not start to heal until more than two decades later.[28]

Kossler was inspector of Coast Guard aircraft at the Hall Aluminum Company in Bristol, Pennsylvania, at the time of the crash. Although he frequently rejected unsatisfactory parts, he believed they nevertheless found their way back into the airplanes over his objections. Kossler was also "very dissatisfied with the Hall Boats and the whole practice of landing aircraft at sea that already cost the lives of several Coast Guard fliers."[29] Because of his guilt over his responsibility as inspector, and because of the loss of his friend Lt. William L. Clemmer, the pilot, Kossler suffered a nervous breakdown shortly after the accident. He was hospitalized for two months and afterwards traveled to Hawaii on convalescence leave where he spent time with Erickson.[30]

During this visit, the seeds for better rescue methods were planted in the minds of the two friends, who first met at the Coast Guard Academy in 1930 when Erickson was a student in Kossler's thermodynamics class. Their early schemes, which resulted from many hours of discussion, dealt with dropping sophisticated packages containing rafts and survival equipment from overflying airplanes rather than having those planes land on the water. Kossler and Erickson felt this equipment offered survivors the means to persevere until they could be picked up by Coast Guard cutters or nearby surface ships directed to the scene by aircraft. Neither man knew of the helicopter at the time.

Their ideas did not rest there, however, nor did their interest lag after Kossler returned to Washington, D.C., in May 1940 for his new duty as chief of the Aviation Engineering Division. The two men continued to exchange ideas, and Erickson wrote numerous letters and articles describing in detail how to drop containers of rescue and survival equipment. All the schemes he devised avoided the dangerous practice of operating airplanes on the sea's surface.

In 1941, before the attack on Pearl Harbor, Kossler—eager to pursue the development of deployable rescue equipment—wrote Erickson suggesting that he might work a transfer for Erickson to the Aircraft Repair and Supply Base, Elizabeth City, North Carolina. There both of them "could work on these problems."[31] The transfer did not take place, however. World War II obstructed any plans the two had. Erickson, caught in the middle of the Pacific, soon became obsessed with thoughts of the newly discovered helicopter. He confided to his wife, Betty, "I bet if we were back in the States I could get in on the ground floor of this development."[32]

Erickson Begins Helicopter Project

In June 1942 Kossler visited Erickson, who had been transferred to Floyd Bennett Field, where he was the executive officer. At the meeting they plotted the helicopter's and their own future. Erickson acknowledged later that he "became a member of the Coast Guard's informal helicopter promotion team" at that time.[33] Thereafter, Kossler frequently visited the Brooklyn air station, conveniently situated about sixty-five miles from Sikorsky's Bridgeport plant. Kossler anticipated a larger role for the New York air station for he planned for them to receive helicopters from the Sikorsky factory. It was a grand plan, and Erickson, an integral part of it, was already in place.

On this particular trip Kossler tried to interest other Coast Guard pilots at the station in the idea of using the helicopter for rescue operations. He confided to Erickson that his helicopter proposal was receiving a "cool acceptance at Headquarters."[34] His proposition made little sense to most of the pilots as well. Academy officers initially rejected the helicopter because of its unknown future and out of a fear that any association with it might be a threat to their careers. Obvious signs of the indifference and outright rejection came from among the aviators later, when the program began.

Further proof of the lack of interest in this new craft among commissioned Coast Guard aviators was demonstrated when eight of the first ten Coast Guard helicopter pilots could come from the enlisted or former enlisted pilots ranks. Senior Coast Guard officers made it well known that they considered the helicopter useless. Some argued that it would fly only short distances and for a limited time; it could not carry any payloads; and it was not suitable for any Coast Guard missions. All of these naysayers' allegations were *true*.

First Operational Helicopter

The YR-4As,[35] with a 180-horsepower Warner Super-Scarab seven-cylinder radial engine, could not carry much more than the pilot and one other person, and that with a limited fuel supply.[36] Often, with two aboard, the radio and possibly even the battery were removed for flight on hot windless days. Though it showed remarkable flight characteristics, this model was a long way from performing any lifesaving role for the Coast Guard. However, the HNS—the Navy's designation for the R-4—was never intended as an operational missions' aircraft. It was built to train a pool of pilots in the unique flight of helicopters. Moreover, it was produced just to develop the principle of the helicopter. Operational missions would be handled by later aircraft already on production lines.

Helicopter Not Accepted

Kossler met rejection everywhere. The Navy's Bureau of Aeronautics was buying aircraft for the Coast Guard during the war, and a "Coast

Guard Admiral" in headquarters told Kossler, "Hell, Bill, the Navy isn't interested in life saving; all they want to do is get on with the business of killing the enemy."[37] Even the Navy's inspector of naval aircraft at the Sikorsky plant was similarly unimpressed.[38] He opposed helicopter development; it interfered with the production of fighter aircraft. (The Vought-Sikorsky plant was then building the popular F4U Corsair fighter.[39]) Even though some Coast Guard officers gave Kossler "lip-service," he sensed they did not really mean it.[40]

Army Begins ASW Experiments

Meanwhile, military strategists grasped at ideas to combat the extraordinary losses the Atlantic convoys were suffering at the hands of Germany's undersea raiders in 1942. Early propositions included the gyroplane or autogiro flown from ships or light scout airplanes equipped with floats and catapulted from merchant ships to ward off submarines. Both the Army Air Forces and the British had experimented during the mid-to-late 1930s with the autogiro.

However, it was from their very first experiments with the XR-4 that the U.S. Army Air Forces recognized the helicopter might have a potential as an antisubmarine weapon. The Army Air Forces was already flying wartime antisubmarine patrols, using fixed-wing patrol aircraft from land bases. The helicopter, some speculated, might be an extension of this mission, and so the Army Air Forces began to experiment with using the helicopter as a weapon in antisubmarine warfare (ASW).

The Army Air Forces added the first helicopter, the XR-4, to its livery on 30 May 1942, following its first cross-country flight from the Sikorsky factory to the Wright Field in Ohio. The 760-mile trip, flown by Morris, took five days.[41]

A few days after the XR-4 arrived at Wright Field, Gregory began to conduct bombing tests with it. He was aware then of speculation by military strategists on the use of the helicopter as an antisubmarine weapon. "Naturally," Gregory remarked, "Army men who had nursed the helicopter to success saw it as the ideal craft for such operations." However, its weapons delivery capabilities were yet unknown.[42]

The experimental helicopter showed obvious advantages in scouting for submarines. The question in Gregory's mind was, "Could it bomb accurately?" Col. Douglas M. Kilpatrick, director of the Bombardment Branch of the Army's Engineering Division's Armament Laboratory, helped Gregory prepare the helicopter as a bomber. "Doug was quick to see the possibilities of this hovering craft for bombing and enthusiastically cooperated in getting the necessary bomb sights and bomb racks fabricated and installed," Gregory recalled. Eager to test the craft, Gregory took Kilpatrick aloft before the helicopter was equipped with those devices. Kilpatrick simply carried a twenty-five-pound practice bomb on his lap. Gregory hovered the helicopter two to three hundred feet over a "sub" outlined on the ground with chalk. Then Gregory "would give Kilpatrick a poke and the bomb would be heaved overboard."[43] Gregory proudly noted that some bombs came within three feet of the target. He conceded with honesty, however, that "others missed by thirty yards."[44]

When the XR-4 was finally outfitted with a pendulum-type bombsight—used on early bombers—and external bomb racks, the bombing results were more accurate. Later, Gregory refined his target, substituting an old piece of oilcloth for the chalk marks. His accuracy became more predictable after he discovered that bombing runs on the target at forty miles per hour provided more consistent results. Thus it was that the bombing capabilities of the XR-4 were among the first operational tests for the machine that Kossler and Erickson envisioned using to rescue those in peril.

For his next test, Gregory had a twenty-by-twenty-foot platform built, which was raised three feet above the ground. This was done, according to Gregory, to make the demonstrations look more convincing to the pilot and onlookers since "an error would mean a crack-up." His plan was to simulate a helicopter deck aboard ship. He and Morris even included vertically mounted two-by-fours to simulate masts just beyond the tips of the rotors.[45] (Having practiced on this platform proved helpful to Gregory, who was chosen to pilot the helicopter for the first actual shipboard demonstrations.)

Gregory started what Kossler and Erickson would later continue; showing helicopter capabilities to senior officers and VIPs who were trying to focus some interest in the novel aircraft. On 7 July 1942, Gregory demonstrated typical helicopter flight maneuvers—vertical, backward, forward, sideways—for General Arnold. Gregory felt Arnold "was greatly impressed," but quite noncommittal. This feeling was dispelled later in Washington, when they discussed possible production of the new and larger helicopters, the R-5s. According to Gregory, before the first experimental R-5 model flew, Arnold said: "The Army Air Forces has taken fliers before with not so much to gain promised. I think we're justified in doing it again in this case." Gregory interpreted this to mean "procure the craft right from the drawings, if necessary."[46]

One day, Gregory was summoned to demonstrate the "ship" while he was out flying around Wright Field. The control tower ordered him to land, adding the comment, "An important officer wants to see you."[47] Maj. Gen. James H. Doolittle, just returned from the Tokyo raid, was waiting at the ramp for him. Boastfully, Gregory greeted Doolittle with, "General, you may have had quite an experience over Tokyo, but this will be one of the tops in your career of flying." Doolittle flew the aircraft and then asked when the Army was getting more. The general had immediately perceived the utility qualities of the craft and expressed his desire to acquire helicopters for "evacuating the wounded, transporting key personnel, and for supplying isolated units."[48]

Erickson Learns from Gregory

Kossler knew Gregory from their association on the Dorsey Board. Later, Erickson was drawn into their collaboration, and he got to know Gregory well. Erickson picked up two quick lessons from the Army test pilot. First, he developed an unrestricted testing program; any idea was fair game. For a military pilot, he had an unusual situation few had before and probably none since. Erickson was virtually open as to what he could do with the aircraft, and he had a close personal working relationship with the key personnel at the manufacturer's. In the military, he was given carte blanche, with apparently no directives restricting his activities. Second, and perhaps the most important lesson passed on by Gregory, was the importance of selling the merits of the craft to influential leaders. Later, these freedoms would become the trap to end Erickson's career and nearly end the helicopter's development.

Conspiracy Begins

In the meantime, Kossler, undaunted by the opposition he experienced from the Navy and from within the ranks of the Coast Guard, orchestrated events with seemingly little to connect them. He needed an ally to push the failing cause, and it was no secret he admired Erickson.[49] He integrated Erickson into the helicopter development program.

This seemingly spontaneous accord was contrived weeks before, with Erickson's orders to New York. Erickson's enthusiasm for helicopters was as unflagging as Kossler's. So it was not just coincidence when, a few days following one of Kossler's visits to New York, Lt. William Kenly, Kossler's assistant, arrived at CGAS Brooklyn. Kenly remarked casually at lunch one day that he had an appointment with Sikorsky and wondered if anyone could fly him to Bridgeport. "I didn't realize at the time that his little pitch was for my benefit," confessed Erickson. "It was the 26th of June, 1942, a day I will never forget."[50]

Erickson was captivated with those he met at the manufacturing plant. "Igor Sikorsky and Michael Gluhareff, his chief Engineer," Erickson later reflected, "were two of the most charming people I had ever met." They spent several hours discussing the possibilities of the helicopter. Sikorsky showed a film of Gregory performing the first tests with the XR-4 at Wright Field. Then Sikorsky gave a personal, "convincing" demonstration in his VS-300. He landed within inches of a given spot. Erickson remembered: "This was something I could really appreciate after my experience of operating a JF-2 amphibian from the CGC *Hamilton* on the Bearing Sea Patrol. . . . What a pleasure it would have been to have an aircraft like that aboard ship."[51]

That night, writing with emotions whipped up by the day's events, Erickson drafted his proposal to the Coast Guard commandant outlining possible future missions for the helicopter. Erickson was well aware of opposition to Kossler's perception of the helicopter as a rescue vehicle and therefore slanted his report in a direction he anticipated the Navy might accept. The idea was perhaps suggested to him by Kossler and Sikorsky and influenced by the motion pictures of Gregory's experiments bombing a mock submarine and landing on a platform. Erickson noted the lifesaving and law enforcement possibilities of the helicopter, but he also introduced—hoping to capture a new interest in the helicopter—the potential capacity for "providing aerial protection for convoys against submarine action." To ensure his participation in his proposed project, he concluded his opening remarks by stressing that the helicopter antisubmarine warfare mission would be "an important function of Coast Guard Aviation."[52]

Erickson's proposal might have had an immediate and vital impact on the war if helicopters were already capable and proven. They were not. In support of his vision for using helicopters in a war against submarines, Erickson cited the statistic that in the month of June 1942 alone, German submarines sank a record fifty-five U.S. merchant ships for a total of 289,790 tons.[53] According to his formal plan, then, the Coast Guard should develop the ASW capabilities of the helicopter. Merchant ships could protect themselves in convoy while helicopters would take off from small platforms built onto the decks of cargo ships and tankers to search for submarines. They might also carry a single depth charge.

Erickson further stressed the ability of the helicopter to operate from ships in convoy beyond the ranges that constrained patrols by land-based aircraft. He argued that helicopters could fly in poor visibility and they could refuel in flight by merely connecting a fuel hose that was lifted from a patrol boat to the hovering helicopter. He was confident that arguments about poor performance could now be defeated. As he wrote the letter, Erickson was already aware of the Army's order for the new more powerful operational model, Sikorsky XR-5.

Though Erickson pitched his focus toward the ASW mission, he did remind the commandant in carefully crafted prose of the helicopter's lifesaving features. "[I]t is also the ideal aircraft for rescuing personnel from torpedoed vessels." Erickson concluded his letter with a brief statement introducing anti-mine warfare.[54]

Erickson was optimistic that his proposed program would be accepted. He was soon to learn, however, that the Navy was not willing to risk resources on an aircraft with no proven value. In Erickson's favor, though, his commanding officer, Burton, favorably endorsed his letter, noting that the Army accepted the idea of helicopters for military use. Burton's remarks suggested that the helicopter had even greater possibilities for service to the Navy. He closed his endorsement by writing, "Unfortunately the Navy has not shown any great enthusiasm for this type of aircraft."[55]

Adm. Stanley V. Parker, head of Coast Guard activities for the Third Naval District, added his endorsement three days later, supporting the ASW concept for helicopters.[56] He also suggested additional missions for the helicopter such as "captain of the port inspections" and "expeditious visits to a number of lifeboat stations in the interest of coordination of beach patrol activities and inspections." Parker concluded with a remark that almost destroyed the strength of his arguments, however, recommending the acquisition of merely two helicopters.[57]

Comdr. F. A. Leamy, a Coast Guard aviation operations officer, concurred with Erickson and gave him a third endorsement. It lacked enthusiasm, however, and offered no additional support. Earlier, Leamy had requested that the Coast Guard buy helicopters, but he was refused.

It was Kossler's final endorsement, advising haste in acquiring helicopters, that brought results. Kossler knew that the Army planned to return its XR-4 aircraft to Sikorsky around the first of January 1943, following the contracted six-month test period. The Army had no other use for it. As Kossler wrote, "[It] would be highly desirable to test the XR-4 helicopter in this capacity as soon as possible." He feared that if tests of the new helicopter were delayed until production aircraft were built for the Coast Guard, there would be a further delay of several months before it could determine if helicopters should be purchased in quantity for ASW. Appearing at the bottom of Kossler's endorsement is a handwritten note: "Operations I concur. HFJ [Harvey F. Johnson, engineer-in-chief]."[58]

The first resistance within the Coast Guard had crumbled. Kossler's superiors would, from this time on, support his actions in acquiring helicopters.

One week had elapsed from the time Erickson first viewed the helicopter in Connecticut to the completion of the fourth endorsement. This swiftness in communications and action was to be the hallmark of Kossler's efforts throughout the succeeding three years he spent driving the Coast Guard's helicopter development program.

WAVE OF ENTHUSIASM

Erickson's Vision and Dedication

With boldness nourished by his conviction, Erickson became assertive. This was not out of character, however. Many who served with him recalled his single-minded dedication to helicopters. Erickson was "a zealot (in the best sense of the word)."[1] To Capt. John M. Waters, U.S. Coast Guard: "Swede was always the salesman, willing to explain the helicopter's merits to anyone who would listen. His visions of the helicopter's future seemed highly extravagant to many of the fixed-winged clan, and his predictions were often ridiculed behind his back."[2]

Erickson's physical size added to his aura of dominance. He looked like a college-football lineman with slightly slumping shoulders—a common characteristic of pilots who sit at the controls of helicopters for long periods. Atop a rather thick neck stood a square face crowned with blond hair. His friends called him "Swede," and it would be easy to imagine him as a Nordic god. Getting his way in tough situations was simple, or so it seemed.

Admiral Parker Views Helicopter's Remarkable Performance

Erickson followed up his favorably endorsed letter to the commandant by inviting Parker, his district commander, to witness a flight of Sikorsky's VS-300. This invitation was the beginning of a long series of promotional flights for VIPs. Erickson would soon establish a close relationship with Sikorsky and could call him personally and make arrangements for exhibition flights.

19

Kossler, just promoted to captain, also attended the demonstration at Erickson's invitation, or so it was made to appear. In actuality, Kossler made the contacts and arrangements behind the scenes; Erickson was the spokesperson, the public figure. Kossler was unmistakably the architect behind the development of the helicopter; Erickson was the developer, vocal promoter, and showman. They worked as a dedicated and unshakable team, both emphatically believing in the helicopter's future. Erickson unabashedly used these demonstrations to try to gain influential backing for his program, and they paid off, for a while.

Parker was ebullient over the demonstration performed by Sikorsky in the VS-300. The hovering and maneuvering capabilities of the frail-looking craft impressed Parker, the Coast Guard's first dirigible pilot. His comments to the commandant were effusive: "It is a remarkable thing. . . . Its control is almost unbelievable." He marveled that it could land both on top of a pile of aircraft engine cases and on the water using its sausage-shaped floats. Parker even related how it "flew along abreast and at the same pace as a tugboat." Parroting a phrase used by Erickson and Kossler, he asked, "Might not the Coast Guard be given the job of showing its application to convoy work?" And Parker strengthened that suggestion by observing: "It is interesting to note that the Navy Department official most closely in contact with this problem has given it very little encouragement. I think he is missing a bet."[3]

The Navy's objections to the helicopter, according to Grover Loening, consultant on aircraft to the War Production Board, "have been largely based on Capt. [Walter] Diehl's thesis that this type of craft could not be built to large enough size to carry a sufficient load to be of any value."[4] Loening criticized the Navy's reluctant attitude toward the helicopter, saying, "In taking positions like this, technical bureaus often overlook that concurrent developments are likely to occur to completely change their forecasts."[5]

British Order Helicopters

Kossler and Erickson worked feverishly, and in January 1943 their fortunes got a boost. The British placed orders for two hundred HO2S/R-5, 450 horsepower helicopters. They were also negotiating for eight hundred of the smaller HOS/R-6, 245 horsepower craft on the strength of Wing Commander Brie's recommendations. In contrast, the Navy had only two HOSs on order. "The fact that the British were so convinced of the usefulness of the helicopter that they placed such large orders in spite of the apparent indifference which seemed to be thwarting Navy developments," wrote Adm. J. F. Farley (Coast Guard

Commandant 1946–1950), "led Commander Kossler to believe that the picture had completely changed."[6]

The huge British order renewed Kossler's optimism and boldness. Kossler wrote the commandant on 8 February 1943, arguing that the Coast Guard was "in a particularly advantageous position to be given the mission of protecting convoys with helicopters." Needlessly he stressed, "It is part of our job." In a rather presumptuous remark, Kossler then reminded the commandant, Vice Adm. Russell R. Waesche—his close friend and former shipboard commanding officer, who wasn't an aviator— that most aviators in the Coast Guard also had extensive at-sea experience. Manpower was no problem; most air stations had "five or more Lieutenant Commanders and Commanders . . . with only a dozen or so planes. It appears now that we have an opportunity to really do an important job for which we are peculiarly fitted." Kossler concluded his argument, "I have discussed this with officers who have just returned from convoy duty and I am personally convinced that the helicopter may well solve the submarine menace without the use of a large number of escort vessels for convoys and may play a decisive role on the winning of the war."[7]

Commandant Waesche Views Helicopters

Evidently, Kossler's arguments were convincing. Waesche asked to see Sikorsky's remarkable helicopter. Erickson again made the arrangements. The commandant visited Sikorsky at the Bridgeport plant on 13 February 1943. Kossler and Erickson attended. Two helicopters flew together: Sikorsky repeated his earlier flight demonstration with the VS-300, and test pilot Morris flew the XR-4. The XR-4 had just returned to the Sikorsky factory from Wright Field, having successfully completed the Army flight test on 5 January 1943.

Both pilots flew precision maneuvers to exhibit the helicopters' warfare possibilities. The demonstration was impressive. "Admiral Waesche was completely sold," Erickson reported, and even the reluctant naval inspector Comdr. Harold Brow casually admitted to the admiral during the demonstration that "the helicopter might be all right—for the Coast Guard." Erickson later summed up the day, saying, "'Igor's Nightmare,' which had been something of a joke around Bridgeport, even among the workers in his plant, was at last being given serious consideration."[8]

CNO Orders Test and Evaluation Program

Immediately upon his return to Washington, Waesche reportedly called on Adm. Ernest J. King, chief of naval operations (CNO). Results of that meeting were instantaneous. King issued a one-and-a-half page directive in Washington, D.C., dated 15 February 1943, to the chief of BuAer ordering a test and evaluation program for helicopters. King supported the thesis "that a helicopter [is] capable of operating from a platform on a merchant ship under normal sea conditions [and] will be of value."[9] (King's actual role in supporting the helicopter is questionable, however. He makes no mention of it in his memoirs, nor is there any discussion of helicopters in his biography. Furthermore, the Coast Guard receives little acknowledgment in his history of World War II.)

The British immediately noted the change of attitude within the U.S. Navy in their secret communications between Washington and London. The head of the British Air Detachment in Washington notified the Admiralty on 8 March 1943: "[T]he helicopter situation has undergone a radical change. The U.S. Naval Authorities are now thoroughly interested in the project and it is understood Admiral King has instructed the U.S. Navy to take over three of the first six YR-4A's built which would include our two."[10]

The first sentence of King's directive, however, opened up controversy. He ordered BuAer to "carry out tests." This was understandable and unavoidable, since the Coast Guard was then under the control of the Navy, and all Coast Guard aircraft were acquired and their operations managed through BuAer. Furthermore, King instructed the U.S. Maritime Commission to make a typical merchant ship available—which they assured him was no problem—but the Maritime Commission was instructed to cooperate with BuAer to develop and construct a helicopter landing platform, a task already assumed by Kossler.

At this time, the helicopter, as a category, was enrolled in the Battleship/Cruiser Section of BuAer. These ships were still using fixed-wing, float-equipped aircraft for patrol work. The commander in charge of the Battleship/Cruiser Section "strongly" opposed rotary-wing aircraft as replacements for those planes. He supported the Navy's 1938 study of rotorcraft, which was based on the autogiros of the time. "Rotorplanes might be of some use in anti-submarine work, [but it is] a minor application which hardly justifies the expenditure of funds at present." He further emphatically wrote that, as long as he was in a position to control development: "Only one machine will be used for evaluation. The others will be run out when the first is broken up." His conclusion was one held even within the ranks of the Coast Guard aviators, namely, "The machines will never pass the evaluation program."[11]

In rebuttal, Erickson reminded him that the British order for "several hundred helicopters" came with an express interest in a joint evaluation program. The commander responded that there would be "no joint evaluation program" and that he was "not interested in what the British thought." Furthermore, as far as he was concerned, "There will be no problem concerning Coast Guard personnel operating machines in convoys because . . . the machines will never pass the evaluation program."[12] Soon thereafter, this commander was terminated from the helicopter program. The reason why was not discovered, but obstructions to Kossler's plans had a way of strangely disappearing without explanation.

Once the tests were concluded on the XR-4, the Army appeared to have no further plans to develop the ASW or seagoing options for the helicopter. They were waiting for delivery of their order for the R-6 from the Sikorsky plant. Therefore, Admiral King requested in his 15 February directive that arrangements be made with the Army Air Forces—through the Joint Aircraft Committee—for the early delivery to the Navy of at least three of the YR-4A helicopters "under procurement by the Army Air Forces." This order was limited "until the effectiveness of this type aircraft has been established," since King's and the Navy's purpose was to determine the helicopter's abilities to operate from merchant ships combating submarines. No mention was made anywhere in King's order of the helicopter's use as a rescue vehicle.

The final paragraph of King's letter eventually became Kossler's trump card in his battles with the Navy. It stated that the seagoing development of helicopters, including their operations in convoys, "will be a function of the Coast Guard." Furthermore, it specified that "Naval Aviators of the Coast Guard will be employed as practicable in the early testing and evaluation of helicopters."[13]

Coast Guard Creates Helicopter Training Program

On 16 February Waesche directed Kossler to undertake the "Coast Guard's part in this program dictated by King." Kossler was ordered to create a training program and "stations" until the "training program has been placed on a routine basis."[14] In effect, the commandant gave Kossler a blank check to direct all divisions in headquarters to assist in his efforts on the project. Kossler lost no time with his new authority. Even though no training program existed, that very day a confidential directive went out to the chief personnel officer soliciting volunteers to apply for training as pilots and mechanics in the new helicopter program.[15]

Earlier, on 14 February, Kossler had contacted Commander Labrot of the War Shipping Administration urging higher "priorities to facilitate production at Sikorsky's" for a speedier delivery of the first YR-4As. So, when Kossler phoned Gregory at Wright Field on 17 February and learned that the "first ships [helicopters] would not be delivered until the latter part of March or April," he could inform Gregory that he had already contacted the War Shipping Administration "and they might be able to do something about that."[16]

Kossler worked with fierce urgency. On 19 February he was in Sikorsky's plant quizzing the staff about "early training and technical matters." Test pilot Morris was drafting a training syllabus. He and Gregory were the only two helicopter pilots qualified to teach helicopter flight. Gregory was unavailable, however; his duties were with the Army test facility at Wright Field. That left Morris, whose time for instruction was restricted. Consequently, only a limited number of pilots could be helicopter qualified.[17]

Kossler next made arrangements with the Army Air Forces and Navy's BuAer for pilot and maintenance crew training. Erickson was selected to be the first Coast Guard aviator to qualify in the helicopter. He anticipated starting training in April. Accompanying him to the Vought-Sikorsky factory in Bridgeport for the mechanics course was Aviation CMM Oliver F. Berry and Aviation MM1 James A. Boone. Kossler was eager to start the program immediately since, despite King's directive, BuAer continued to stubbornly resist the helicopter program. Kossler's project was moving ahead now at a fast pace, he thought.

BuAer Assumes Helicopter Development Role

Conflicts began within a week. The Coast Guard was moving aggressively, assuming the role of developer for the helicopter in the antisubmarine mission, but with their own charges in mind. BuAer, nudged to alertness, asserted it was *their* assignment, based on King's orders. Previously, however, the Navy had not interfered with the Army's development of the helicopter, claiming it was not their job. The Navy was not justified, according to Loening, in "butting in." In rebuttal, the Army said it had no authority to pursue the antisubmarine role even though at that time it was conducting antisubmarine patrols from coastal air bases with fixed-winged bombers.

Loening, exasperated by more than a year's delay in advancing the helicopter, and observing this apparent adolescent behavior between the services, denounced the Navy's participation in helicopter development through a sharply worded confidential report to the War Production Board. He began his attack:

> The Navy's statements on the load limitation, the lack of initiative on their part, the fact that Navy officers did not ever ride in the helicopter

in the original demonstrations by Col. Gregory in June of last year, all sum up to the fact that the Navy which is charged with exerting every possible ingenuity and effort to combat the submarine menace has failed to take advantage of the possibilities that were offered in this development. . . . We have a Navy Bureau of Aeronautics technical staff that is wholly unfamiliar with helicopter development, has never taken any serious interest in it, hardly ever flown in this type of aircraft, and therefore can be excused from having anything further to do with it. The particular Naval officers involved in this lack of action in the last year are Capt. [Walter] Diehl and Capt. [Leslie C.] Stevens, and should of their own free will withdraw from any further consideration of helicopter development.[18]

Loening, in disgust, recommended that any directives having anything to do with the further development of the helicopter should "emanate from the Maritime Commission, the War Shipping Administration, *from the Navy through the Coast Guard,* and not through the Bureau of Aeronautics."[19]

Despite the stinging rebuke, activities continued within BuAer, showing some enterprise to further delay helicopter development conducted by the Coast Guard. Comdr. George W. Anderson of the bureau's planning section told Kossler on 22 February, however, that he was aware of a helicopter project but had not received any instructions regarding it.

Then events began occurring, coupled with some "misunderstanding" in the wording of King's directive, that nearly wrenched the project away from Kossler. Perhaps these misinterpretations came from a new perspective toward the helicopter gained by Rear Adm. John S. McCain, chief of the Bureau of Aeronautics, during a secret visit to Sikorsky's plant. At least his sojourn was a secret to Kossler who, up to this time, appeared to orchestrate the program and personally usher every witness to Bridgeport. Navy personnel were prohibited by the Army from visiting Sikorsky's factory, apparently in retribution for troubles between them and the Navy the past year over helicopter development. Consequently, Kossler did not learn for nearly two weeks that McCain had witnessed a helicopter flight demonstration. The timing of McCain's clandestine trip was noteworthy; it came immediately after Waesche's visit and about the time Waesche was meeting with King.[20]

BuAer suddenly saw the development of shipboard helicopters as their responsibility. Comdr. James S. Russell, U.S. Navy, director of Military Requirements, and Morton K. Fleming Jr., of the bureau, privately informed Kossler of *their* interpretation of King's directive. The Coast Guard's role was minor, subject to the bureau's needs.

Kossler Tries to Regain Control of Program

In a sudden act of protectiveness, Waesche immediately fired off a memorandum to McCain—authored by Kossler. It pointedly reminded McCain of King's orders, namely, for the bureau chief to give "such assistance to the Coast Guard in this early testing, evaluation and seagoing development as the Coast Guard may desire."[21] A battle of wills ensued.

McCain's ardent response to the commandant asserted, "It is not my understanding that this bureau would assist the Coast Guard but this bureau will conduct those early tests and will utilize the services of Coast Guard Naval Aviators during these tests."[22]

Kossler dug in to save his program. He and Erickson needed the helicopters to develop their search-and-rescue capabilities. Accepting the antisubmarine warfare project was only an ill-concealed means to this end. They made no secret of it.

During the next two days Kossler wrote two memos to his superior, chief of the aviation engineering section, enclosing with the cover memo a suggested letter from the CNO to the commandant. The letter— intended to be over King's signature—clarified the CNO's 15 February order, establishing the test and evaluation program for the helicopter, interpreted, of course, in favor of Kossler's intentions. Kossler clearly defined the Coast Guard's role as dominant and in control of liaisons with the War Shipping Administration, the Bureau of Aeronautics, and other undefined agencies also interested in helicopter development. Furthermore, Kossler elaborated, the Coast Guard would provide personnel to operate and maintain the helicopters "in connection with ocean convoys, when helicopters in quantity are available."[23]

Whether or not these memos and letter were ever delivered is unknown. No letters from King were found reflecting the comments written for him by Kossler. Nevertheless, Kossler's wrath did reach appropriate offices, for the climate at BuAer changed suddenly. The Navy's objections, for a short period, seemed to have abated.

A week later, on 11 March, Kossler requested from the commanding general, U.S. Army Air Forces, approval to send "a few pilots and mechanics as soon as practicable to the Sikorsky Aircraft Corporation, in a liaison capacity so that they may become familiar with the construction, maintenance, tests and operation of helicopters as soon as possible."[24] The next day, Kossler received a telephone call from Commander

McCoffrey, U.S. Navy, newly assigned at BuAer to the helicopter project. The stymied bureau was taking a new tack: it was drafting a letter
to Adm. Percy Noble, head of the British Admiralty delegation, proposing a joint committee to evaluate the helicopter. Members of that
committee would be the British, the Coast Guard, and BuAer! The
"machines to be used will be those from the present Army procurement program now assigned to the British." Kossler was pleased,
apparently, summarizing in his follow-up memorandum to the commandant, "This begins to sound like sense."[25]

Introduction of "Dipping Sonar"

Soon thereafter, Kossler received an unexpected letter. It began simply,

> My dear Captain,
> I have been informed that you were recently in Miami in connection
> with the development of helicopters for use against submarines. I
> endeavored to get in touch with you but found you had returned to
> Washington. I think I have some information for you that may be of
> interest.[26]

The information that followed the understated introduction contributed more to the development of the helicopter over the next
seven years than any other wisdom. Lt. Comdr. George D. Synon,
U.S. Coast Guard, working as a researcher in the Navy's headquarters,
Gulf Sea Frontier, Miami, described in his letter a sound recording
device "specifically designed for use in a helicopter." It was created by
Dr. Harvey C. Hayes and described as an echo-ranging device. The
device would be attached by a special cable to the helicopter and lowered into the water while the helicopter hovered over a particular spot
in the ocean. Synon noted that the "gadget" permitted a helicopter to
locate and hold a submarine under "almost any circumstances." Hayes
felt the device had "tremendous potential value," but he had been
unable to discover any helicopter program in the Bureau of
Aeronautics where it could be developed. Synon humbly concluded
his letter with, "May I hear from you on this?"[27]

Kossler's reaction was as weak as the letter's presentation, and
Erickson delayed for more than a month before following up this
remarkable query. They were reluctant, in part, because this concept
could only work if helicopters could fly reliably over water, carry
weapons, and had the ability to land on ships. At this stage in their

evolution, only two helicopters could fly (the prototype VS-300 and experimental XR-4), with limited abilities, from land and calm water.

Helicopters Aboard Ship

Erickson would eventually pursue the idea of the helicopter-borne sonar device, but only much later, when his project lost support and was in jeopardy of closing. Meanwhile, he was still attempting to prove the helicopter compatible to operate off surface vessels. In April he took a photo to Sikorsky and Morris that showed a tanker broken in half after being torpedoed off the New Jersey coast. What interested Erickson about the photo was a platform for cargo built on deck amidships. Morris, as the test pilot, had already landed on a platform at Wright Field. They agreed an XR-4 could operate from that type of platform despite the obstructions of rigging and superstructure fore and aft. Erickson then passed this information to Kossler. Armed with this assurance, he contacted R. W. Seabury, president of War Cargoes, Incorporated, at once. Kossler propounded the concept of helicopter protection for convoys. Seabury was interested.

Kossler then arranged a quick meeting between Seabury and Sikorsky. Sikorsky asked Seabury if a ship might be made available for testing an XR-4. Without a moment's pause, Seabury telephoned Captain Conway, in charge of the War Shipping Administration's office in New York. Conway assured Seabury that they would have a temporary deck installed immediately on a tanker. "If the test proves successful," Kossler reported, "a production order will be immediately given to Sikorsky by Cargoes Inc." Seabury met with Rear Adm. Ralph Davison, Bureau of Aeronautics, and Kossler was assured "everything is straightened out." The shipboard landing trials would be conducted the first week in May. As further evidence of his enthusiasm and assurance that he once again was in control of the project, Kossler reported, "It is understood and agreed by the Bureau of Aeronautics that the Coast Guard will operate the production machines for War Shipping."[28]

It must have been an exciting week for Kossler. He learned BuAer was stepping aside and turning over to the Coast Guard two of the bureau's YR-4As for tests and training. The best news for Kossler was that the make up of the proposed joint evaluation committee would change and "the Bureau of Aeronautics will be out of the picture."[29]

This news came at the heels of another blow to the Navy's obstruction-ism issued by Senator Harry S Truman's special committee investigating the National Defense Program. That committee recommended in its report of April 20, that "the Navy be less conventional and conservative in its thinking, that it spend less time propounding explanations as to why unfortunate situations have occurred, and that it devise and use such substitutions and new methods as are necessary to obtain production."[30]

Optimism was high at the new Sikorsky Aircraft factory, which had become a separate division of United Aircraft Corporation on 1 May. The Army accepted it first YR-4A on that same day. The Army was assigned production helicopters one, four, and seven; the Navy was to get numbers three, six, and eight.

Kossler, meantime, was meeting almost daily with the Maritime Commission, detailing his needs for a helicopter landing platform and scheduling the first operational tests. Lurking on the sidelines, unbeknownst to Kossler, was Capt. H. B. Sallada, U.S. Navy, of BuAer. He wrote a letter to the chairman of the Maritime Commission dictating the bureau's unilateral specifications for the shipboard landing platforms. The bureau was creeping back into the helicopter project over a different horizon.

On 4 May, just three days before the scheduled test, Rear Adm. R. S. Edwards, U.S. Navy, chief of staff, U.S. Fleet, authored a letter for the CNO and sent to BuAer modifying King's orders of 15 February. Admiral King's new order designated the Bureau of Aeronautics as the coordinating agency of a joint board. Members for this board would represent the CNO, BuAer, Coast Guard, British Admiralty, and the Royal Air Force.

The justification for proposing such orders was the Navy's ship-based operational background plus its ASW experience. This pretext ignored the Coast Guard's experience, which equaled—and in some cases surpassed—the Navy's in shipboard and airborne antisubmarine operational exposure. A handwritten note on the bottom of a letter in Coast Guard files, probably penned by Kossler, says, "This was put out when the Bureau got wind of the first trials sched. 6–7 May."[31]

First Shipboard Helicopter Landings

A deck built amidships on the SS *Bunker Hill* had only seventy-eight feet of clearance between obstructions. The ship lay at anchor near the airfield off Stratford Point, Long Island Sound, on 6 May 1943. As Morris acquainted Gregory with the helicopter's latest changes for the test, he turned to him, pointing out the ship, and asked, "See that little pilot-house there amidships?" Gregory nodded. "Now see that mast a few feet the other side of it?"

"Sure."

"Well, Colonel, in between those two you're going to land the XR-4."

"Are you kidding? . . . You mean somebody else is going to land in that space—not me."[32]

A painted fifty-foot square on the deck had an eight-foot bull's-eye in the center. Approaches to the landing space were only possible from the sides of the ship. The modified XR-4 appeared in new battle dress for its most important test to date.

The entire helicopter project now rested on the XR-4's ability to land on a ship. It had a new, more powerful engine—180 horsepower instead of the original 165. New rotor blades extended to thirty-eight feet in diameter. "U S ARMY" was stenciled on the fabric-covered fuselage—painted a shiny aluminum—just forward of the white star in the blue circle, the standard Army Air Forces aircraft marking of the period. For shipboard landings, the helicopter returned to its "all-purpose landing gear—a big pair of rubberized floats thirty inches in diameter and thirteen feet in length which looked like a couple of oversized hot dogs."[33]

Gregory was a reluctant participant. He was "very unhappy at first."[34] After all, he had not flown the helicopter for nearly six months, and his "shipboard" experience was limited to the stationary twenty-foot platform on the grass at Wright Field. Adding to his discomfort was the fact that the new rotor system's controls were sloppy.

Gregory approached the ship for his first attempted landing; fifty pairs of eyes watched. The next few moments would determine military careers and the very future of Sikorsky, his new company, and his helicopter. From the helicopter, Gregory noted:

[T]he space on the deck looked even smaller. . . . It didn't look at all as if the helicopter would fit. The cabin superstructure towered up like a big two-story building, and the people on it all had that "it can't be done" look on their faces. . . . Yet that big white bull's-eye stuck out like a target. . . . The XR-4 came true to the white marker as though being pulled by a powerful magnet, and a minute later the floats touched the deck.[35]

Despite a cobweb cross hatching of shock-cords and two-by-fours lashing the floats to prevent bouncing, the "XR-4 bounced a bit" then "she shook a little and then relaxed, her fuselage covering the white center. . . . I disengaged her rotor, shut off the engine and she eased back on her haunches, satisfied and pleased."[36]

Gregory practiced all that afternoon, with the ship both at anchor and under way. Ninety-seven guests arrived aboard the SS *Bunker Hill* the next morning—7 May—for the formal flight demonstration. Flight conditions on the sound were poor; fog obscured the ship.

Despite those conditions, at the scheduled time observers on the ship suddenly saw the helicopter loom from the gray mist, circle the ship, and land on the water alongside. Even before its important test, Gregory proved to the gathered witnesses that the helicopter excelled any aircraft in its ability to fly in restricted visibility and alight on the sea with ease.[37]

Without question, Gregory proved that day the ability of the helicopter to work aboard ships. He landed the XR-4 while the ship cruised at speeds up to fifteen knots and in relative winds up to thirty-five knots, although the tests were performed in the protected waters of the sound, not the open ocean. Consequently, a few Navy observers spoke derisively about the helicopter, but in defending the project over these objections, Farley later pointed out, "The degree of control available and the relative slowness of roll or pitch of a vessel this size did not seem to warrant the skepticism of some of the observers."[38]

In the boat ferrying the guests ashore following the demonstration, the Navy's aerodynamist, Diehl—in an apparent change of attitude toward helicopters—confided to Erickson that if he had seen a film of that day's demonstration, "he would have been sure that it was faked."[39]

New Interest in the Helicopter

The first documentation to support Kossler's and Erickson's pursuit of the helicopter as a rescue craft came in Loening's report of the shipboard-landing test. Having watched Gregory, Loening noted: "[A]nother obvious use that was demonstrated as a secondary matter in the tests of May 7 was the use for lifesaving. The ability of the helicopter with flotation bags to land and take off on the roughest water was evident in the way it plops in and pulls out of the sea with no forward velocity whatever." He went on to describe "the helicopter is much better on the water than a duck." Loening declared openly that "its rough water lifesaving possibilities, particularly for the Coast Guard, are completely convincing, even to such an extent to warrant a helicopter being stationed at a beach side for use by a lifeguard instead of a boat."[40]

Loening, excited over the prospects of helicopter aviation, and in obvious disgust over the Navy's obstruction of helicopter development, ended his report by warning, "[T]he successful demonstrations are apt to cause an additional hindrance to its logical and quick development." He predicted "a rush for bandwagon seats which at present in our governmental organization means half a dozen different bureaus and authorities taking a hand in it, with resulting inconclusive arguments, delays and decisions, etc." Therefore, Loening admonished that a single authority was necessary to "see that submarines are sunk by helicopter— that is the end product; the rest of the steps are incidental."[41]

Loening's dire predictions came true even before they were finally written. Just three days following the shipboard demonstration, Hayes called Kenly, Kossler's assistant, informing him that the Army Air

Forces wanted the submarine listening equipment under development for installation in the helicopter.[42]

Then, on 17 May, a conference was held in the Maritime Commission office during which plans were presented for building a landing platform on the Coast Guard's SS *Governor Cobb,* a former coastal passenger ship, for continued testing and, later, for convoy work. (The General Ship Repair Company of Baltimore converted the vessel to a helicopter test ship, and on 2 August 1943, its name was shortened to the *Cobb.*[43]) The discussion concentrated on installation of helicopter platforms on Liberty ships because they represented the greatest tonnage in convoys. Seabury "did most of the talking and outlined his plans for the whole helicopter program, all of which was logical, straight-forward, and just what we want."[44]

Once More, BuAer Takes Charge

Russell, representing BuAer, injected in the proceedings the news that a board was being formed by representatives of various government agencies to aid in the adoption of the helicopter for wartime needs. Seabury immediately suggested that he should represent the War Shipping Administration. Comdr. Stanley C. Linholm, U.S. Coast Guard, disclosed later in a confidential memorandum, "I don't believe Mr. Seabury will be invited by the Navy to be a member of the board."[45] Linholm misjudged the power behind Seabury, however.

On 18 May 1943, the Navy Department sponsored the first "Combined Board for the Evaluation of the Helicopter in Anti-Submarine Warfare" meeting. The Coast Guard sent Linholm—not Kossler—and Lt. Comdr. William E. Sinton. Kossler's best work was still behind the scenes, manipulating events. Capt. Leslie C. Stevens, U.S. Navy, senior representative of BuAer, assumed chairmanship of the board. Once the lengthy name for the board was selected, the following item was settled without discussion: "It is the understanding of the board that the agency conducting the tests of the helicopter is the Bureau of Aeronautics."[46]

BuAer and the Navy were back in command of the helicopter project.

Noted by their absence were representatives from the Army. The Army Air Forces, from the beginning, was designated as the agency to develop the helicopter under the terms of the Dorsey Act, and it had not been relieved of this responsibility. But BuAer insisted that one aircraft be tested at the Naval Air Station Anacostia, D.C., by Navy Flight Test, and a second one tested for comparison by NACA. This Navy-controlled board strangely overlooked that the one qualified military helicopter pilot was Gregory, from the Army Air Forces, and that the only helicopter in existence belonged to the Army Air Forces.

The Navy's one concession to the Army concerned procuring helicopters. Though the initial production helicopters were assigned to the Army, Navy, and the British, they were purchased from Sikorsky under an Army Air Forces contract. In order to meet the projections of the committee and to facilitate arrangements with the contractor in an Army-controlled aircraft manufacturing plant, the board asked the Army Air Forces to appoint a liaison officer from the Office of the Chief of the Material Division at Washington. This officer would be an adviser concerning the purchases of helicopters and would "be available on short notice to sit with the board at such of its deliberations as may be appropriate." He would have no voice in board matters, however. The Navy thus intended to keep the Army at arm's length on its helicopter policy.[47]

Three other agencies vital to the mission of developing the helicopter were missing from this board: the U.S. Maritime Commission, the War Shipping Administration, and the British Merchant Shipping Mission. Each of these agencies were most interested and earnestly working to get helicopters immediately for the protection of their convoys.

These apparent oversights were readily resolved by Captain Stevens, who informed the organizations that the "Bureau of Aeronautics, as the coordinating agency in arranging the details of the installation of flight platforms and servicing facilities on the various types of merchant ship, would provide sufficient liaison and coordination" and therefore, their representation on this board "was unnecessary."[48]

Nevertheless, Seabury was added to the board later as a representative of the War Shipping Administration, following a directive to BuAer from the CNO on 5 August. Seabury had influence, and he used it. He was not to be slighted.[49]

The board was then told that two ships were being readied as helicopter landing ships. The first was the *Governor Cobb*, three hundred feet in length and already undergoing conversion. The second was the seven-thousand-ton British freighter SS *Daghestan,* which had formerly been used for autogiro tests and already had a platform on the stern. It would be ready for trials in U.S. waters in July.[50]

A Lot of Helicopters in a Hurry

Sikorsky was delivering helicopters, cargo ships were being readied, but the Navy and Coast Guard had no qualified pilots or even provisions for training them. As a result, Russell and Buckley and Linholm and other members of the committee met with Col. H. Z. Bogert, U.S. Army

Air Forces, and Gregory at Wright Field on 1 June 1943. At this meeting the Army agreed to permit the training of *one* Navy pilot and two mechanics at Sikorsky's plant. The costs would be charged to the Army Air Forces' contract. The Coast Guard had long anticipated this agreement and already had orders ready for Erickson to train with test pilot Morris, with Berry and Boone attending the mechanics' course. The Navy was not prepared and had no one scheduled for this assignment.

The Army designated five YR-4A helicopters for the training and evaluation project: numbers two, three, five, six, and eight. These modified orders allowed for the training of additional pilots at the Sikorsky plant during the delivery of the first eight aircraft. BuAer's plan was to shift the training to NAS Anacostia, using the original Navy pilots trained as instructors.[51] It issued specific instructions to the commanding officer, NAS Anacostia, detailing the helicopter test program. The aircraft would move to Anacostia upon the completion of initial training at the Sikorsky plant.

Ships and Helicopters, But No Pilots

Erickson, expecting to start training in helicopters, finally followed up on the letter from Synon. He wrote, "[A] number of officers have questioned the usefulness of helicopters on the grounds of their limited range and load carrying capacity." He pointed out that the principal advantage of helicopters versus fixed-wing aircraft was in their flexibility of control. He justified the frail craft saying, "They can be operated under some weather conditions when conventional aircraft cannot, especially during periods of low visibility or with very low ceilings."[52]

Erickson stressed, "The detection of enemy submarines is the greatest problem facing anti-submarine forces." The role of the helicopter in solving that problem was "not as a killer craft but as the *eyes* and *ears* of the convoy escorts." He suggested that Hayes's detection gear, helicopter borne, could possibly become those "eyes" and "ears."[53]

Erickson showed Russell a draft of that letter and later wrote to Linholm that Russell "is anxious to present it to the board."[54] The board accepted Erickson's idea immediately, and on the strength of this approval, Hayes stopped his work on sonar for blimps at the Naval Research Laboratory in Anacostia and began developing dipping sonar for helicopters.[55]

Loening, in a May 1943 plea to Charles E. Wilson, executive vice chairman of the War Production Board, disclosed his urgency to acquire helicopters. He wrote, "We want lots of helicopters and we want them in a hurry." He acknowledged plans yet unpublished for "extensive

production of Sikorsky helicopters," and expressed, "a wave of enthusiasm will result probably in an order for almost 2,000 of these craft."
However, he stressed, it was vastly more important to have fifty by the
next September. "We will be much better off therefore to have 200
more or less made by hand at *once*, than to have 2,000 delivered by the
end of 1944."[56]

o THREE o
FIRST MISSION

Military Helicopter Flight Training Begins

Four U.S. military helicopter flight students began training early in June 1943 at the Sikorsky plant. Erickson remembered, "It had been nearly a year since I had submitted my proposals for using helicopters for anti-submarine warfare, so I was eager to get started." Morris used Sikorsky's original XR-4, modified for the sea trials and called the XR-4A. To Erickson it "proved to be a rather unstable machine," a common feeling among fixed-winged pilots flying a helicopter for the first time.[1]

Erickson caught on to helicopter flying quickly. Morris let him fly solo with less than three hours' total flight instruction. All four students soloed on 16 June 1943, a week after starting.[2] They continued instruction according to Morris's syllabus as four more students started the training. Commander Brie had already soloed the XR-4 at Wright Field in September 1942. He was back for a refresher course with countrymen Lt. Comdr. E.A.H. Peat, Royal Naval Volunteer Reservists, and Flt. Lt. F. J. "Jeep" Cable, Royal Air Force. The fourth student, James Ray, a former autogiro test pilot, was a civilian test pilot for Platt-LePage, builders of the XR-1.[3]

The Navy's trainee, Comdr. Charles T. Booth, dropped out of the qualification program almost immediately after his solo flight. He was involved in moving the Navy's flight test facility from NAS Anacostia to the Naval Air Test Center at Patuxent River, Maryland. Erickson thus remained the only "naval aviator" qualified in the helicopter.

Erickson Crashes First British Helicopter

The number two YR-4 was delivered to the British trainees at the Sikorsky factory on 2 July 1943. It was to have a short life.

Erickson recalled that the three British pilots nearly "flew the rotor blades off it during the next two days. By 4 July, they had their fill for a time." Rather than let the aircraft sit idle, Erickson took it out for a solo flight.[4] The helicopter started vibrating violently on approach to his first landing. Entering a hover, and with the aircraft nearly uncontrollable, Erickson "dropped the collective pitch and the helicopter fell to the ground in an upright attitude." On impact, the still rotating blades drooped far enough to strike the tail boom. "This shredded the main rotor blades," as Erickson remembered, "leaving a dismal mess" of the new British helicopter.[5]

The three British officers rushed across the field to the still wobbling wreckage; they were relieved to find Erickson okay. Earlier that day, Peat had tried to hover at five hundred feet, a maneuver he described as "belting it all out!" Discovering Erickson to be okay, Peat exclaimed, "If it had to happen, I'm glad it bust with you at fifteen feet rather than with me at five hundred feet!" Relief brought levity. The three accused Erickson of celebrating the Fourth of July with a strike back at the British Empire by "pranging" Britain's only helicopter.[6]

The accident occurred when one of the two tail rotor blades struck the framework supporting the tail rotor gearbox, breaking the blade off. The tattered tail rotor blade was discovered about a hundred yards from where the helicopter crashed. Erickson received no blame for the accident.[7]

Helicopter Shipboard Trials

The newly discovered tail rotor problem jeopardized the scheduled shipboard trials aboard the U.S. Army transport ship *James Parker* scheduled for 6 and 7 July. Quick action by Sikorsky engineers had the XR-4's and number one YR-4's tail rotor systems modified in time for the demonstrations on Long Island Sound. This time, the newly trained pilots were landing on a forty-by-sixty-foot platform built over the stern. This permitted approaches through 270 degrees. The two helicopters had room enough to operate together.

Many guests from the *Bunker Hill* demonstrations two months earlier were aboard again as observers. This was the first time, however, that BuAer's Russell witnessed helicopters landing aboard ship. His later report to BuAer was positive after watching the 162 landings by pilots

with less than a month's experience. Furthermore, his confidence was bol-
stered after riding aboard one for a takeoff and landing, with winds over
the deck at thirty knots. Low ceilings and visibility did not hamper flight
operations, although rain did damage the wood and fabric rotor blades.

Following the demonstration, Russell supported the opinion that
R-4 type helicopters could operate from platforms on merchant ships
"in all weather in which an escort carrier could operate conventional
airplanes" and that they could make patrols of up to two hours and
thirty miles away from their home ship. He was aware, however, that
Grumman TBM/TBF Avenger torpedo bombers were already flying
from escort carriers in convoys for up to four hours, at 160 knots, and
carrying four five-hundred-pound bombs or a single torpedo. The
Avengers were also armed with 30- and 50-caliber machine guns for
defense against the antiaircraft fire of the heavily armed German submarines. These escort carriers were already turning the tide in the battle against the submarine menace in the Atlantic. If the helicopter did
have any advantage at all, it was that every merchant ship could have
one on board, thus reducing the need for defensive naval elements.[8]

Problems Plague New Helicopter Deliveries

BuAer followed Russell's report with orders for the purchase of 173 helicopters.[9] But just when the project appeared to be on track for Erickson
and Kossler, problems started plaguing the first production aircraft.
Helicopter number three, the Navy's first HNS, was delayed. Then,
within two weeks of Erickson's crash, a more serious accident happened
to helicopter number one, which belonged to the Army and was piloted
by newly designated Army helicopter pilot Lt. Frank T. Peterson. On 15
July, during an approach to the Allentown, Pennsylvania, airport, it lost
a main rotor blade while thirty-five feet above the ground.[10] The Army
immediately grounded all helicopters and stopped deliveries until problems with the blades were solved. This seriously threatened the time
schedule for continuing the ASW program.

New blades were manufactured for helicopters number three and
four. To support the Navy's project, the Army released to the Navy
helicopters six, eight, and nine; helicopters number five and seven
went to the British.

Erickson Takes Charge of Navy Helicopter Program

The Navy still had no qualified helicopter pilot except Erickson, however, and he was using the ASW project solely to further his own goals
of a rescue vehicle for the Coast Guard.

In the summer of 1943, Erickson took charge of the Navy's helicopter development project. BuAer requested on 3 September that he
submit weekly reports to the bureau on the aircraft plus the pilots'
training progress. These reports were to "include . . . technical information . . . [that] might have a bearing on present or future operation
of this type of aircraft."[11] It was thus a way for the Navy to spy on the
Army's helicopter program. Erickson responded by writing his first
report the next day.

All flight training had ceased because of the lack of aircraft, so
Erickson used his time at the Sikorsky factory to take charge of helicopter development. He began what would be a career-long pursuit of
gathering experts to examine the helicopter, then devising changes to
improve its capabilities. Since aircraft numbers five and six were not
planned for delivery until about 11 September, on the second of that
month he held the first of many conferences that would follow
through the next few years.

Landing Gear

Landing gear was Erickson's first focus. Weighty, conventional aircraft
tires had been used from the beginning, but Sikorsky experimented
with floats as an optional undercarriage. Although Gregory successfully
used floats on his shipboard landings, Erickson wanted something
more than the wooden two-by-four and bungee lash-up on the floats
to prevent rebounding when landing. Floats caused a resonance—an
interaction with the rotor system—when they contacted the ground.
The resultant "bouncing" could ultimately destroy the aircraft.[12]

J. F. Boyle, president of Air Cruisers (the company built floats), met
with Sikorsky engineers and the British officers to discuss Erickson's
proposed modifications. The solution they soon accepted was a low-
pressure tube, extending along the bottom, that would be connected
through a "chimney" to a similar one on the top of the float. Erickson
ordered one set to test on a Navy HNS. The British, on the other
hand, favored landing wheels with emergency pop-out floats. These
inflatable bladders, attached to the sides of the hull, were proposed to
save the aircraft and crew in the event they were forced down at sea.

Erickson argued that the pop-out floats were untenable. Whereas
airplanes have wings that keep them afloat until the crew can escape, a
wingless helicopter would sink so fast, a pilot might, like a British airman whose autogiro ditched at sea, surface only "after being forced
down to great depths."[13]

Erickson prevailed with his plan for floats over the inflatable bags.
(Later, however, he spent considerable time developing inflatable bags

for emergency flotation, an item still used today on modern helicopters.) At the time, Erickson emphasized advantage. Floats raised the helicopter fuselage higher above the ship deck, providing greater clearance for the tail rotor if the ship was rolling during a landing. This advantage, they soon discovered, was still not enough, however, and the British insisted on ordering a set of inflatable bags for testing.

Landing skids—later a common configuration on most Army helicopters—were also proposed at this conference. Skids eliminated the weight of bulky landing wheels and rubber "sausages," a real advantage for the underpowered HNS. But it was the wheels and brakes that caused the next HNS accident.

Another Crash

The British finally received helicopter number five on 23 September, but four days later, Brie crashed on landing. This had been their only operational craft. After the accident, fellow British pilot Peat remarked, "Poor old Reg was pretty down the drain about his helicopter flying. . . . I remember him looking up from the wreckage and saying, 'What did I do wrong that time?'"[14]

Brie's helicopter accident resulted from old habits. Earlier in his career, he had successfully flown Cievra autogiros. In January 1935 he again succeeded in flying one on and off the Italian cruiser *Fiume* in the Mediterranean. Still later, in May 1942, as a pioneer in rotary-craft shipboard operations, he flew a Pitcairn PA-39 "jump take-off Autogyro" from a stern platform erected on the British merchant vessel SS *Empire Jersey*. This first flight took place in the Chesapeake Bay off Annapolis.[15] Just before the crash, Brie "made a good approach, but carried some forward speed when he touched down as was customary in autogiros. This would have been all right if he had not forgotten his wheel brakes."[16] He landed with them locked.

A New, Larger Helicopter

The new-generation helicopters soon appeared. By the week ending 11 September 1943, the first XR-5 was capable of flying an hour and a half. Erickson expected the XR-6 to be ready to fly during the first week in October, but progress at the factory was slow, delaying its delivery.[17] Perhaps most significant for helicopter development was a load-lifting test conducted with the XR-5. Critics at the time were constantly denigrating the aircraft because it could lift little more than the crew. Often in the HNS, the fuel load would be adequate for only a few minutes' worth of demonstration flight. This successful load-lifting test of the R-5/HO2S proved that a helicopter could do more than fly backwards and lift off vertically. The XR-5 flew with a useful load of 1,836 pounds, and by the end of September, it increased its load to 2,120. The testing period suddenly ended, however, when the helicopter crashed on 12 October due to a tail rotor failure. The Sikorsky test pilots were uninjured.

With the arrival of a Navy lieutenant known simply as Hogan, and Lt. (jg) Stewart R. Graham, U.S. Coast Guard, on 25 September, training began. But because no Navy aircraft were available, Erickson had them attend a short engineering course at the factory. Berry, the Coast Guard's first helicopter mechanic, supervised the course for the new pilots.[18]

The British received their third helicopter on the last day of September. Erickson and the British pilots resumed flying. It was just over two weeks—16 October—before Erickson accepted delivery of the first Navy helicopter, number 46445. Erickson was thus able to begin flight instruction with his first two students, Hogan and Graham.

A Near Crash for Kossler and Erickson

On 21 October—a cold autumn day—Kossler visited the factory and took his first helicopter ride. With the Navy helicopter once more temporarily out of service, Erickson borrowed the British craft for the flight. In many aircraft engines of that period, hot air was ducted through the carburetor to prevent icing, which could ultimately lead to engine failure. Its use, however, reduced the power available from the engine. So, with carburetor heat applied, the HNS had insufficient power to take off. Therefore, lift off was necessarily performed without it, even in conditions leading to probable icing. Once stabilized in flight at reduced power settings, heat could be applied. The first production HNSs had the carburetor heat control lever located behind the pilot's seat, compounding the pilot's problem. During the takeoff and immediately after, the pilot was too busy with the helicopter's cyclic, collective, and throttle controls to have a free hand.[19]

These were a few of the obstacles Erickson faced when he took off over the factory's parking lot, where workers were going to and from their cars during a shift change. The engine immediately lost power. Carburetor ice. He spun the aircraft in a steep left turn to line up with the axis of a nearby canal, planning to ditch in the water while "pumping the throttle." Erickson still had the helicopter in the left turn when the carburetor cleared itself of ice.

> Suddenly we had full power. Before I could compensate for the increased tail rotor torque, we were in a steep climbing turn heading toward the buildings across the canal. We just cleared the roof of the first building, but I could not roll out of the turn without running into the structure supporting a large water tank. So we just continued in what amounted to a "wing over" and dove out over the canal again. By that time, I had the helicopter under complete control. It was a frightening experience, but it didn't even ruffle Kossler.[20]

Kossler evidently showed great composure and hid his true reactions to the helicopter acrobatics. Shortly afterward, however, he wrote in his flight log book—the longest comment he ever committed for any entry—"First flipper turn ever made in helicopter. Almost crashed! due to pilot forgetting he was in a helicopter & taking evasive action on some stacks."[21]

These early experimental flights revealed to Erickson and other pioneers flaws in early design assumptions that had no benefit of empirical knowledge. Some of these oversights produced unexpected flight conditions which ultimately led to changes in the aircraft or its operating guidelines. In this case, the carburetor heat control lever was repositioned in the center of the cockpit next to the mixture control lever convenient to both pilots.

Helicopter Flight Training Officially Begins

Coast Guard/Navy helicopter flight training officially started later that month. On 20 October, Graham became the syllabus's first student to solo and was designated Coast Guard helicopter pilot number two. The week ending 23 October, Booth, returning to resume his training interrupted in July, logged five and a half hours of solo time following a refresher flight. No records show that he ever completed the course for his helicopter designation, however. Hogan completed two and a half hours of instruction—plus soloing—during the last week of October, but he withdrew or was ordered from the training program without explanation. Lt. Comdr. John Miller, U.S. Navy, an autogiro pilot, replaced Hogan on 21 October and had his familiarization flight the following day. The Navy had no list established for helicopter pilots, so Miller did not receive an official designation despite having finished the training program with Graham.[22]

The second and third Navy helicopters arrived from the Sikorsky factory the week ending 30 October. The date for the scheduled shipboard trials was too soon thereafter, though, for the pilots were not yet trained. So Erickson recommended a delay. This additional time gave him the opportunity to test the new landing-gear floats and flotation gear and to buy the spare parts he thought essential to shipboard operations.[23] Erickson also took advantage of this time to begin some experimental work.

Underwater Sound Recording Equipment Ready

Information about the developments of underwater sound recording equipment appeared slow in getting to where it was beneficial. An undated report written by Hayes, weeks old from references in the text, did not reach the Coast Guard until 5 November. In the ten-page report, Hayes briefly reviewed the history of the development of his sound devices. He described the equipment and illustrated its ability by revealing remarkable test results carried out by his lab in actual experiments in the Chesapeake Bay. Hayes ruled out lighter-than-air craft and emphasized helicopters as the ideal machine to bear the device.

Further, he wrote, the "equipment will be ready for tests on or before October 10, 1943." This date was nearly one month before the Coast Guard received the letter. No documents or actions taken by Erickson were discovered to show a follow-up by him or Kossler on this announcement. It appears the plan was deferred by Erickson now that he had other projects more dear.[24] Also possible was that Erickson received information, undocumented, that Hayes's unit was not ready for testing. Some evidence points to this conclusion, but it can also be conjectured that Hayes stopped development because of no response to his strangely delayed letter.

Helicopter Training Moves to New York

Meanwhile, training operations with five HNS/YR-4s crowded the space at the new Sikorsky plant. The main buildings that were to house the HNS/YR-4/R-6 production and the R-5 experimental assembly lines were not ready, so both shared a small shop, resulting "in very serious congestion."[25] Helicopters were now moving rapidly off the production lines. The Navy was still moving from Anacostia to Patuxent River and apparently not yet ready to accept the new helicopters and the training program.

Consequently, Kossler suggested to Erickson that he request permission immediately to move the Navy and British helicopters, along with the training program, to the Coast Guard Air Station at Floyd Bennett Field. The Naval Air Station's commanding officer, Capt. Newton H. White, had no objections. The Coast Guard air station was a tenant on the Navy base. BuAer, after their flurry of directives in May, June, and July, seemed to withdraw from the project. This was a time in the war when the Navy—especially BuAer—was preoccupied with supplying the fleet with hundreds of TBM, TBF, F6F and F4U aircraft each month, and the pilots to fly them. The Navy's urgency of a year earlier for helicopters capable of operating from ships in convoys was over. The helicopter was no longer needed.

The CNO approved and designated the Coast Guard Air Station Brooklyn as a "Helicopter Training and Development Base" on 19 November 1943. But Erickson did not wait for this approval; he had moved the three Navy helicopters and students to Floyd Bennett Field the first week in November. The first helicopter flown there by Erickson was received with less than an enthusiastic welcome. Graham, who piloted the craft, with Erickson along on the flight, remembers that, after landing: "We weren't received or greeted with open arms. The Air Station personnel looked at the machine, then at us, in bemusement, as if to say, 'Better you guys in that contraption than us.'"[26]

Erickson wrote of the move, "Captain Kossler was instrumental for having this station designated as the first Military or Naval helicopter base."[27] The timing of the move to New York and the needed arrangements seemed to fall easily in place, thanks to Kossler. CGAS Brooklyn had been flying wartime antisubmarine patrols and convoy escorts as well as coastal search and rescue. A Navy patrol squadron had recently taken over all the ASW patrols from the Coast Guard. Suddenly, without any apparent plans, all missions except harbor patrols ceased and a helicopter training station emerged. Most fixed-winged aircraft, pilots, and crew were transferred. Under the circumstances, nearly all regular Coast Guard officers welcomed a transfer; most did not want to be involved with helicopters. Some enlisted pilots, including newly commissioned ones, remained behind to train in helicopters. They did, however, only after not-so-subtle motivating by Erickson and Graham. These new recruits became the nucleus of the instructor pool and project test pilots.

Flight training continued without interruption. The two Army officers Erickson had taught returned to Bridgeport on 5 November to train further in Army aircraft coming off the Sikorsky production lines. Ens. Walter Bolton, U.S. Coast Guard, began flight training, the first aviator so instructed at Floyd Bennett Field.

The suddenness of the major change in the status of the air station without any known paperwork shows again the probable chicanery practiced by Kossler. Thus, with intense maneuvering by Kossler and Erickson, aided by some providence, CGAS Brooklyn became the Coast Guard and Navy's—and the world's—first helicopter training base on 1 December 1943. Erickson, as commanding officer, received his promotion to commander later that month.

Coast Guard and British Pilots Qualify Aboard Ship

The next phase of the ship/helicopter trials took place between Wednesday, 24 November, and Sunday, the twenty-eighth, aboard the *Daghestan,* in Long Island Sound, and at sea, off Block Island. One Navy HNS helicopter, Bureau Number (BuNo) 46700, equipped with special floats that had low-pressure chambers designed by Air Cruisers, and one British YR-4A Hoverfly,[28] on floats designed by Goodyear, flew aboard Wednesday afternoon.[29] The British pilots Brie, Peat, and Cable, along with American pilots Erickson, Miller, and Graham, practiced that day and through the next preparing for the demonstration before the "Combined Board."

It was not easy. Miller and Graham had just three weeks' experience flying helicopters. Peat won a coin toss to be the first British pilot to land on the British ship. On the morning they were to fly to the ship, he remembered, "It was blowing 30 knots and snowing." Charles Loder, the RAF ground engineer, "shook hands" and wished him luck. Peat recalls thinking, "God, he thinks it's dangerous, and my heart sank into my boots!" Nonetheless, Peat managed to land successfully but could not return to Bridgeport by boat; the seas were too high to allow the tender to get alongside the ship.[30]

With improved weather two days later, the board, including Seabury, witnessed landing demonstrations.[31] Some members of the board even rode the helicopter in these shipboard landings. One of them in particular, Gen. Frank E. Lowe, U.S. Army, "Military Executive of the Special (Senate) Committee Investigating the National Defense Program" (commonly referred to as the Truman Committee, named for its chairman, Harry S Truman), was later influential in helicopter development.

Open sea trials on Sunday concluded the exercise. Erickson reported the "most difficult conditions under which operations were conducted": namely, the relative winds to 42 knots over the deck and the vessel rolling four degrees. The deck moved vertically five feet. The pilots, combined, logged 27 hours flight time and made 328 landings: 162 for the British and 166 for the Americans. Two conclusions were garnered from the tests. First, starting and stopping rotors in high winds was a problem solved only by the ship running downwind. The crew planned for a temporary wind barricade for the next phase. Second, landings with a deck roll greater than ten degrees would require a "special means of hooking the aircraft on landing."[32]

Phase three, the Atlantic crossing, was just over a month away.

First Students and Visitors to the New School

The Navy's first helicopter training class began with Lt. Comdr. W. J. Lawrence, U.S. Coast Guard, Lt. Comdr. James Klopp, U.S. Navy, Lt. W. V. Gough, U.S. Naval Reserve, and Capt. E. S. Greg and Lt. C. P. Miller, U.S. Army Air Forces. The school trained the two Army pilots as repayment for the Army's having instructed Erickson and Booth. Interest in the new school was high, as evidenced in the steady stream of visitors it entertained.

Lowe, who had first observed the Navy HNS from the *Daghestan*, was among the earliest such visitors, and he even flew with Erickson in the helicopter. Next came Lt. Col. Charles J. Hubbard, U.S. Army Air Forces, rescue officer for the Air Transport Command, and Maj. Joseph Phillips, U.S. Army Air Forces, of the Emergency Equipment Section. Erickson showed them rescue equipment already being developed by him and his crew. One piece was a stretcher adaptable to the helicopter and the other a net Erickson explained was "intended for use in scooping up survivors from the open sea." He was apologetic, saying it was not "a practical device, but it was the first step in adapting the helicopter for rescue at sea."[33]

Some of these adaptations were quite crude. In one instance, in an attempt to get a stretcher inside the HNS cabin, the left pilot's seat was removed. The remaining space was still too narrow for the stretcher, so a mechanic working with Erickson took the steel-tube and wire-mesh litter over to the hangar door, wedged it into the gap, and closed the door, pinching the litter. He then returned to the helicopter to check its fit. He repeated the process until the slightly crushed litter could be squeezed into the cockpit.

Loening, chairman of the NACA subcommittee on helicopters, flew on a flight demonstration.[34] Other visitors entertained by Erickson in December were several executives and engineers from the "Rotary Wing Aircraft Industry."[35] These demonstrations paid off handsomely later on when Erickson needed support to push his struggling rescue helicopter program, but it was this popularity outside the Coast Guard that, in part, cost Erickson his career.

With the unit just ten days old, Erickson had accumulated a total of 108.2 hours helicopter time and Graham, now designated an instructor pilot, had 48.1 hours.

Problems Flying the HNS

The HNS posed a peculiar problem for the new instructors. Modern helicopters with side-by-side seating—featuring complete sets of controls for both pilots—have a "cyclic" stick for the pilot's right hand and a "collective" lever with a throttle occupying the left. Sikorsky's HNS, however, provided only one collective control, with its motorcycle-grip throttle. This craft reversed typical airplane cockpit convention and shifted the pilot's seat to the right-hand side. The copilot or observer shifted to the left. This feature continues as a standard in helicopters today. Shifting seats permitted an airplane pilot trained to control flight attitude with the right hand to continue the practice in the helicopter. In the case of the HNS, the instructor moving to the left seat had to suddenly learn to maneuver "a very sensitive cyclic," as described by Graham, with his left hand and to roll the throttle backwards while lifting and lowering the collective with his right. "The functions performed by the right and left hands," according to Erickson, "were so different that the pilot had to learn to fly all over again when he shifted from [the] right to the left seat."[36]

No Students

The school had plenty of helicopters and official attention, but it did not have students. During the first weeks at Floyd Bennett, Erickson, "became snowed under with paperwork and public relations in the attempt to interest VIPs in the rotary-wing aircraft." Meanwhile, Graham, a new instructor without students, began "luring fixed-wing pilots to the rotary-wing aircraft." Initially, he captured no one's interest. Graham alleged, "I was looked upon as not having all my marbles, was ridiculed beyond belief among my fellow flyers, that I would jeopardize my well-being to fly such a contraption." Slowly, over time, "some of the ex-enlisted pilots would approach me in groups of three or four with questions concerning the helicopter. Never would they lower themselves to be seen speaking to me alone in fear of being ridiculed by the so-called die-hards." (Their initial attitude would prevail among young fliers for nearly the next thirty years.)[37]

Graham further related that, ultimately:

The ice was finally broken one Saturday afternoon when Ens. Bolton and I had the flight duty at the Air Station. In the past he and I flew together quite often on anti-submarine patrols in our fixed-wing aircraft, so it was a lot easier to convince him to take a ride with me in the helicopter. Of course it was after duty hours, no other pilots were aboard [that is, at the air station] except the senior

duty officer, hence Bolton must have felt that he was not embarrassing himself to fly with me. Now that I had him strapped in the
seat beside me, he was completely under my control.

It was up to me to put him at ease. I endeavored to make the initial take-off and forward flight as smooth as possible so as not to fright-
en him too much. It didn't take long before I noticed he was beginning to take interest of the control movements and etc. I allowed him
to follow me through holding the cyclic control stick as I made several approaches to a hover and landings. When I felt he was quite
relaxed I demonstrated backward take-offs into the wind, right and
left turns over a spot on the ground and flying sidewards, all to his
amazement over the precision control I had over the machine.
Needless to say he was convinced and indicated his desire to be
checked out. He eventually became my first student, soloed and
received helicopter pilot designation number three. That was the
genesis—other ex-enlisted pilots were showing their interest in the
rotary-wing machine, they were August Kleisch, Loren Perry and
David Gershowitz whom all became instructors.[38]

Curriculum and Extracurricular Experiments

Erickson instituted a helicopter mechanics course at CGAS Brooklyn;
the first class met on 27 December. Lt. A. N. Fisher, the station's engineering officer, supervised instructors Berry and G. F. Lubben. The
two-month course began with sixteen students: fourteen Coast Guard
mechanics from the air station and two Navy mechanics from the new
Patuxent River test center.

Erickson continued to busy himself with developing the helicopter
for rescue purposes. Before the second week of the new program had
expired, he flew a helicopter with a stretcher suspended under the fuselage. The dangling stretcher proved to be no problem in forward
cruising flight, hovering, or landing with the floats astride. The plane
flew with both seats filled and two hundred pounds of ballast in the
suspended stretcher. The object of the tests was to develop a method
of plucking survivors from seas too rough to land upon.

The First Mission

Destiny was on Erickson's side. A catastrophic event occurred on 3
January 1944 that inaugurated the helicopter in the humanitarian rescue
role. The Navy destroyer USS *Turner*, anchored off Sandy Hook, New
Jersey, suffered an explosion shortly after six in the storm-darkened

predawn hours. The blast was felt fifteen miles away and was followed by a second explosion forty-seven minutes later, which sank the ship. Many survivors were brought to the hospital at Sandy Hook. Large quantities of plasma were urgently needed, but a blizzard blocked all aircraft and hampered ground delivery.

A northeasterly storm sweeping the Atlantic coast with snow and sleet driven by twenty to twenty-five knot winds impeded rescue operations. All airfields in the region were closed. Admiral Parker, from his Third Naval District headquarters, "called Erickson to ask if it would be practicable for a helicopter to pick up blood plasma at the battery and fly it to Sandy Hook." Erickson responded with a booming, "Yes, sir!" Neither he nor the helicopter had performed together in stormy conditions, but this was his chance to prove his dream to the world. Erickson, with Bolton as his copilot, lifted off CGAS Brooklyn in Navy BuNo 46445. The dark blue helicopter disappeared almost instantly in the swirling snow whipped by gusting winds.[39]

Visibility was so low that Erickson observed, "We practically had to 'feel' our way around the ships anchored in Gravesend Bay." He battled the roiling winds in a steep approach over pilings along the shoreline to a landing in Battery Park. Bolton, who had qualified as a helicopter pilot just three days before, reluctantly left the aircraft to allow for two cases of plasma to be strapped to the landing floats. To take off from the park, Erickson noted, "[the] only way to get out was to back out"; the trees blocked his way forward.[40]

Sitting in the helicopter's pilot seat parked next to the Barge Office on New York's waterfront, Erickson, with his left hand, rolled the hand-grip throttle. Gradually he raised the collective lever, coordinating the twisting motions of his left hand and rising arm, closely watching the engine RPMs. His hands, arms, and feet moved in an uncoordinated cacophony of motion. Anticipating needed rotor blade pitch for balance, he moved the cyclic stick with staccato movements with his right hand. Simultaneously, with deftness, but gently, he alternated foot pressure, gradually applying left rudder pressure to counteract the torque, keeping the nose pointed straight ahead into the park.

What looked like a strange dance of the seated helicopter pilot was influenced by the irregular rhythm of the sudden and variable wind gusts that were pummeling the frail fabric and steel-tube structure. Steadily Erickson kept the shaking helicopter in place and level as it struggled to rise into the battering winds. "Igor's nightmare,"[41] bouncing on its sausage floats, then suddenly leaping, rose vertically. Slowly, still climbing, it backed out over the pilings before Erickson finally spun it around to the right and headed downwind toward Sandy Hook with the lifesaving cargo. Paradoxically, but appropriately, the helicopter started its first historical mission flying backwards.

According to Erickson, the "weather conditions were such that this flight could not have been made in any other type of aircraft." He nonchalantly commented, however, that the flight was "routine for the helicopter."[42] The casualness of his comments did not escape the press. The New York *Times*, in an editorial dated 6 January, echoed, "It was indeed routine for the strange rotary-winged machine which Igor Sikorsky has brought to practical flight, but it shows in striking fashion how the helicopter can make use of tiny landing areas in conditions of visibility which make other types of flying impossible."[43]

The editorial went on to accurately predict the role of the helicopter for the next five decades. "Nothing can dim the future of a machine which can take in its stride weather conditions such as those which prevailed in New York on Monday."[44]

With only six months of experience in this novel rotor craft, Erickson, fighting the weather and concentrating on the mission, probably could not have noted the irony of this fourteen-minute flight. The first operational mission for this much-maligned flying machine was a rescue sortie—Kossler and Erickson's dream. Erickson had rushed lifesaving aid to a crew of the U.S. Navy, the very organization that had found little use for the helicopter.[45]

Two days later a lieutenant, junior grade, with less than three months' experience in helicopters, began an adventure aboard a British ship in the North Atlantic winter's tempest that would bring further creditability to the ridiculed flying machine.

· FOUR ·
DECEPTION

Helicopters Go to Sea

Two days before Erickson's mission of carrying plasma to the Navy victims, phase three of the ASW helicopter evaluation began. "The British Helicopter Unit," wrote Graham, "loaded two helicopters aboard *Daghestan* on 2 January 1944." The Navy's aviators, Miller and Graham, joined the group as the Navy and Coast Guard pilot-representatives of the evaluation board. Lt. Comdr. James Klopp, U.S. Navy, accompanied the group representing BuAer. The plan for the third phase was to operate helicopters from the fifty-by-ninety-six-foot wooden platform built on the vessel's stern twenty-two feet above the water. Their task was to conduct patrols, seeking enemy submarines during the convoy's Atlantic crossing. The wintertime North Atlantic was a poor time for experiments, however, especially one involving inadequate craft and pilots with essentially no experience.[1]

The British freighter sailed from New York on 6 January 1944 in a convoy of twenty-six freighters, one British aircraft carrier, and three British escort destroyers, plus one oceangoing tug—a helicopter rescue vessel—bound for England. A winter storm battered the eastern seaboard. The convoy's speed was set at nine knots to accommodate the slowest ship, the *Daghestan*, which was also the smallest, at ten thousand tons. It rolled constantly ten to twenty degrees. The vessel yawed excessively, and its deck rose and fell about thirty feet. "My cabin-mate, Giles Montgomery, who had the lower bunk, was forced to sleep elsewhere because seawater was constantly flowing into our quarters, and with every roll of the ship, water would splash up on his bunk soaking the bedding," Graham chuckled as he remembered conditions in the British freighter.[2]

It was impossible in these conditions to make any type of shipboard helicopter landings. Flight operations were thwarted.

Four days out from New York through constant freezing rain, heavy snow showers, and strong winds from the northeast, the convoy joined thirteen Canadian vessels bound out from Halifax, Nova Scotia.

On the sixth day at sea, sounds of explosions had crews scrambling to abandon-ship positions. The grain-laden vessel with its special "highly secret classified" deck cargo went unsteadily to General Quarters. U-boat torpedoes had struck two freighters directly astern. Later, flames on the horizon confirmed the deadliness of the German attack. By dawn, three more ships lay on the Atlantic seabed. "After this torpedo attack," Graham recounts, "the crew of the good ship *Daghestan* began to realize and appreciate how lucky we were to be aboard a vessel, small, slow, and relatively inconspicuous among the much larger freighters and tankers in the convoy. We were probably overlooked by the German submarine captains as being insignificant and not worth wasting torpedoes on."[3]

A major storm struck the next day. Waves, driven by winds exceeding eighty knots, flushed three men off the nearby rescue tug *Perth*. On the *Daghestan* tumultuous seas swept critical helicopter parts in two crates from the decks, along with some ship's life rafts. Many of the lost helicopter parts were on loan, taken off Navy helicopters sitting at New York. The *Daghestan* was taking rolls of forty-five degrees when seas crushed a forward hatch, flooding a hold and soaking portions of its eight thousand tons of cargo. Water-swollen grain put the wallowing ship in a permanent five-degree port list, which added to the hazards of using the ship later as a helicopter launching stage.

Waves tumbled over the stern, drenching the two new Hoverfly helicopters lashed to the wooden flight deck. A stack of lumber on deck ruptured its bindings, and the loose timber ripped a hole through the fuselage of Royal Navy helicopter FT-834. A splintered two-by-four continued its ricocheting path through the airframe, damaging the rotor head. The jagged spear ended its trajectory by puncturing the port-side float and deflating the rubber pontoon.

The weather finally moderated northeast of the Azores on the tenth day at sea. This was an opportunity for the select crew to make their first try at shipboard/helicopter ASW operations. Helicopter development hung on fragile threads. Any failure now would be a perfect excuse to drop plans to continue with its development.

Graham First to Fly from Ship

Richard Garnett, a British commander on board,[4] asked each pilot, individually and "in private," if he thought the weather permitted flight operations.[5] Graham, then a twenty-six-year-old former U.S. Lighthouse Service Surfman, later discovered that he was the only one who thought flying from the ship was possible in the prevailing conditions. Furthermore, he was the least experienced helicopter pilot on the ship—with a mere sixty-five flight hours to his name—and had only qualified to land helicopters aboard the *Daghestan* the last week of November.[6]

"It was late afternoon," Graham continued, "when I made the decision that a successful flight could be accomplished." Even though the weather had abated, conditions were still harsh. Moving the float-equipped helicopter into position for installing the main rotor blades was a problem. "Wheeling" the helicopter in position with the vessel rolling fifteen degrees was dangerous. So instead of using the specially designed cart, sixteen men handed the twenty-two-hundred-pound craft into position.[7]

Next, the launching crew erected a precarious wind screen before attempting to install the rotor blades. The screen was a row of wooden two by fours, raised vertically and stuck down in the gap between the deck planking. The timbers reached up about seventeen feet. Darkness was approaching because of delays preparing for launch. Graham hurriedly "started the engine and engaged the rotors, revved up the engine and with the magnetos checked satisfactory," was ready for the "okay to take off" sign from the signaling officer. In his summary of the flight, Graham wrote simply: "I was airborne and proceeded to patrol along the columns of vessels in our convoy. Upon completion of the patrol I returned to the *Daghestan*."[8]

The operation was not quite as simple as Graham made it sound. He ended the flight by landing athwartships, into the relative wind, then on the ship's starboard beam. The ship, with its offset cargo, had a roll of up to fifteen degrees to port and ten to starboard. Graham flew the approach over the port (lee) quarter where he could see his target: the twenty-, thirty-, and forty-foot painted squares emanating from the center of the deck. After several attempts, Graham finally set the helicopter down off the lee corner of the deck, the tail boom hanging out over the ocean. This was the only way he could keep the tail rotor from striking the deck.

A flight on the following day established that helicopters could operate from cargo ships, but "Jeep" Cable, whom Graham describes as "a typical Britisher, great big walrus mustache, jungle boots and a real nice fellow," experienced the same difficulty in clearing the deck that Graham had had.[9] The helicopter's 180-hp engine was insufficient to follow the pitching deck on lift off. Then, Cable's final landing, following his thirty-minute flight around the convoy, "took skill to prevent the tail rotor from striking the deck. He ran into the same problems due to the rolling of the deck as Graham [experienced]."[10]

At-Sea Tests Inconclusive

The two British Hoverflys arrived in Liverpool, England, on 22 January and flew to a small airdrome on the city's edge. They were immediately covered with canvas tents, and armed guards were posted. The plan was to use the helicopters in picking up pilots downed in combat over the English Channel.

The Combined Board's formal evaluation concluded by calling for "some orientable gear for securing the helicopter to the deck immediately upon making contact during the landing." Further, they felt some form of capture and securing equipment was essential before shipboard landing operations could "be conducted efficiently with a minimum ground crew."[11]

Even the helicopters' promoters were in doubt about their effective use against submarines. "It had become evident by this time," noted Erickson, "that a suitable anti-submarine helicopter would not be ready in time to play an important part in the war effort."[12] And later, he confessed, "I suggested helos for anti-sub weapon because we had to develop that idea in order to get them." And as the project advanced, Erickson "thought about how easy it would be to blow yourself up with your own depth charges" if a submarine could even be located.[13]

Submarines at that time typically operated on the surface at night and during periods of low visibility. Helicopters could fly only in daylight and in reasonable visibility. The frail craft, extremely vulnerable to the antiaircraft weaponry mounted on German submarines by 1944, could not carry the armor plating already protecting the Avenger torpedo bombers, which were also able to deliver a two-thousand-pound ordnance load.[14] For the war against submarines in the Atlantic, the helicopter was too little too late. By May 1943 the wolf pack menace was ended—seven months before Graham's first test of an ASW mission from a ship at sea.[15] By July 1943, the Navy had already backed off in its support of the helicopter.

Kossler and Erickson's interest lay only in developing the helicopter's rescue potential. Now, by default, they were back in control of its development. Ultimately, however, it was the ASW role that kept helicopter development alive. Erickson later shifted his scheme, desperate to keep the program alive, to using the helicopter as a searcher for rather than a destroyer of submarines.

These events would come in the future, far after the war was over. In the meantime, CGAS Brooklyn was becoming a major helicopter training base, and Graham returned from England to continue as a helicopter instructor and experimental test pilot.

FIVE

MORE THAN
SATISFACTORY SUCCESS

Floyd Bennett Field, January 1944

G raham returned from England to Floyd Bennett Field to resume his job as helicopter instructor. Training of the second group of students was already near completion.[1] Erickson— flushed with earlier successes, his program moving along without interference—now had time to train students who would be instructors when the school opened formally to classes in the spring. He was free too to devote time to pursuing experimental work in developing rescue systems.

Public attention swept Erickson along as well. The many news articles generated by the blood plasma delivery in the days immediately following the *Turner* disaster roused the interest of Navy doctor Capt. J. D. Benjamin to the possibilities of using the helicopter as a flying ambulance.[2] Erickson seems to have anticipated this and others' interest. He certainly flew carefully contrived demonstrations to the widest audience possible. Very early on, he grew quite skillful as a promoter of the helicopter, principally through his devotional belief in the craft, which fired his overwhelming enthusiasm.

The air ambulance mission could hardly come as a surprise to anyone at Floyd Bennett Field. The daily exploits of Erickson and his "flying palm trees" were a constant curiosity wherever they flew.[3] A month before the doctor's sudden interest in the flying ambulance, Erickson had already practiced carrying the stretcher about the airport.

A flight test with the little trainer loaded to maximum weight began within days after Dr. Benjamin sent a letter to Capt. J. Adams, U.S. Navy Medical Corps, Division of Aviation Medicine, proposing that helicopters be used as air ambulances. Load-lifting tests in which the ballast stretchers were mounted externally proved satisfactory. The maximum useful load reached 865 pounds each on the two aircraft tested. "This aircraft could have flown away with this load," Erickson noted with reservations, but "this was nearly the maximum which could be handled under these conditions." Erickson's own weight accounted for 206 pounds of that total weight. The fuel and oil accounted for still more, leaving a small remainder for the stretcher and patients.[4]

Later on, Erickson found these results optimistically misleading because conditions at the time of testing were ideal for helicopter flight: at sea level, the temperature at freezing, with a high barometric reading. The hot muggy days of New York in summer, however, caused Erickson to doubt the helicopter's abilities. On those days he was forced to do a little creative thinking when he demonstrated the helicopter. Besides removing radios and batteries, he often used just enough fuel for the few minutes planned for the flight. (Ordinarily, standard fuel load for takeoff with two people on board was fifteen gallons, or about ninety pounds.)[5]

On one occasion on a hot, windless day, Erickson had a heavy passenger aboard, and he could not get the machine airborne. It sat lightly on the floats, bouncing and shuddering, but not flying. He shut down and swiftly departed the cockpit, leaving a slightly bewildered passenger in the left seat as he raced away toward the hangar, tossing back the excuse of needing to make an important phone call. Erickson sent Graham, at 135 pounds, out to successfully fly the weighty VIP.[6]

Another example of struggling with hefty passengers occurred because of the concern of Rear Adm. DeWitt C. Ramsey at BuAer about the helicopter's hovering performance. Earlier in the summer, Ramsey rode in an HNS at the new Naval Air Test Center, Patuxent River. It was hot on the western edge of the Chesapeake Bay, without helpful breezes, but even under those marginal circumstances, the craft flew. So on landing, Ramsey asked the pilot to take his aide up. "The aide weighed about 250 pounds," according to Erickson's version of the event. The helicopter did lift off and was airborne, and it immediately passed slowly over a building excavation. It did not have forward speed sufficient for translational lift,[7] however, and lost the ground cushion[8] as the ground abruptly dropped away. The overburdened helicopter ungracefully settled at full power, landing in the pit.[9]

A Year of Great Promise

The new year of 1944 began encouragingly. Erickson had his command, a helicopter training base, and a promotion. Next he selected a close friend, Lt. Comdr. W. J. "Red" Lawrence, as his executive officer and began training him with the first group of pilots. Years later, Erickson wrote: "Red and I were more than just good friends. You might say we were conspirators in putting across our schemes for these wonderful new flying machines that we had gotten our hands on. I had not had any support from any Academy grads before Red came along, but he was so eager to get going that I started giving him instruction when he showed up."[10]

Lawrence became the first Coast Guard officer from the academy to qualify as a helicopter pilot at the new school.

The first signs of trouble for Erickson came, though, within days of Lawrence qualifying and becoming chief flight instructor. Another officer with the name Lawrence, Lt. Comdr. J. G. "Joe" Lawrence, who outranked Red Lawrence, was ordered to the CGAS as executive officer. Erickson and Joe Lawrence were not friends. Because of this unexpected personnel assignment from headquarters, Erickson had to reassign Red Lawrence to training officer. These orders for Joe Lawrence began a strange chess game of officer assignments. It is not difficult to surmise that Kossler exerted his mastery in manipulation—this time in headquarters—for Joe Lawrence was transferred a few months later after qualifying in the aircraft he did not want to fly.

Coast Guard Fights Helicopter Development

Erickson and Kossler did not have to fight the Navy any longer; the Navy no longer tried to wrest projects away from Erickson. In fact, BuAer appeared to be most cooperative. It was the Coast Guard now that became his biggest enemy. Personalities clashed.

The Coast Guard was still a small organization despite the tenfold expansion through the war years. Starting in 1925, the Coast Guard initiated an aviation program that boasted fifty qualified aviators by 1937. That number swelled with new pilots and aviators by the close of World War II, but those in command were from the original small cadre of fifty and well known to each other. Erickson's critics came from among this group, and he knew it. Years later, he wrote, "I thought [Comdr. Stanley C.] Lindhom, who was Chief of the Aviation Operations Division, had sent Joe to check up on me and report back to him, although we didn't even come under Operations." Adm. Carl B. Olsen, at the time a captain working in Operations with Lindhom and for Adm. Robert Donohue,[11] said, "Frankie [Erickson] had a persecution complex. He always kept saying, 'the SOBs are after me.'"[12]

Technically, the helicopter training and development programs were under the direction of the Aviation Engineering Division in headquarters, which meant Kossler. Since he and Erickson both knew Operations was against the project, Kossler could avoid that headquarters branch and still have control through Personnel, obtaining assignments he desired. Kossler's position protected him; Erickson was exposed and vulnerable. As a result of this circumvention of the normal military chain of command, the helicopter training command eventually became a pitfall for Erickson that ensnared him in clashes with former academy classmates in an arena where he could not prevail.[13]

Plans for British Unit at Floyd Bennett

Meanwhile, training for the British staff began. Maj. J. Richardson of the Royal Army started flying with the second group of Coast Guard aviators and pilots beginning the third week of January 1944. He became the first of thirteen British officers who were eventually inducted for training by the Coast Guard for the Royal Navy and the Royal Air Force.[14] The British modified their plans to train about thirty Commonwealth (that is, Canadian, New Zealand, and Australian) pilots in the United States, in addition to the thirteen RN and RAF aviators trained by the Coast Guard. Their aim was to use the first trained as instructors for three, two-month-long classes of ten students each, starting in May and ending in about October 1944. Then the helicopter training would move to England to handle the Commonwealth trainees.

Among their schemes was a plan where some of the earliest helicopter qualified British pilots would assist in the upcoming flight instruction while others would return to England to establish the new course there by October. This British plan to leave the United States was based, in part, on information relayed in secret documents from the British Air Commission in Washington, D.C., to the Admiralty in London. The classified message divulged information that the Coast Guard was proposing to move the helicopter training school to Florida about the end of September. According to the British document, there was "insufficient space at Floyd Bennett Field and no other sites are available." Where this information came from was never disclosed. There were no confirming documents concerning a move to Florida; Erickson was unaware of the impending move, nor did he even suggest a move from New York.

Further pressure leading to the British departure was exerted when a written agreement with the Navy elapsed authorizing them to remain only through December 1944, and then only with a restricted enrollment. So the Coast Guard's helicopter training school, to begin in the spring of 1944, was doomed to close—at least that portion devoted to the support of the British—before it began. Erickson and Kossler appeared to be manipulated once again, this time by unknown forces.[15]

Even the alternate British training plans did not gel. Tardy production of aircraft at Sikorsky, plus mechanical delays with the delivered fleet, slowed the project. Furthermore, Erickson was devoting substantial time to his rescue helicopter research and training *his* cadre of new instructors for an expected surge of Coast Guard and Navy flight students. The British eventually felt that the Coast Guard would not fulfill the British goals for trained pilots and proposed that after the first of the pilots were qualified, the British would take over and set up their "own training unit at Floyd Bennett Field," instructing British and Commonwealth aviators, "but working with and under the direction of the U.S.C.G. unit."[16]

Recruiting qualified pilots from the ranks of Commonwealth subjects soon became a problem, however. All qualified pilots were needed for the air war over Britain at the time. To remedy this shortfall, the RN proposed to adjust the strict physical requirements and to increase the maximum age from thirty to thirty-five. "In the D.N.A.D.'s [Director of Naval Air Division's] opinion, it would be extravagant to convert fully qualified pilots for these duties, except possibly for a few instructors." Moreover, this opinion was "supported by the R.A.F."[17]

No one in a supervisory position yet knew of the physical requirements for helicopters, nor were they aware of the inherent dangers associated with flying the new experimental craft. Consequently, the Admiralty director suggested "flying pay at a slightly lower rate than for fully qualified pilots should be granted."[18] These presumptions met with a countering opinion from someone by the name of Boyd (only signature legible):

> We are introducing into the Naval Service an entirely new type of flying machine which, if successful, may have a very great effect on our anti-submarine warfare. This flying machine will have to land on a small platform in a ship under conditions which will call for very great skill on the part of the pilot. If, therefore, we are to make a success of this operation, I consider we shall require a pilot who is very much alert and has a high degree of skill. He will not be carrying an observer, and his responsibilities whilst engaged on anti-submarine patrols, and returning to land on the ship after a tiring flight, will be similar to any other, or so it appears at the moment. We may find we can accept men of lower standard later on, but we should not start with that idea.[19]

Notwithstanding this viewpoint, the early British fliers experienced difficulty completing the course. Of the 102 aviators and pilots undergoing training, eight did not finish. Training was terminated for three of the original contingent of thirteen British aviators. Only one Coast

Guard aviator did not qualify in the group of seventy-one trained. Four others from the group of Navy, NACA, CAA, and manufacturers' test pilots withdrew for other reasons (see appendix C). One additional student, with no previous aviation training qualifications, or experience, completed the course satisfactorily.

Erickson's and Graham's earlier experience working with the British at the Sikorsky plant led to an amiable and cooperative relationship between the allies. One minor incident occurred just as the Coast Guard began training the British, however, which showed a conflict in military customs between the two nations. Erickson recounted, "one of our nonconformist British autogyro pilots was approaching . . . for a landing over a concrete sea wall." The helicopter fell short of the intended touch-down spot and settled awkwardly on top of the wall, with the landing gear hooked on the fore side which thus prevented the aircraft from tumbling back into the bay. "It just sat there rocking back and forth with its tail over the sea wall." Upon seeing this, Red Lawrence— "a good man in an emergency"—rushed from the operations office, crawled into the left seat, and flew the helicopter out of its predicament. Lawrence quickly discovered that the British pilot was drunk. "The station had a wardroom beer mess that was supposed to be closed until after working hours," declared Erickson, "but some of the students were having a few after breakfast. That was the end of the beer mess."[20]

Rescues and Simulators

Erickson was soon able to display the rescue capability he was developing. Bolton flew an HNS with simulated stretcher patients strapped to the sides for the 30 January 1944 demonstration for members of the Truman Committee. General Lowe was again at this demonstration. The weather made the demonstrations even more spectacular, for Bolton was flying in winds that gusted to forty knots. Erickson laconically reported, "All flights were conducted with more than satisfactory success."[21]

When he began his helicopter flight training, Erickson asked BuAer for training devices to aid in teaching the unique task performed by the helicopter pilot. As with the helicopter itself, no precedent had been established on which to base this work. Erickson asked for a landing platform that simulated the rolling and pitching of a ship's deck and for a second device, namely, a flyable cockpit simulator—something that was not built again until nearly two decades later, with the advent of computer-controlled simulators.

As a result of Erickson's queries, Donald Dodge, of the Atlantic Elevator Company, and Lt. (jg) E. K. Smith, U.S. Navy, BuAer Special

Devices Division, toured the Brooklyn air station the last week in January 1944, conducting research for the design of a helicopter synthetic trainer. They flew aboard an HNS to experience the flight characteristics needed in a mechanical device, and they measured space in the hangar where the trainer would be suspended.[22]

Earlier, when Erickson was still flying at the Sikorsky factory, Navy commander Louis De Flores, chief of the Special Devices Division, BuAer, responding to Erickson's request, visited Bridgeport to determine what devices might be needed for the new helicopter school at New York. The episode that followed illustrates the tasks Erickson had to undertake to overcome the conflicts between the Army Air Forces and the Navy.

Visitor access to the plant was still under Army control at that time. Consequently, Erickson revealed, "There was considerable friction between the Army and Navy at that time regarding helicopters." De Flores "was unable to get in the plant to examine an R-4." So Erickson flew the helicopter alone on the short flight to Seaside Park, where De Flores boarded—away from the plant and the Army's control—for a one-hour-flight demonstration.[23]

Settling into a Routine

Preparation for the convening of a formal school to train pilots and mechanics continued through the winter and spring of 1944. Pilots were trained, then qualified to teach others in just a few weeks. Mechanics learned to maintain the aircraft used in the immediate training and did the experimental work; they also qualified as instructors for the maintenance ground school offered to the enlisted mechanics. "Because of the lack of suitable books on helicopter subjects," Erickson explained, "it was necessary to write the required texts from data then available, much of which had been gained from personal flight experience."[24] Lt. Comdr. O. R. Smeder, U.S. Coast Guard, in charge of the ground school, wrote most of the texts.

The Navy was still leaving Kossler and Erickson alone in the helicopter development project. They appeared to maintain only a token effort in accepting the helicopter. For example, only eight Navy officers were sent to qualify during the entire program, whereas seventy-one pilots and aviators were assigned from the Coast Guard. One Navy officer was dropped—or withdrew—almost immediately, and two others never completed the course. Even Erickson's weekly progress reports were too much of a bother for BuAer.

From the project's start, Kossler directed Erickson to report weekly on progress while he was at the Sikorsky plant. The plant had no Navy or

BuAer representative as a result of the Army's exclusionary policy toward the Navy, which came about because of the earlier conflicts over helicopter development. As a result, BuAer requested Erickson as their insider to provide a summary "outlining the progress made on the various model helicopters; estimates of completion; trial and delivery dates." BuAer also sought "such other technical information determined from time to time which has or may have a bearing on present or future operations of this type of aircraft."[25]

Erickson typed this report each week even after he moved to CGAS Brooklyn. He noted the hours flown, named each student, and summarized their progress, plus he recorded the total time on each aircraft. Likewise, he noted reoccurring maintenance discrepancies and his problems acquiring parts, along with other minor matters. He briefly summarized who had visited and the results of tests, plus the status of research. Chiefly, his efforts were to configure a rescue helicopter, but his research did include performance evaluations typically done at the Navy's test center. Normally, these reports were concise, not longer than two pages.[26]

No documents from the Coast Guard or Navy containing responses, questions, or a request for additional specific information raised by his reports have been discovered. Erickson's correspondence also indicates no responses to unrecorded queries. This evidence perhaps shows the general apathy to Erickson's helicopter development scheme within both services. It was not too many weeks after Erickson began filing these reports before Russell at BuAer bluntly noted, "[A] semi-monthly report is sufficient for this office."[27]

The British pilots arrived in March 1944 at Floyd Bennett Field. Erickson graduated three more of his Coast Guard pilots as instructors to assume the load which, by the middle of that month, rose to twenty-one students.[28]

Another In-Flight Emergency

It is strange to imagine that two people so important to the development of the helicopter should ever choose to fly together, especially when they had had a near disaster only six months earlier, but fly together they did. Erickson reported in his usual indirect writing style, "Kossler and I had an unforgettable experience."[29]

The event was the flight to deliver a Navy HNS to the new Naval Air Test Center at Patuxent River, Maryland, on 21 March. Kossler went because it was convenient transportation back to his office in Washington, D.C. The weather was "beautiful," but they ran into a rain shower just out of Baltimore. "We knew that the fabric on the leading edge of the main rotor blades was not properly protected, but our efforts to get something done about it were in vain." Erickson landed the helicopter in Baltimore "to have a look." They both agreed the "fabric showed definite signs of wear." However, Kossler pushed to continue the flight when the rains diminished. He expressed his disgust "that a little rain could ground us when the solution to the problem was so simple." Sitting in the helicopter waiting to go, he snapped, "If the damn blades can't take it, it's about time people found out about it!"[30]

They resumed the flight, and near Fort Meade, over a heavily wooded forest, they heard the sound of a loud crack through the steady engine roar and transmission whine. A section of fabric on one blade ruptured. The imbalance in lift from the damaged blade fed back into the control system with such force that Erickson could barely hang on to the stick slapping itself around the cockpit. "There was a small clearing ahead," Erickson recalled, "but Kossler, who was very cool in emergencies, calmly said, 'There is a bigger field over here,' and pointed to a spot on his side that was slightly aft of the helicopter. Somehow I managed to keep the stick from getting away as we circled, then made a straight-in approach to a clearing that turned out to be a Soya bean patch."[31]

The landing was successful, but the danger was not over until the damaged flapping-blade stopped. The cyclic control stick, wrote Erickson, "continued to whip around until the rotor came to a stop." The missing fabric near the blade's tip created a giant whistle. The loud quavering screech caused by the air passing over bare spar and ribs spinning near the speed of sound "brought people from miles around the area." A two-foot section of fabric had torn loose from one blade; the fabric was nearly worn through on the others.[32]

One pleasing result of this near catastrophe was that the long-awaited protective strips arrived immediately afterwards. They were quickly installed on all the helicopter blades in service.[33]

Shipboard Landings and Expanded Training

On 1 April the Coast Guard accepted the helicopter training deck, christened USS *Mal de Mer* and built by the Special Devices Division of BuAer. It simulated the conditions landing aboard a ship at sea by rolling five to ten degrees with a period of ten seconds. Soon, actual landings aboard the cutter *Cobb*, the first U.S. vessel to be outfitted with a deck designed for helicopter landings, began. The *Cobb* was assigned to the Coast Guard Training Command at Manhattan Beach.

The former coastal passenger steamer acquired from the War Shipping Administration had its superstructure cut down and a thirty-eight-by-sixty-three-foot flight deck added aft. Other major modifications and the addition of armor to the then-thirty-eight-year-old ship fitted the vessel out for a role in coastal antisubmarine warfare. It had been recommissioned on 20 July 1943, but, due to aging engines and weak framing, the cutter saw little duty except to serve as a training ship for helicopter landings.[34] The first landings aboard the new helicopter deck took place on 15 June 1944.[35]

Erickson's empire was in control and growing beyond his dreams. He had only just qualified as a helicopter pilot nine months earlier and now he was in command of a rapidly growing training unit with major research and development projects. A further boost for his dream came in early April when Waesche testified before the House Appropriations Committee in support of the 1945 Navy Department appropriations for 210 Coast Guard helicopters for that year. Waesche disclosed in his arguments to the committee that the "Coast Guard has been assigned the duty of carrying on extensive experimentation in connection with the use of helicopters, both aboard ship and at coastal stations in connection with both anti-submarine warfare and air-sea rescue operations."[36] While this might have been an overstatement, and the first official recognition of the SAR (search-and-rescue) role, it was exactly what Kossler and Erickson wanted.

The only order for helicopter development was still the CNO directive of 15 February 1943 to BuAer for ASW development. No documentation was ever found that ordered any experiments or development in anything but ASW for the helicopter. But Erickson unhesitatingly conducted experiments in other areas where he and Kossler thought the helicopter might be useful as well. Most of these activities were mentioned but briefly in his "Progress Reports." He did not mention experiments conducted in ASW until months later. No one checked his adventurism, so he continued his course and grew bolder. But quiet grumblings were beginning to pass between Coast Guard officers along the passageways in headquarters.

Erickson accelerated his already fast pace. The Coast Guard augmented the training program to supply the pilots and mechanics needed to support the 210 helicopters expected within months. Erickson also had to train enough instructors for the British so that they could, in turn, train the pilots and crew needed to operate the 250 helicopters they had on order.[37] The British established a separate flight syllabus with their instructors but attended the Coast Guard's ground school directed by Smeder.

Erickson formalized the flight curriculum. The first classes of the six-week training course for aviators for U.S. military service began on 4 June

1944. Thus, service-wide operational training in helicopters began just six months after the formation of the helicopter training school.[38] Only three flyable helicopters were on hand, however, when the one Navy and five Coast Guard aviators, plus seventeen Coast Guard aviation machinist mates, reported for training on 1 June. On the same date, Peat took command of the British shore-based unit named as a ship, HMS *Saker*.[39] That unit began with its own four aircraft in separate spaces. One British helicopter, however, the FT-839—the only one equipped with floats—was shared. As the need arose later, the two schools shared other helicopters.[40]

Training Slows as Summer Progresses

Warm summer weather suddenly revealed problems. Erickson explained, "Training during the period was slack, first because of lack of aircraft and second because of poor performance of these available." He went on to clarify, "During the calm, hot, humid weather dual instruction could not be carried out." The only aircraft on floats crashed due to the hot weather and "inattention by the pilot." Most of the training craft were stripped of radio equipment and side doors to reduce weight.[41]

The unit received six more new helicopters by 20 July. Training flights accelerated, thus permitting the first class to graduate on schedule. The second regular class of twelve pilots, all Coast Guard, reported on 1 August and did even better by completing the course in five weeks. The third regular class, again all Coast Guard, reported on 4 September. No one ever recorded comments about the lack of the Navy's participation in training, and Erickson did not broach the subject or ask for Navy pilots for his school.

The Navy, in the summer of 1944, recognized it had more urgent needs for pilots in seats of combat aircraft. It was also beginning a planned reduction in the number of new pilots in training. The slowly developing helicopter was not ready, nor would it be, to assist in the war effort. Grumman was then manufacturing more than five hundred F6F Hellcats a month, and General Motors was producing nearly three hundred TBM Avengers in the same time. More than ten thousand of the famous "Corsairs" were built throughout the war. These figures are only partial numbers of the cockpits that needed filling each month from all aircraft manufacturers. In June 1944 the chief of naval operations issued plans which called for a "drastic reduction in the pilot training program."[42] The Navy just did not have pilots for a rather insignificant helicopter project.

Two more helicopters arrived in New York from Sikorsky on 8 September, bringing the total number of Navy helicopters to eleven.

By this time, the Royal Navy Helicopter School was operating six of their own from the station. Seventeen helicopters buzzing between the Coast Guard air station, the training field at Rockaway, the *Mal de Mer*, and the *Cobb*, cruising the waters of Long Island Sound, "resembled the flitting of a swarm of dragon flies."[43]

Kossler opted to qualify with the first class in helicopters and completed the course on 1 July, becoming Coast Guard helicopter pilot number twenty-five. He moved his office from the headquarters in Washington, D.C., to CGAS Brooklyn, "where he could remain in closer contact with current helicopter developments."[44]

This move may have been a mistake, because he was thus removing himself from the halls of power in headquarters where dissension among officers against the helicopter and Erickson was mounting. In his single-minded effort to establish the helicopter as a rescue craft, Erickson maneuvered recklessly around in the military chain of command. He did work through Kossler, and Kossler did go through his superior to his close friend Commandant Waesche, but this streamlined routing missed important offices in Coast Guard headquarters. This simple expedient for Erickson and Kossler soon started a crack within the Coast Guard aviation ranks that later swelled into a major schism. Strong feelings and polarization among officers eventually led to a conflict between rotary-wing proponents and seaplane advocates.

Erickson established an excellent rapport with influential dignitaries. When called on—and they were—these Erickson supporters outside the Navy and Coast Guard commands could assert substantial influence in getting Erickson what he wanted. (The ire this raised among his detractors was intense, feelings that are still apparent half a century later in interviews among individuals who were involved with Erickson. On the other hand, few remember Kossler or any role he played in helicopter development.)

Erickson's direct approach to influential leaders inside and out of the military was unabashed. On one such occasion, for example, Erickson offered to fly a U.S. senator—on a visit to evaluate the usefulness of the helicopter—to Manhattan to catch his train. Because the winds near the Battery were gusting to forty knots, making that landing spot "extremely turbulent in the lee of the buildings," Erickson continued up the Hudson River and landed in Riverside Park, where the senator hailed a cab to the train station. This should have been the end of the anecdote except that the park commissioner learned later of the helicopter landing and threatened legal action. One day, when he appeared at the Coast Guard air station to request a ride to view one of his projects from a helicopter, Erickson "gladly made the flight in the interest of better relations with the city and as a 'favor to the Commissioner.'"[45]

On another occasion, Erickson sent photos of helicopters landing on the *Cobb* to the Coast Guard's director of public relations with information for an article. He suggested, "[W]e have the material for a really good story in one of the major magazines, perhaps *Life* or *Collier's*." He further noted, in an ironic tone, "We have had such excellent cooperation with the Bureau of Aeronautics that I believe the story should be a joint one giving fully as much publicity to the Navy as to the Coast Guard."[46] Actually, at the time that statement was probably true. BuAer no longer tried to control helicopter development as they had attempted to a year earlier. They were cooperating with some of the experiments and providing experts when Erickson sought them.

A further example of Erickson's attempts to draw attention to his helicopters was when he had two HNSs fly around the Statue of Liberty. A photograph of a helicopter just above the statue, "marked a change," he later wrote, "in the Navy's [reluctant] position on helicopter publicity."[47] Language in Erickson's correspondence late in the summer of 1944 reveals his optimism, recorded in lighthearted phrases. He was on top now; he was getting his way. Of that promotional photo he remembered:

> The occasion was a Fourth of July War Bond rally. Red [Lawrence] was in charge of the flight of two helos taking part. I suggested that one helo line up just back of and slightly above the torch so it would appear . . . that the torch was actually supporting the helo. They came back with a remarkable photo which I thought had been made according to my suggestion. Some years later I was explaining to a group how that photo was obtained, when Rebel Berry, who was then a warrant officer, spoke up and said, "Hell, Captain, we were right over the torch, so close I could have spit on it!" . . . In fact I'm glad I didn't know because the Army Colonel who was responsible for the protection of the statue threatened to have me court-martialed for endangering the Statue of Liberty, so it was just as well I didn't know.[48]

In an unusual request, General Lowe asked Erickson if he, the general, might "devote most of October and perhaps the first week or two of November, if necessary, to a course of instruction on helicopters." He explained he wanted to "be more intimately acquainted with the characteristics of the beast," in order to make his recommendations to the Truman Committee. The general wanted just a small room and expected no social activities on his behalf. "It would suit me perfectly if I could be quartered and subsisted there in your main building, providing this could be done without inconvenience to anyone. I know you will be frank in telling me whether or not this is at all agreeable to you."[49]

The fifty-nine-year-old general, a nonaviator, did go through an abbreviated syllabus. He did not solo but satisfied Graham he could fly a helicopter alone. Erickson flew the general on most of the earlier training flights. However, as each man weighed more than two hundred pounds—Lowe was "way over"—Graham stood in as tutor on warm-weather days when the helicopter refused to budge off the tarmac with Erickson and Lowe aboard.[50]

As a result of their earlier meetings and time together in the training environment, both men acquired a strong admiration and respect for each other. This esteem grew into a friendship quickly, with both "Franks" on a first-name basis. Although Erickson knew Lowe's position could catapult him and his program, and so it was in his best interest to use his relationship with the general, he did not, out of deference to that friendship.[51] Lowe saw in Erickson a man with dedication to a dream with promise, and though he had significantly more important matters to occupy his time during the war, he supported Erickson.

Lowe introduced Erickson's project to several high-ranking Army officers. One was Brig. Gen. William "Wild Bill" Donovan, chief of the Office of Strategic Services (OSS, forerunner of the CIA), who flew to Floyd Bennett Field to examine this new flying machine. Donovan told Erickson he had an urgent need for helicopters but was unable to get them from the Army Air Forces. Shortly following his visit with Erickson, Donovan asked the Navy for a Coast Guard helicopter detachment, to be assigned to the OSS. Lowe later wrote Erickson confirming that Donovan's request "was approved by Admiral Horne, the Chief of Naval Operations," but Erickson heard nothing more about it.[52]

Lowe was quick to praise and praise heartily. Immediately following his return to Washington after qualifying in the helicopter, Lowe called Admiral Waesche to tell him: "I had a most pleasant and impressive experience. I haven't run into anything in my years of amateur and professional service that made a stronger appeal to me than that entire activity and the way it is administered."[53] The old Army man was bewildered by the conduct of the sailors in Erickson's command. "I was dumbfounded to find that they had no brig in the station [and] that they couldn't remember when they had had any arrest. I never saw a man under any influence of alcohol or under any other untoward circumstances. Dammed if I ever saw anything like it. I never saw anything work so."[54]

Furthermore, Lowe was flabbergasted to learn that only three of the officers were "regular" Coast Guard. "The rest of those young officers were all enlisted men that you [the commandant] brought up through the ranks, and I was tremendously impressed with that staff."

Finally, the old general revealed, "I had quite a considerable bit of experience in the Army in schools of instruction in the last war and this and I never saw a better designed, better prepared, or better executed course in my life." His praise echoed through empty halls, however.[55]

The School's Demise

Erickson continued to be optimistic. The aviation training was being accomplished without major mishaps and on schedule. The quality of instruction both in the classroom and in flight was excellent, even though he was teaching an entirely new subject and had no precedents to follow. New helicopter pilots were receiving seventy to eighty hours of flight training to qualify.[56]

The Royal Navy Helicopter School departed for England in December, taking their aircraft with them. The first leg of their journey was flying twelve of their thirteen Hoverflys from Floyd Bennett Field to Norfolk, Virginia. There they boarded a carrier and sailed for England. The British training unit's former commanding officer, Peat, stayed on a few more weeks in New York to evaluate the new R-6 helicopter coming off the production line.

This was the beginning of the end for the new helicopter training base in Brooklyn. The joint operation at Floyd Bennett Field that had benefited both countries ceased. The early British interest in helicopters and the Royal Army's willingness to buy great numbers were the most important elements boosting the Coast Guard's position on acquiring helicopters at all. The helicopter pioneers trained at Floyd Bennett Field later "were destined to play important roles in the development of the new helicopters that emerged on both sides of the Atlantic during the post war period."[57]

All helicopter training was terminated when the sixth regular Coast Guard class graduated on 6 February 1945. The school was closed.

THE ROAD AHEAD

January 1944

Concurrent with the opening of the new helicopter school, Erickson began to engage in development and promotional activities that had not been directed or authorized, all in pursuit of his goals to create the rescue helicopter. Frequently, as some who worked with him at Floyd Bennett Field remembered, he would dash out of his office shouting out a new idea to try.

Erickson collected individuals from his cadre of pilots and either outlined projects for them to pursue when they were not teaching, or he would round up his aircraft mechanics and explain what new device he wanted fabricated. Now that he had the chance to prove his dream for the perfect rescue vehicle, Erickson did not hesitate to involve his aircraft and fledgling crews in experiments.

The first task toward his goal proved quite simple. He substituted a helicopter for the fixed-wing aircraft used on missions already performed by the Brooklyn air station. The air station sent airplanes out daily on harbor patrols. These planes were usually twin-engine JRF or J4F Grumman amphibians deployed to deter sabotage and check vessel movement in the busy wartime New York port.

The limitations of an airplane flying harbor-patrol missions at 85 to 120 knots were obvious. Just as obvious to Erickson was how much more the helicopter could do. Fitted with a loud hailer, it could "speak" any vessel in the harbor, overcoming strictures imposed by a conflict in radio frequencies available between units, radio silence in wartime, or no radios at all. Helicopters could transfer confidential messages or special equipment directly to or between ships even while they were under way. A helicopter was also an excellent platform from which to detect oil-contaminated waters and to readily recover samples.[1]

The first example of a now common mission was when Lt. David Gershowitz, U.S. Coast Guard, flew an inhalator to a vessel in Long Island Sound that was surrounded by ice, which blocked surface craft from approaching with aid. On another occasion, Lt. (jg) Barney Mazonson lowered Lt. Comdr. James L. Baker, the Coast Guard air station's medical officer, to a vessel at sea so he could treat crewmen who had been injured in a shipboard explosion.

Not unexpectedly, the helicopter's greatest advantage over the airplane in port safety and security came from its ability to land on the water or land in the immediate vicinity of need. Because of this proximity, crews could be on hand to thwart or investigate questionable activities, or they might lend timely assistance in crucial situations. For example, one helicopter delivered a fire extinguisher to Jamaica Bay and lowered it to fire fighters unable to get their equipment to a Long Island Railroad trestle fire.

Erickson installed a loudspeaker on an HNS, and in tests it proved to work better than one on an airplane. As a result, Erickson proposed, in his eclectic justifications, that the helicopter would "be of value in directing landing operations or gunfire without the necessity of resorting to radio, or for directing either waterborne vehicular traffic, or be of service in hurricane and disaster warning duty."[2]

"There was just one use for the helicopter Frank did not think up," Graham remembered. That was its use as a plane guard aboard a Navy aircraft carrier.[3] New pilots training in Erickson's school in 1944, however, were told "a helicopter could take off from a carrier, pick up the personnel of planes shot down in combat and return them to the carrier without requiring any ships in the group to stop."[4]

Erickson as Visionary

The modern Coast Guard helicopter pops up frequently on television news programs showing its use in flood relief throughout the United States. It is a common but nevertheless spectacular and highly effective mission. This function was envisioned by Erickson in the helicopter's embryonic development period and was mentioned in the first school's course material.[5] Erickson's instructors suggested more than nineteen other uses for the helicopter now essential in today's society.[6] Many went on to influence the policies of the Federal Aviation Administration, manufacturers, the Army, the Navy, and the Coast Guard years later.

One such operation entails coordinated maneuvers between the ship and its own helicopter. Young Coast Guard officers learned that the "searching range of a cutter could be greatly increased and made more effective if correlated with a helicopter."[7] Consequently, most Coast Guard and many naval ships today have permanent helicopter landing pads.

Among his early successful schemes was Erickson's use of helicopters for torpedo recovery work in testing and practice runs. Erickson's enthusiastic summary claimed that the helicopter could remain with the torpedo throughout the run, regardless of its course and speed. The helicopter became so effective that eventually one HNS was assigned to the Naval Torpedo Range, Newport, Rhode Island.[8]

The helicopter's future, however, was still threatened by its own flight limitations. The general instability of the aircraft required the pilot to constantly refer to the physical surroundings. He had to see outside to maintain attitude control. Night flying was possible only with clear visibility and a well-lighted landing area; the aircraft did not have landing lights.[9] Instrument flights were not possible. This restriction, along with the helicopter's limited capacity to carry weight and its short range, kept this seemingly remarkable machine from being anything but a novelty.

Erickson was well aware of these restrictions and set his priorities accordingly. He began immediately to equip the aircraft with standard flight instruments borrowed from fixed-winged airplanes. He also attempted to design some form of automatic pilot. The nature of controlling a helicopter in flight at that time demanded the constant deft use of both the pilot's hands and feet. As student Lt. (jg) S. A. Constantino cleverly described it:

Remember when you first learned to ride a bicycle? You kept wiggling the front wheel in radical motions from left to right to keep your balance. And remember when you first learned to ice skate? Your ankles wiggled, you were afraid to take long strides, your arms waved wildly about, and occasionally you'd get a little confidence—too much—and fall on your fanny. And the first time you tried to park the car on a steep hill—well—what I'm getting at is that there's a striking similarity between learning to fly a helicopter and learning to ride a bicycle, to ice skate and to park a car on a steep hill all at the same time. And you might throw in a fancy rumba with that too.[10]

The *Pilot's Flight Operating Instructions* states: "This model cannot be flown 'hands-off' since there are no centralizing forces created by the main rotor. The stick must be held all the time during rotor operation, both on the ground and in the air."[11] The simple task of tuning a radio was impossible without releasing a control and possibly jeopardizing stable flight. Morris describes helicopter flight best when he writes, "It is a strangely slippery feeling." The test pilot and first helicopter instructor further noted, "[I]t feels like trying to balance on top of a beach ball in the water." [12]

Erickson soon determined from his early trials that "control of helicopters on airplane-type instruments without reference to ground contact has proven fully practical."[13] It would be many years, however, and the addition of various forms of automatic stabilization designed into the helicopter's control system before this statement was meaningful and not just an optimistic boast.

The Sperry Company, at Erickson's invitation, made an extensive study to develop an automatic pilot for helicopters, but its early trials failed despite Erickson's encouragement and cooperation. So he began experimenting on his own and later designed and patented a mechanical flight control system that provided the pilot some hands-off control in forward flight. Sikorsky later designed a synthetic stabilization system, which included the critical hovering maneuver, to be operational in all flight modes. Although Erickson's design did not get past his early experiments, it did show his uncanny genius for understanding the helicopter and his ability to do something under the pressures of time constraints and criticism from experts. His contemporaries ignored him and refused to speak to him because of his outspoken staunch position, which they considered useless.[14]

Variations on a Theme

One of the schemes coming from Erickson's office in New York was a plan to have Coast Guard helicopter air stations spotted along all U.S. coastlines, their coverage overlapping. This was not a new idea; Erickson just revised one that had been implemented by the Coast Guard's earlier components. The Life-Saving Service was "the foundation upon which the U.S. Coast Guard's reputation in rescue rests."[15] As a person deeply devoted to clutching mariners from hazards of the sea, Erickson's ideas built on past successes. Congressman William A. Newall of New Jersey authored an amendment to a lighthouse bill in 1848 that provided for "surf boats, rockets, cannonades, and other necessary apparatus for the better protection of life and property from shipwrecks."[16] This ten-thousand dollar appropriation was the beginning of a federal network of lifesaving stations that eventually came under the Treasury Department's Bureau of Revenue Marine.

In 1871 a veteran Treasury Department employee, Sumner Increase Kimball, took over the poorly managed Revenue Marine. He also inherited a badly run network of lifesaving stations. Over the next seven years, he whipped the stations into order and, in 1878, became the first, and only, General Superintendent of the U.S. Life-Saving Service, still under the Treasury. The lifesaving stations covered much of the coastal sections of the United States. In 1915, the U.S. Life-Saving Service amalgamated with the U.S. Revenue Cutter Service to form the U.S. Coast Guard.[17] Erickson's idea was to re-create this now obsolete coastal rescue service, replacing the famous "surf boats" with helicopters.

Erickson's proposition did not stop with service to mariners in peril. He felt "helicopters assigned to Coast Guard Stations on the West Coast could, along with 'life boat' service, provide assistance to the Forest Service in fire patrol work" as well.[18] Like many of his early schemes, however, it was never acted on.

Helicopters Begin Work for the Navy

At a time when BuAer was being lethargic, some people in the Navy Department expressed interest in procuring help from Erickson's helicopters. The Brooklyn Navy Yard asked for one helicopter, half a day, once a week, to be used as a target to calibrate ships' fire-control radars. Conventional methods using surface targets were insufficient for the new challenge posed by Japan's kamikaze threat, which was mounting in the Pacific. A controllable airborne radar target for calibration became essential. Requests for radar-calibration flights increased almost immediately after the first helicopter flights in mid-April proved so successful. A "wire mesh screen" was installed on the bottom of the aircraft "to improve reflecting qualities." According to Erickson's report to BuAer, "The radar office at the [Brooklyn] Navy Yard reported excellent results."[19]

It was on one of these missions that this impotent fighting machine, in its battle for recognition, accidentally upset Navy protocol. Normally, when working with Navy warships, the helicopter pilot communicated via radio directly with the ship. On occasion, however, a pilot would fly directly from a training mission to the ship. Often on dual flights—where the instructor and student flew together—the radio would be removed from the aircraft. This was the situation when "Lt. (jg) Barney Mazonson took off without a radio to calibrate the fire control radars on the newly commissioned aircraft carrier USS *Bennington*," anchored in Gravesend Bay.[20]

Typically, calibration flights required a helicopter to remain over a fixed position on the ground at an altitude between five and six thousand feet.

This was virtually impossible for the HNS with two pilots aboard if the winds at altitude were less than fifteen knots. Flying at speeds less than this, the helicopter is hovering, an impossibility for the HNS in rarefied air.

Mazonson was flying with Comdr. R. E. Doll, U.S. Navy, who would soon be assigned to BuAer as a rotary-wing design officer. Without a radio with which to conduct a briefing with the ship's CIC, Mazonson elected to simply land aboard the aircraft carrier's vast empty flight deck for the briefing.

"All hell broke loose," Mazonson told Erickson, "when the helicopter touched down!" He was rudely informed that the landing of the first aircraft aboard a carrier is an occasion calling for a special celebration. "[A] slick combat airplane is afforded this honor. But when an insignificant looking helicopter settled down on the deck, it was too much for the captain." Neither the commanding officer, nor the executive officer, nor the operations officer was aware of the scheduled radar calibration, at least that it involved a Coast Guard helicopter. The captain refused to talk to either Mazonson or Doll and gave orders for "flight quarters" to clear the deck of this aberration. The flight deck was then prepared for a normal launch of fixed-winged aircraft. Mazonson unceremoniously "lifted the helicopter clear of the deck and took off backwards over the side." An amused Erickson wrote, "I think the captain got the point!"[21]

(Ten years later Coast Guard helicopters again landed on the *Bennington*. An explosion followed by fires below decks wracked the aircraft carrier while it was cruising about seventy-five miles off the New England coast.

The Navy had only experienced one peacetime disaster in which the loss of life had been heavier. When word of the disaster reached the First Coast Guard District, two HO4S helicopters from the Salem Air Station were immediately dispatched to the scene. The helicopters, piloted by Lt.'s Thomas G. Condon and Richard M. Underwood landed on board the *Bennington* and began shuttling badly burned personnel to the Naval Hospital at Newport, Rhode Island. A total of thirty-four, who were in the most urgent need of attention, were flown ashore."[22])

Mazonson's landing on the *Bennington* "was the only misunderstanding" during the two years the Coast Guard provided the radar calibration service. Moreover, it was the success of this operation that eventually forced the Navy to accept the helicopter into service. The Brooklyn Navy Yard commandant, gratified with the early success credited to helicopters, wrote the CNO with the recommendation "that the helicopter service be continued without interruption."[23]

The helicopter's reputation as a target spread. Soon the shipyards at Philadelphia and Boston as well as New York sought Erickson for this service. On one occasion a helicopter even journeyed on board a Navy ship to Norfolk, Virginia, to complete calibration while under way in the ship's urgent run to combat. After the helicopter school closed, CGAS Brooklyn continued to support the calibration flights until the Navy formed its first helicopter squadron, VX-3, which was commissioned at Floyd Bennett Field on 1 July 1946 and moved to Lakehurst shortly thereafter. This squadron then assumed the role that the Coast Guard was abandoning.[24]

In summary, Erickson concluded that the radar calibration activities "saved time and money . . . by expediting radar calibrations. . . . It is probable that it paid for the helicopter activity at Floyd Bennett Field several times over."[25]

One accident occurred to a Coast Guard HOS-1 helicopter during these calibration flights. It is noteworthy because of the circumstances. On 25 September 1945 Ens. John Greathouse and AMM 3/c John Smith were flying a radar calibration mission near the Philadelphia Navy Yard, climbing to five thousand feet. Scattered thunderstorms were building in the area, and the helicopter encountered turbulence. A sudden jolt, accompanied by a tearing sound, caused Greathouse to look up; what he saw was the helicopter's main rotor system flying off, unattached. Both men were now passengers in a spinning flightless hulk.

Ordinarily, crew members of the time did not fly with parachutes. In this instance, however, Greathouse was flying for the first time "above 700 feet," and he claimed that was the highest he had previously flown helicopters, and then only on those rare instances to practice autorotations. He "just decided it was a good time to wear a parachute." Smith flipped his seat belt release and was thrown through the Plexiglas nose, cutting himself only slightly, as the fuselage proceeded to free-fall. Smith never reached the ground; his parachute snagged the top of a two-story building and he was left dangling against the wall. His broken leg came later, when eager helpers cut the parachute shroud lines from above, thus speeding his belated journey to earth abruptly.

Greathouse was ejected through the side of the fuselage where the door had been. As he rode the parachute down, he watched the loose forty-eight-foot-diameter rotor whirling, wandering in lazy circles, nearby, "looking and sounding like a helicopter." He landed unhurt in downtown Philadelphia at the intersection of Broad and Bigler Streets.

Miraculously, the falling wingless bird did not injure pedestrians on the street next to the bus stop where it dropped.[26]

The Hoist

Erickson wrote to BuAer on 13 July 1944 proposing an external "hydraulically operated hoist" for picking up or landing personnel— perhaps the most significant development for the helicopter. Included in the letter was a list of other tasks a hoist might perform such as the mounting of the spray equipment for BuAer's upcoming malaria control experiments.

Erickson's interest in some form of mechanical lifting device had been growing since April, when Army Air Forces made a dramatic rescue using a helicopter. Three Army Air Corps fliers were downed in enemy territory in the mountain jungles of Burma. A disassembled R-4A was loaded on board a twin-engine Curtiss C-46 Commando transport and flown halfway around the world to a base in Burma. The helicopter was reassembled and Lt. Carter Harmon flew three flights into the jungle, bringing out one survivor on each trip. "This became the first rescue made by a helicopter in combat."[27]

It was this early Army Air Forces operation that fired the small group of dreamers at Floyd Bennett Field with "something to think about. If a helicopter could be whisked across an ocean in a transport airplane to perform a rescue behind enemy lines, why not go a step farther and carry one fully assembled piggyback on the wing of a large seaplane?" Erickson mused further, "If the rotor could be allowed to windmill in flight like an autogiro, it seemed quite probable that the helicopter could be launched from the plane in flight. It might even be capable of returning to the plane and landing on it. Thus it could serve as a flying lifeboat for the seaplane."[28]

But before the helicopter could be teamed up with a large plane in this manner, much would remain to be done in equipping the helicopter for rescue operations at sea. Some means had to be found for lifting a "survivor" from the water or, if on shore, from wherever the aircraft came down. This device would have to be capable of pulling the survivor up to the aircraft in hovering flight, to be brought inside for first aid treatment and covered with blankets.[29]

An early concept for a hoisting device was created for the yet-to-be-delivered HO2S. Sergei Sikorsky, Igor Sikorsky's son, working for Erickson, modified the design to have the doors hinged at the top, "so that they would wing outward and up into the open position. Each door supported a hoisting unit, which was also swung out when the door opened." The hoist was a motor driving a shaft with two hoisting cables on drums. The cables attached to bridles at the head and foot of a Stokes litter wound on a common shaft to keep the litter level.[30]

Erickson was eager to start with this plan, but "the Coast Guard did not have an HO2S helicopter at that time, and would not have one for at least a year." He lamented: "Besides, some of the aviators thought the idea farfetched. It was unlikely that such a major modification could be sold even if an HO2S had been available. The only practical approach was to devise something simple that could be demonstrated on the HNS."[31]

This "something simple" turned out to be the foundation for the modern hoist mechanism used today, more than fifty years later, on all helicopters. Carrying stretchers proved the ability for the helicopter to act as a rescue vehicle, though in a somewhat limited capacity. The helicopter, as envisioned by Erickson, had to have the ability to hover over a ship or lifeboat and, without landing, lift survivors into it. While a test version of the twin-cable hoist did work, he switched his concept to a single-cable hoist. The stretcher proved awkward and difficult to manage. A harness or sling had to be devised to work with it.

Recalling a lesson from his seagoing career as a young battleship sailor in the Navy, Erickson devised a single whip hoist similar to those used aboard ship when working aloft. He felt it "would just be necessary to pull the survivors up level with the door and let them crawl in by themselves." He tested the idea by attaching lines toting weights at various locations about the airframe where he might later attach a hoist, then flying the craft to test for controllability. "The HNS proved to have adequate control with weights in excess of two hundred pounds attached to an arm that extended about one foot from the side of the cabin." Erickson was the weight "in excess of two hundred pounds": Graham flew the aircraft around the field with Erickson bound in a parachute harness attached to the end of a line.[32]

It was a chilling ride. According to Graham, Erickson nearly froze in the blast of wind as he dangled twenty feet below the helicopter.[33] The thrill of the ride and the success it promised pushed aside the discomfort, however, and Erickson proclaimed, "[I]t was more comfortable than swinging in a boatswain's chair one hundred feet above the deck working with 'one hand for the government and one for himself' hanging on to keep from falling out."[34]

This was just one example of the risks the "Commanding Officer"—as Erickson usually referred to himself in reports—would take to prove his helicopters worthy. And of his men, including Sergei Sikorsky, who had enlisted in the Coast Guard in order to serve with helicopters, he asserted, "[They] thoroughly enjoyed these experiments."[35]

Erickson's engineering methods might be described as scrap yard mechanics. The first motor he accepted for his proposed lifting crane was a bomb hoist that came from a "crashed bomber." Erickson's machinist scoured "the junk shops on Canal Street in New York where [they] picked up a lot of odds and ends that still failed to work."[36] The motor was too heavy. More searching yielded a lightweight electrical rotary actuator. With a gear ratio of approximately a thousand to one, it could lift the expected load—slowly, very slowly.

Machinist Mates Berry and George Lubben designed the hoist boom for mounting on the side of the helicopter cabin and a winch drum driven by this rotary actuator. Initially, the pilot controlled the up movement with a switch mounted on top of the cyclic stick. A block of wood buoyed a hook at the end of the cable, keeping it afloat for a survivor in the water to grab. To complete the system, the air station's parachute rigger designed and built a ring type floating harness for a swimmer to slide into easily.[37]

The first experiments with the electric rescue hoist on HNS 39040, in July 1944, "worked even better than had been anticipated, except for one minor deficiency. The magnetic brake was apt to slip when the load on the cable got up to about 195 pounds." Red Lawrence hoisted a crewman and stopped the hoist when the "volunteer" was even with the door. "Suddenly the brake let go." The volunteer dropped about ten feet onto soft turf, unhurt.[38]

Despite the brake failure and risky mechanical devices, Igor Sikorsky himself volunteered to act as a survivor and was hoisted during a visit to Floyd Bennett Field on 14 August 1944. He was not the first in the Sikorsky family to be lifted by the new device, however. Sergei had been an earlier guinea pig. His role as "survivor" had a double meaning: he played survivor while they tested the hoist and various concepts of harnesses, and he survived swinging in space beneath the helicopter cabin "hundreds of times."[39]

Overall, though, experiments with the hoist and slings were disappointing. The first electric hoist motor had only one switch which could be activated by the pilot. After it was turned on, it could be shut off only by depressing a contact switch just under the motor with the hoist collar at the upper limit of travel. This created one unexpected problem, which Erickson soon demonstrated.

He took Igor Sikorsky as passenger aboard an HNS, and they "tried hoisting an overweight Coast Guard aviation machinist mate first class named Carl Yanuzzi from the water just off the station's seaplane

ramp." Comdr. John Redfield, U.S. Coast Guard, witnessing the
event, further recalled years later:

> Yanuzzi was in swim trunks in the water off the ramp. Our heroes moved
> off the ramp in HNS-1 [BuNo] 040, lowered the hoist collar . . . to [the]
> waiting Yanuzzi. What they overlooked was that they were almost at
> max. gross [weight] for the [aircraft] and it was a hot day. They started
> the hoist, and as soon as the slack was taken up, that little motor—about
> the size of your fist—started to crank the helo down into Jamaica Bay.
> No, Yanuzzi wasn't a first class for nothing, and he immediately saw he
> would either see two famous aviators take a bath or have a bird helicopter
> come down on him like he was a chick in a nest. What he lacked in finesse
> he made up for in speed in evacuating the sling.[40]

An Interested Party

In the meantime, the Army Air Forces sustained interest in Erickson's
activities at Floyd Bennett Field. Gregory made frequent trips to
Brooklyn during the year to watch Erickson's projects develop. He
expressed concern about the poor performance the Army was getting
from helicopters. Erickson's equipment was a little more satisfactory.
They finally concluded that the long hot humid summers around
Wright Field sapped the ability of the helicopter to lift. Erickson's aircraft flew better because of the cooler air from ocean breezes.[41]

What really caught the Army Air Forces' attention, however, was
the hoist development. They ordered twelve units, based on Erickson's
reports, and had their engineers—together with engineers from
Sikorsky and Kellett Aircraft Company—visit CGAS Brooklyn to
"copy the details of the installation in BuNo 39040." Leo Brzycki, a
chief aviation machinist mate from the Coast Guard air station, then
went to Wright Field with a boom and hoist to help the Army install a
hoist on one of their helicopters.[42]

Into the late summer of 1944, Sikorsky continued to deliver helicopters fast enough for Erickson to meet his needs for training and to
expand his development programs. This excess gave him the opportunity
to move in yet another direction, namely, emergency assistance in
extreme weather. On 9 September, just a few days after Erickson
received the last two HNSs from the factory, an emergency arose where
Erickson could use the trainers. The scope of this mission, combined
with the novelty of the "agitated palm tree," again brought extensive
public attention to the helicopter and to Erickson as its promoter.[43]

A hurricane hit North Carolina, sweeping the coastline and passing into New England. Forty-six people were killed in its path, a deadly course that sank one Navy destroyer, a minesweeper, two Coast Guard cutters, and one lightship, taking an additional 298 lives.

On the morning of 15 September, Capt. Eugene Osborne, U.S. Coast Guard, commander of the Long Island section, called Erickson to ask for aircraft support to conduct an immediate survey of hurricane damage. All land communications were out on the eastern end of Long Island; an aerial inspection was necessary.

Normally in such cases, fixed-winged amphibians had been used. That day, however, Erickson substituted helicopters for airplanes. He took Kossler in one HNS and led a flight of three others. One JRF fixed-wing amphibian accompanied the helicopters. They flew to Osborne's headquarters at East Moriches, where "the task that awaited," Erickson's crew, "was made to order for the helicopters." Osborne, who had come up through the ranks from the lifesaving branch of the Coast Guard, "immediately recognized the lifesaving possibilities of the helicopter."[44]

Osborne's summary of the recovery from the hurricane's devastation spoke glowingly of the helicopter's importance as a rescue craft. He cited specific instances where helicopters performed in minutes what boats would take a day to accomplish. His report, however, like so many others, smacks heavily of Erickson's influence, and propaganda. With the convincing powers of both Erickson and Kossler at each elbow, Osborne could hardly refuse recording that, "the helicopter was indeed astonishing, and the ease with which observation of all the damage at any special point could be quickly ascertained was gratifying."[45] The summary continued; the words flowed in Erickson's familiar prose, however, suggesting that Osborne probably did not compose it at all.

Erickson's battle was becoming more desperate within the Coast Guard. The British were leaving, the Navy was not sending students to his school, and he was under heavy pressure from headquarters to desist from his extravagant ways. Even Kossler's support, as will be seen, was diminishing. So Erickson manipulated Osborne, a senior officer, in an attempt to buy allies. Few were buying his repeated arguments, so any unsolicited endorsements were encouraged.

Osborne concluded his report by mentioning aspects of the helicopter that were not even demonstrated on their missions for him that day. He suggested that helicopters stationed at strategically located points along the coast, such as important lifeboat stations, would prove to be of inestimable value in connection with work then being performed by Coast Guard units. This would be particularly true of other lifesaving phases like lifting personnel from the water or ground to the plane through the use of an electric winch, which, when perfected, should prove a most useful attribute to the other Coast Guard facilities.[46]

Breakthrough on the Hoist

Erickson continued his work on the hoist after the storm. He discovered a hydraulic motor, an off-the-shelf item available from Vickers. It could drive a winch on the hoist boom and be controlled by the pilot with a valve switch on the collective lever. The unit could hoist four hundred pounds at a rate of two-and-a-half feet per second. Erickson committed himself to the purchase of two units, not knowing where he would get the money. "But something was needed in a hurry to replace the electric installation."[47]

As the summer closed, the helicopter pilots at the station had a chance to develop their techniques picking up weights with the original electric hoist. They were ready for the new units when the "Vickers Aircraft Field Service Supervisor arrived with new hydraulic units on the afternoon of 23 September." Berry, Lubben, Carl Simon, a chief metalsmith, and their crews worked through the night. Early the next morning they had the unit installed on HNS BuNo 39040. A test flight was flown immediately; several hoists were done. "The equipment worked perfectly." It was ready for a Navy air-sea rescue exhibit at the Naval Air Station Lakehurst, scheduled just five days after the Vickers motor and pump were delivered. This was the opportunity Erickson hoped for. He could now finally demonstrate the rescue capabilities of the much-maligned helicopter.[48]

The air-sea rescue exhibit was delayed until 2 October. Erickson used the extra time to drill his pilots in picking up crewmen from life rafts. He asked that the *Cobb*, with its helicopter deck, participate to demonstrate the ship/helicopter concept, an as-yet untried idea.

This important show for Erickson took place at sea just off Manasquan, New Jersey. Kossler, ever present at helicopter demonstrations, was aboard the *Cobb* as a witness, along with Erickson's now-staunch supporter General Lowe. Erickson and Graham flew HNS BuNo 39040 with its new hydraulic hoist to NAS Lakehurst, arriving well before the show's 0930 opening. Later, they flew out to the *Cobb*. According to Erickson, success at this most important demonstration of its early career would assure a doubtful Admiral Ramsey, chief of the Bureau of Aeronautics, that the HNS—with its new hydraulic hoist—could make pickups at sea.

Erickson felt confident of success in his unrehearsed demonstration because he could expect a breeze at sea to bring cool temperatures, which always helped improve the helicopter's hovering ability. The Navy had relegated Erickson's part of the program to the end of the performances, time permitting. Demonstrations that started at 1345 were dragging on; for more than three hours Navy rescue units demonstrated parachute drops, survival equipment in the water, and simulated rescues by carrier-based aircraft.

In the late afternoon, the needed wind died. Even if Erickson got his chance, the aircraft might well prove the doubters correct. The lightweight Graham was substituted to fly in Erickson's place. The radio, battery, and anything that could be taken off was removed. Graham loaded aboard only ten gallons of fuel.

Finally, at five minutes before five—the time slated for the exercises to conclude—four men were set adrift from an aircraft rescue boat in two Mark II life rafts. Each man wore a life jacket fitted with a rescue sling that could be snapped to a hook on the hoist cable. The boat pulled off, leaving the men drifting by themselves but surrounded by the small fleet bearing demonstration-weary observers. Curiosity, or perhaps a premonition by the naysayers of obvious failure, kept them there to watch what would surely be a dismal attempt by an ill-fated aircraft.

Graham lifted the 39040, later dubbed the "4.0" (a Navy grading term for excellence) off the *Cobb*'s deck. He tested the hoist by lifting a man from the deck and setting him back down. Observers in the flotilla saw it. Then concern over what appeared to be an accident on board the *Cobb* swept through the nearby vessels. Boats got under way, charging toward the *Cobb*. Confusion reigned. A journalist later wrote that observers thought someone tangled in gear was being dragged off the ship. This unexpected distraction drew a large, now-attentive, and curious crowd. A fresh breeze stirred the water's surface.

Graham flew away from the ship and circled the rafts. He approached one from downwind. He hoisted one man while hovering at about fifteen feet and sped to the ship, where the hoist lowered him safely to deck. He repeated the trip twice more. On the final trip to the raft, Graham lifted into a hover off the *Cobb*'s deck, then flew the helicopter *backwards* to the raft, where he picked up his last "survivor." He completed the four pickups within ten minutes.[49]

The skills of a showman, a little chicanery, and luck had given Erickson what he needed to push aside some doubts about the helicopter. But there is little evidence to show that this exhibition gained any more support for him than he had already. He did proudly claim, however: "Admiral Ramsey was very impressed by the demonstration. From that day on, the helicopter program had his unqualified support." Furthermore, Erickson expressed delight that "the exhibit and tests also received very favorable coverage in the press."[50]

Publicity, he knew, was his strongest ally, and he used it. In the end, though, it was this battle for recognition of the helicopter through his showmanship and public exposure that eventually doomed his career. A bitterness toward Erickson began to swell in the ranks of his contemporaries. It was Erickson, not the helicopters, that soon came under attack.

Erickson Designs New Helicopters for Rescue

Erickson examined the first XHOS-1, still at the factory, with a critical eye, based on the victory at the air-sea rescue show. His recent experiments provided him with a list of configuration changes he proposed for the new aircraft to improve it as a rescue vehicle. Erickson sought BuAer's approval to make certain changes; BuAer approved. He then cleared the changes with Sikorsky.[51]

Erickson's crew installed a hoist immediately when the first XHOS (R-6) helicopter, BuNo 46447, arrived at Floyd Bennett Field. For his first rescue helicopter, Erickson cut the fuel tank, located in the rear of the cockpit, in half, using the space for folding seats for passengers. The fuel tank was removed from the production HOSs, and gasoline was carried in external tanks. The crewman's seat also folded up, opening up space through which to pull a person into the aircraft. The hoisting equipment was installed, with a new operating switch on the cyclic lever. Following the first tests Erickson claimed that it "operated as well as the installation in the HNS 39040."[52]

The Sikorsky's company immediately proposed that Erickson's modification be made on all Army Air Forces R-6s. The plan was accepted, along with the addition of one more feature common to modern helicopters—a sliding door.[53]

The first test involving this newly configured XHOS took place on 29 November. The planned extended evaluation ceased suddenly, however, when the aircraft crashed in shallow water three days later. Lt. August Kliesch was the pilot, Lt. W. E. Prindle the copilot. Graham was a passenger in the rear jump seat. He was injured slightly and hospitalized for a week. The other two escaped injuries.

A mechanical failure had caused the crash, thus emphasizing the still highly experimental stage of helicopter development. "The main pitch actuating bearing failed," Erickson reported, "allowing the azimuth plates to drop over the main pitch activation fork, jamming the azimuth plates in neutral." As a result, the pilot lost all ability to control the aircraft. The new helicopter, with a mere total of 18.2 flight hours, was "damaged beyond repair."[54]

On 15 December 1944, Erickson requested that BuAer order thirteen hoists to be installed on the HNS helicopters. Ramsey, in response, summoned Erickson to discuss the entire Navy helicopter program. Erickson's will for introducing a rescue helicopter prevailed.

The Navy's order for its first one hundred HOS helicopters as 1945 began was cut to thirty-six aircraft. Even so, Erickson was still optimistic; the future for helicopters "looked very promising." According to his memoirs, Erickson received "verbal instructions" from Ramsey to have the Naval Aircraft Modification Unit, Johnsville, Pennsylvania, modify the new helicopters "to the configuration Erickson developed on the XHOS." Most important for him and the future of the helicopter was the "installation of the rescue hoist" and the sliding door "that could be opened in flight."[55]

Ramsey told Erickson that he wanted all Navy helicopters to be equipped for rescue work, and to that end he ordered Erickson to Johnsville to discuss the modification of the new HOS helicopters with Capt. Ralph Barnaby, U.S. Navy. A request for modification required the usual routing through "channels," however. The work might be accomplished if Barnaby was willing to take on the task, despite the pressure on his facility for warplane modifications.

Erickson, knowing how to sell his helicopter persuasively, flew a helicopter to Johnsville, where he lifted Barnaby with the hoist-equipped HNS, flew him around the field, then lowered him back in his tracks at the starting point. Erickson remembers that "[H]e was very eager to get started. This was reminiscent of some of Barnaby's own early experimental work, when he became the first Naval aviator to fly a glider from a dirigible."[56]

Barnaby favorably endorsed Erickson's request; the Navy could do the work. Opposition to the modification, however, came from Coast Guard headquarters.[57]

Donohue, as the newly appointed chief air-sea rescue officer, approved only twelve HOS modifications in his endorsement since, "anticipated deliveries of operational models in 1945 do not exceed that number." Erickson was delighted that BuAer disregarded this endorsement. "By so doing, [BuAer] insured that both the Navy and Coast Guard would have enough helicopters to initiate development programs when the services began taking a new look at helicopters" the following year.[58]

Kossler Has an Idea

All new ideas regarding helicopter use were not coming from Erickson alone. Kossler initiated a project to develop an aerial spraying capability for the aircraft. It was Kossler's expressed concern that malaria-carrying mosquitoes were causing more problems for the U.S. troops in the

Pacific than the enemy forces. He proposed that helicopters should spray DDT on the Pacific Islands. Time was running out for this plan to go to war, however, so he extended the idea to add an insect-killing mission to Erickson's coastal helicopter station concept. To get something started, Kossler created a joint Navy/Coast Guard–Department of Agriculture malaria control project. His proposal outlined the creation of a force to combat mosquitoes infesting the aquatic regions of the United States. Coast Guard helicopters would work in cooperation with the U.S. Public Health Service in carrying out the plan.

The Navy provided the project officer, Lt. Joseph S. Yuill, an entomologist from the Navy's Bureau of Medicine and Surgery. Yuill, who had worked with the Department of Agriculture before the war, had several years of experience with aerial spray projects. He joined Erickson's force on 11 October 1944 and immediately drew plans for spray equipment that could be attached to helicopters. Berry was the machinist who configured the helicopter to carry a thirty-gallon tank to hold the spray, an engine-driven hydraulic pump, plus piping and spray heads. The left pilot's seat was removed to create space for the tank, which was positioned just behind the seat's usual position. Passengers were still carried sometimes; they sat on the floor, leaning back against the tank. A spray boom extended fifteen feet each side of the hull, just ahead of the tail rotor. The equipment was completed and tested by 1 November.

Experiments with spray equipment were conducted throughout Long Island. The crew traveled in a van with a big yellow cross painted on top. Since malaria mosquitoes were absent in New England, Japanese beetles became a substitute target, as did domestic mosquitoes. The Coast Guard sprayed the Yale bowl a day prior to a pop concert, and the Hudson River Valley was another target in the Coast Guard's war on mosquitoes.[59]

More experiments were conducted in Florida; one helicopter and two crews were transferred to the Coast Guard's air station in St. Petersburg. They worked throughout the winter in the tropical region of Florida in collaboration with the U.S. Department of Agriculture, Laboratory of Entomology and Plant Quarantine, in Orlando.[60] Although aerial spraying did not become a Coast Guard mission, the techniques and equipment these few men developed later became the basis for a worldwide industry.

Good News and Bad

With the war still raging, air shows were rare. But Erickson kept pushing for any opportunities. One came. On 9 November 1944 Erickson and Bolton flew HNS BuNos 39040 and 39043 from New York to Naval Air Station Glenview, near Chicago, to attend a show for the Navy's Sixth War Loan Exhibition in Chicago. There the two demonstrated for the public the new hoisting ability of the helicopter by lifting a man from the cockpit of a previously wrecked Navy single-engine dive-bomber, an SBD Dauntless floating in the Chicago Canal. Twenty hoists of the simulated "downed pilot" were demonstrated. One hoist became a true rescue, however, when the Dauntless rolled over, pitching the pilot into the frigid water. The pilot in helicopter 39040 saw the plane capsize, rushed to the scene, and snatched up the real victim, placing him on the pier where he received first aid.[61]

Sandwiched between the training, radar calibration, and major projects, Erickson would squeeze in a seemingly endless string of minor tasks he or his crew felt the helicopter was capable of. Early in October 1944, for example, he branched out, based on his helicopter experiments. He mounted a helicopter hoist on a thirty-six foot Coast Guard rescue boat. He proved two men could pick up a helpless person from the water in less than thirty seconds, while it took four men three minutes to handle the same victim aboard.

During this period he also had a device made by his crew whereby "dispatch cases" might be flown from ship to ship by helicopter. The case was rigged with a ring to snap into the hoist hook. The hook was modified so the pilot could release it with one hand. It was years later before the Navy used this idea to haul slung cargo nets for delivering supplies from ship to ship. Coast Guard boats a half century later still manhandle survivors aboard.

As the first year of his helicopter school drew to a close, Erickson was subjected to a series of unfavorable events. The sixth class reported for flight training on 2 January 1945, but it was to be his last group trained. Erickson's school was terminated. Depressed by the sudden changes, Erickson lamented, "It started out with all the promise of the classes that preceded it, but before the class was over their future in helicopters was looking very bleak."[62]

His attitude toward using helicopters in the Coast Guard was now troubling many. Erickson was quoted frequently as saying, "The road ahead [for the Coast Guard] is helicopters only."[63] This prediction, oft shouted with the optimism of a seer in an overwhelming crowd of doubters, finally led to Erickson's critics referring to him and other helicopter pilots derisively as "rotor heads."

SEVEN

A DREAM DIES

Changes Coming

 yet unnoticed erosion in Erickson's helicopter program had actually come in late spring 1944, just as the formal helicopter training classes were beginning. A major restructuring was taking place within the Coast Guard, and because of that change, Erickson fell into an inescapable trap.

The National Air-Sea Rescue Agency was officially established by the secretary of the Navy in March 1944. The Coast Guard, based on its history of search and rescue, combined with its extensive communication network, was the natural administrator of this new organization. Under the new plan, Coast Guard aviation would simply extend through its air stations "a new organization similar to the long-established life-saving system begun by the Revenue Cutter Service in 1790." This was similar to Erickson's plan, with one exception: he envisioned it as helicopter stations only, not bases with a mixture of all the aircraft types flown by the Coast Guard. This new program also blended in successful principles devised by the World War II British Rescue Service, wherein coastal rescue boats were directed to casualties at sea by airplanes.[1]

With this change, the Coast Guard commandant became the head of the Air-Sea Rescue Administration, whose members represented the Coast Guard, Navy, Marine Corps, Army, and Army Air Forces. Erickson's problems began with the selection of the assistant coordinator assigned to aid the commandant in the capacity of chief of the Air-Sea Rescue Office. This officer was responsible for the administration, planning, and execution of all operations of the agency.[2] Capt. Carl B. Olsen was appointed the first assistant coordinator. Although he was succeeded a short time later by Admiral Robert Donohue, Olsen continued to work for the agency under Donohue. Their goal was to build a maritime aviation search-and-rescue organization around the long-range seaplanes, land-based airplanes, and amphibian aircraft. They saw no use for the helicopter, and, according to Erickson, they were rankled "because of my supposed over enthusiasm for helicopters."[3]

Erickson was later to reflect, "Unfortunately, the fixed-wing advocates had taken over at [headquarters] and the whole helicopter program folded."[4]

At that time the Coast Guard considered its principal rescue planes to be the PBY-5A Catalina amphibian, the PBM Mariner seaplane, and the PB1-G (B-17) Flying Fortress. These military airplanes were stripped of their wartime complement of armament and outfitted with nearly twelve hundred pounds of rescue and survival equipment. The Fortress, since it could not land on water, could carry a twenty-eight foot Higgins airborne lifeboat against the contours of the plane's underbelly. When dropped, its descent to the sea was retarded by three forty-eight-foot cargo parachutes.[5] There are no reports of any actual cases in which rescue boats were so dropped.

Though the amphibian Catalina had many successful landings at sea during the war to rescue downed aviators, landing in an open sea was still a dangerous practice authorized only when extreme circumstances overrode the risks to the aircraft and crew. And the Mariner, being wholly a seaplane, was usually restricted to landings and takeoffs from seaplane facilities typically located on protected waters like rivers, harbors, and bays.

Early tactics had these three airplane types working with air-sea rescue (ASR) boats in near-coastal locations. The aircraft would direct the boats to the distress sites, then provide survivors with equipment such as "Gibson Girl" emergency radios, shipwreck kits, dye markers, smoke and light buoys, and "provisional bombs" by dropping it from the plane.[6]

A Coast Guard ASR unit returned to CGAS Floyd Bennett Field in December 1944 along with three PBY-5As and crews to support them. At that time, Erickson was commanding officer over all of them. This created more problems for him, however, because he insisted that all pilots serving under him become qualified in the helicopter. The new seaplane pilots rejected such heavy-handedness. They were there only as SAR pilots, and the helicopter did not perform SAR missions. The unit's arrival coincided with the departure of the British, so the helicopter school kept on a steady schedule. The new year began with ambitious plans for the Coast Guard's newly acquired ASR service.

After examining their upcoming obligations, including law enforcement missions, the Coast Guard calculated that they would need eighty-four fixed-winged aircraft to carry out their work. This proposed increase raised the personnel ceilings from 587 to 691 commissioned aviators to meet the pilot needs of the expanded fleet. Since the Coast Guard was still a part of the Navy, it was the Navy who approved the increases. On 19 March 1945 it approved boosting the ceiling to 715 "aviators." The distinction was made between aviators and pilots during this period because the Coast Guard used both enlisted and commissioned officers. Commissioned fliers were officially classified as "aviators"; enlisted men doing the same task were designated as "pilots."

At war's end, about 25 percent of the total number of fliers were permitted to be these enlisted pilots.[7] Many, however, when eligible, took examinations to qualify for commissions, and were absorbed into the ranks. Some of these eventually reverted back to enlisted status in order to remain on active duty during postwar cutbacks.

With the arrival of the three PBYs and their crews, problems arose almost immediately with the fixed-wing SAR unit. Erickson was running two units: his helicopter training school, with its unofficial helicopter rescue research and development program, and the much larger and significantly more important (for headquarters, that is) SAR unit conducting ASR (with boats and planes used in combination). Erickson, however, as has been shown, was "all helicopter. He didn't worry about anything about command when he had his helicopters."[8]

Furthermore, he insisted that *all* his pilots fly helicopters, even the newly assigned patrol ASR crews. His primary concern as 1945 began was to develop the search-and-rescue helicopter, and he devoted most of his time to working on the hoist, rescue slings and basket, skids, and floats and operational techniques for that aircraft. According to William Coffee, former student of Erickson's, "[He] didn't oversell the potential of the helicopter."[9] But this is a viewpoint clearly seen from hindsight; that was not the way Erickson's activities were viewed in Coast Guard headquarters late in December 1944 and into the new year.

The aircrews for the fixed-winged SAR aircraft were required to stand alert duty in addition to the normal work routine. That meant that at least once every three days, for a twenty-four-hour period, they were on duty. Not so with the helicopter crews, however. They stood the duty once every five or six days. Tensions soon erupted between the two camps, and word of this situation made its way to headquarters. Erickson's antagonists finally had the cause they long sought.

Tragic Ends

The helicopter school was terminated. Unknown to him then, Erickson was just days away from losing his command also. As the sixth and last class started training on 2 January 1945, Erickson thought, innocently, that the school was being "suspended as no personnel have been assigned" for subsequent classes.[10] By the time that class completed its program on 6 February 1945, Erickson was less than a month away from being relieved by Comdr. Arthur J. Hesford.

As Erickson saw it, Hesford was the man sent by Olsen to replace Joe Lawrence as a headquarters' spy in Erickson's camp. In this new situation, Hesford outranked Erickson. Hesford claimed he was sent to CGAS Brooklyn by Donohue and Olsen "to get that mess cleaned up."[11] It was also common knowledge around headquarters, according to Hesford, that "Donohue hated Erickson's guts."[12]

Strangely, Erickson was not transferred, as is customary with relieved commanding officers. Nor was he reverted to executive officer or any other position in the chain of command. His junior, Smeder, who had become Erickson's executive officer when Lawrence left earlier, continued on as the XO to Hesford, forcing Erickson out of the line. Erickson was just relocated to a "small back office." He was provided space in the wardroom and the small room formerly assigned to visiting officers for his quarters. He now had only an ill-defined helicopter development project to run.[13] Moreover, nearly all the helicopters were either shipped away to other agencies or stored.

It was an "embarrassing" position for both the new commanding officer and Erickson. Hesford was "uncomfortable" having Erickson, the former commanding officer, on his premises as a tenant with no staff or crew.[14] Nevertheless, life was somewhat pleasant for Erickson, considering the circumstances; this was largely because Hesford was an outstanding and very considerate leader. Erickson still appeared to have an opportunity to pursue his helicopter projects with little interference.

But acrimonious feelings between Erickson and staff members in headquarters persisted. In one accusatory statement, Erickson maintained that he was relieved of command of the Brooklyn air station because Olsen and Donohue "claimed that I was pushing the helicopter program too much to the detriment of fixed-wing aviation." Feelings were so intense that Erickson claimed, "Olsen promised me that he would see to it that I never again [held] a responsible job in CG Aviation."[15] And Erickson never did.

For his part, Erickson warned the Coast Guard aviators who supported fixed-winged seaplane operations to the exclusion of the helicopter; he repeated, as though chanting a mantra, "frozen winged, frozen minded."[16]

Erickson's fall accelerated. This time, contrariwise, his professional disintegration was not contrived by those opposed to him and his helicopters. His friend and ally, Kossler, asked the Coast Guard commandant to transfer the helicopter development project from the

Office of Engineering to "regular channels." Kossler's emotional disorders, from which he had suffered previously, resurfaced in March. A reluctant Waesche acquiesced when Kossler was later hospitalized. Kossler surrendered his office at the Brooklyn air station just when, as Erickson later wrote, the helicopter project was "crashing down around our ears."[17]

Moving the helicopter project out from Kossler's protective mantle gave headquarters the authority they could not get before. Kossler could no longer bolster Erickson or his cause, running interference as he did so successfully.

A few months later, Kossler had a complete "nervous breakdown and died over the project." It was "awfully hard on Frank [and he] went through hell."[18] Then, within a few months of Kossler's death, Admiral Waesche was hospitalized and died on 17 October 1946. The loss of these two essential supporters left Erickson virtually defenseless against the opponents of helicopter development. Kossler had been, as Erickson affirmed,"the spark that kept the program going during those early days."[19]

Helicopter development for Erickson and the Coast Guard died with the death of Kossler.[20] Erickson soon lost the backing of even his supporters because of his stubborn single-mindedness. Erickson's disgrace was magnified when he was denied recognition for the task he had accomplished. The record shows that on 28 January 1945 Kossler wrote a recommendation to the commandant asking that he award Erickson a Distinguished Flying Cross (DFC), citing the successful 3 January 1944 rescue mission. Kossler noted that this "First Mission" was "distinctly hazardous and can be classed as heroic." Furthermore, he wrote:

> It was the first time in history that a helicopter had been flown under such conditions. In addition, it contributed greatly to the advancement of aviation in the rotary wing field. The enclosed editorial of the New York *Times* of 5 January 1944 is only one example of the attention and interest the flight created, not only in aviation circles, but in general. It has already been mentioned in several books and will go down in the history of the development of the helicopter. It reflected credit on the service and increased the prestige of the Coast Guard.[21]

Kossler concluded, "It is not only my own opinion, but also the opinion of others cognizant of the facts, that this flight merits more official recognition than a mere letter of commendation."[22]

General Lowe read Kossler's letter before it was submitted. The general received it in the mail along with a copy of Erickson's January

1945 "Progress Report" from an anonymous contributor—probably Kossler. Lowe wished to add his own recommendation to Kossler's. In a private note to Erickson, Lowe queried him if it was appropriate for him "to make known to Admiral Waesche, informally of course, that I know about this citation and have long been of the opinion that your act rated a Navy Cross or at least a Distinguished Flying Cross."[23]

Tragically, no further correspondence on this matter has ever been uncovered. Erickson's one recognition was a Letter of Commendation from the Coast Guard's assistant commandant, Chalker, dated 6 March 1945. Kossler also received, posthumously, a Letter of Commendation in recognition of his work in developing the helicopter. That recognition came from a different and surprising quarter: Secretary of the Navy James Forrestal presented the Navy's award to Kossler's widow, Lois, and son, Jack, in May 1946.

Over the past half century, Kossler has never received recognition from Coast Guard headquarters for his energies and original ideas that went into creating modern Coast Guard aviation or his efforts in pushing forward helicopters as an accepted vehicle in the international field of aviation. A few years after his death, however, the American Helicopter Society did recognize and honor Kossler's contributions by establishing an annual award named for him.[24] The Ancient Order of the Pterodactyl also honored Kossler by installing a plaque commemorating his deeds in the Coast Guard Aviation Hall of Fame at the Aviation Training Center, Mobile, Alabama.[25]

No Place for Erickson

This period at the beginning of 1945 was, for Erickson, the start of a long slide downward in helicopter development. His losses at this time—piling on each other as they did—were tragic ones. He not only lost a close friend but also the support Kossler alone could give. Erickson was stricken. "The training came to a halt, except for . . . Navy personnel so they could commission their first squadron." Even worse, Erickson lamented, "The entire program went down the drain including the synthetic helicopter trainer and the USS *Mal De Mer*, both of which were dismantled and junked."[26] The trainer had not even been put into instructional service.

Hesford, still looking for some solution to his problem of housing Erickson, made personal calls to other commanding officers asking if anyone might take Erickson off his hands. It was nearly a year and a half later when the commanding officer at CGAS Elizabeth City offered a space. What he could furnish was an abandoned Navy hangar last used to house sheep. As Graham remembers, they had to use snow shovels to clean the hangar deck, so deep was the manure.

So it was that this ungainly rotary-winged phoenix eventually rose in an almost literal sense from a noisome pyre.[27] Beginning in March 1945, without Kossler, a command, a school, or a staff, Erickson retreated to the promise that brought him the helicopter project originally. The long-ignored ASW program would provide the single fragile thread that would keep the helicopter alive.

EIGHT

SERENDIPITY

Experiments in Helicopter ASW Sonar

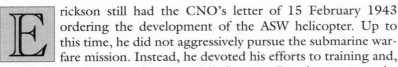

rickson still had the CNO's letter of 15 February 1943 ordering the development of the ASW helicopter. Up to this time, he did not aggressively pursue the submarine warfare mission. Instead, he devoted his efforts to training and, specifically, to his quest for a rescue helicopter. Development on the original Hayes equipment was shelved at the Naval Research Laboratories (NRL) in favor of other, higher priority projects, perhaps in part because of Erickson's lack of focus on ASW.

Erickson's stubborn no-compromise position continued to endanger developmental progress for the seagoing rescue helicopter at a time when there was no longer an obvious wartime-generated urgency for any missions. The only operational commitment Erickson had to acquit was the helicopter's use in the ships' radar calibration flights; the Navy would soon absorb this mission.

The sound-sensing equipment Hayes was so eager and ready to install on helicopters in October 1943 languished until December 1944, when a Navy reserve lieutenant, Roy Rather, serving on board a destroyer and harboring a strong interest in the design, obtained orders as project engineer to reopen the earlier effort. Dr. J. J. Coop was drawn back into the project on 1 January 1945 to assist Rather. Although their orders gave them only a brief time to solve the problems plaguing this equipment, in two months they had a unit ready to install in a helicopter.

Meanwhile, Erickson accepted the second XOS-1, BuNo 46448, on 9 January; it replaced the first one, which had been destroyed in the crash a month earlier. Rather and Coop arrived at Floyd Bennett Field with the sonar equipment early in March, ready to begin testing the sounding gear on board that XOS-1.[1]

On 12 January 1945, the CNO directed his vice chief to make the Hayes sound-detection equipment available to the Navy's Anti-Submarine Development Detachment, Atlantic Fleet.[2] The timing of this order is suspicious, coming just when all helicopter development and training stopped. King's order, moreover, bears some language indicating the probable maneuverings of Kossler in his effort to nourish his helicopter project, which was being starved by Coast Guard headquarters.

In this new directive, the Bureau of Ships (BuShips) and the NRL were directed to provide technical assistance for the evaluation and testing of helicopter-borne sound recording devices for submarine detection in the following declaration: "*The Coast Guard* will provide the helicopter and crew" (emphasis added).[3]

The Navy at this time had their own helicopters and trained pilots at their flight test center at Patuxent River. The Coast Guard was not essential to this plan, yet, in this new order, they were specified. Furthermore, the project was labeled a priority assignment that headquarters could not interfere with.

The XHOS was saved from the fate of most of the helicopters at Floyd Bennett. It was designated for testing the Hayes submarine sound-detection equipment.[4] Chief Machinist Oliver Berry began to alter the XHOS and to install the equipment brought by Rather and Coop. He experienced a "lengthy process of modifying the small cabin of the craft to accommodate all components. . . .[he was the] magician who fitted it all in."[5] Coop once remarked with admiration on Berry's skills in getting any job done; if Rather wanted something, Berry got it. Coop also noted, however, that "the supply department later had some problems in obtaining the proper papers to confirm actions taken."[6]

While the sonar gear was being installed—it took six weeks—Erickson and his crew went to the P. V. Engineering Forum's helicopter plant at Sharon Hill in Morton, Pennsylvania, to view the rollout of the experimental XHRP-1 helicopter.[7] This was the world's first successful tandem-rotor helicopter and the largest one up to this time. It was named "Rescuer." The tandem-rotor Piasecki helicopter had the capacity to haul eight passengers, or six stretchers, plus a two-pilot crew.

Progress on creating the XHRP-1 was rapid. Frank Piasecki had received a Navy contract to develop the utility transport and rescue helicopter from the Navy on 1 February 1944. The tubular structure was completed and all of the major components were installed in less than a year, but when it rolled out in March 1945 for its first flight, the framework was not yet covered with fabric.

When he first saw the spindly tubular structure, Erickson declared, "[It] looked like a huge skeleton." Piasecki and his test pilot, George Townsend, who graduated from Erickson's school in September 1944, completed the ground run-up tests. This momentary success with the engine and rotor systems working properly, fed by the crowd of interested viewers, led them, perhaps a little too eagerly, to the next step. They decided to lift it off in hovering flight.[8]

Erickson reported that "[in] the first few seconds after lift off, the XHRP went through some wild gyrations." Each pilot in this wildly slewing skeletal apparatus suddenly realized they were both on the controls trying to fly the helicopter, thus canceling out each other's efforts. "Somehow they got together, and the aircraft brought under control. Everyone cheered wildly when the helicopter made a safe landing on its full swiveling landing gear."[9]

The success of this demonstration led to a production contract from the Navy in June 1946 for ten fabric-covered HRP-1 "flying bananas." This was one of the few helicopter contracts not canceled at the end of the war. Having these helicopters in production became an important issue in helicopter development in the immediate postwar years.[10]

Erickson's crew finished installing the sonar equipment in the XHOS early in April. Preparations were then made through the Navy's ASW development detachment to operate from the *Cobb*. Earlier, preliminary tests using the sound recording devices had been completed in Jamaica Bay, New York. From these tests Coop determined what noise the helicopter rotor down-wash transmitted into the sea below. These tests were passed quickly; the low readings justified moving ahead and installing the sonar equipment.

The first in-flight test of the dipping sonar in the XHOS took place on 14 April 1945 off Block Island. As planned, the helicopter was flying from the *Cobb*, which had sailed out of New London, Connecticut. Erickson and Graham took turns flying with crew members Coop and Rather, using the dipping sonar while the aircraft hovered over the water's surface. Graham discovered their first real problem was not technical but one of human spatial orientation.

The pilots had difficulty remaining stationary over one spot without a visual reference point on the water. This was essential for keeping the suspended sonar cable vertical and motionless. The surface of the ocean, beaten by the high winds of the rotor down-wash, gave no clues to the helicopter's horizontal speed or direction. Moving waves also contributed to the feeling of being in motion while still. A cockpit instrument was required, and Erickson immediately began to work on it. But for the present, they tried incendiary float lights, colored smoke, and dye markers. Each proved unsatisfactory. Down-wash from the rotor blades swept away the float lights, blew smoke, and scattered the dyes over a wide area, making precision hovering impossible.

Graham remembers the simplicity of the solution when it finally came: "[We] found that a sheet of the Sunday newspaper comics worked best as a reference. The brightly colored paper soaked up enough water to keep it from blowing away, and could be easily seen at a flight altitude of 20 to 25 feet." As a result of their preliminary work, the group proved that helicopter-borne sonar equipment had sufficient potential for locating and tracking submarines, thus warranting further development efforts. Enthusiastic, Coop immediately began redesigning the sonar equipment at NRL to use in helicopters.[11]

The sonar dipping tests were not without the unexpected, however. One episode occurred when Erickson, as pilot, flew in a hover over heavy seas while Coop operated the sonar head fully extended. Deep swells would roll by one moment, nearly touching the bottom of the helicopter's floats, and seconds later, Erickson felt "[W]e were hanging over a trough about fifteen feet deep." Suddenly, the helicopter's engine began to misfire. Immediately, Erickson started flying toward the nearby *Cobb* without waiting for Coop to reel in the approximately sixty feet of cable to which the sonar head was attached.

The engine began to run smoothly again as Erickson climbed to make his landing approach to the ship. However, Coop had the sonar head only halfway retracted when the helicopter made its final approach to the deck. Erickson continued on a high approach, hoping the sonar head and cable would clear the side of the ship. "As the helicopter settled in for the landing . . . the engine gave its last gasp." The XHOS fell the last five feet to the *Cobb*'s deck; luckily, the helicopter and the sonar escaped damage.[12] The carburetor air intake for the HOS was on the bottom of the aircraft, and in this case, where it had hovered low over the water, the down-wash created a water spray that was sucked into the engine.

In March Erickson, always seeking a suitable role and acceptance for his maligned helicopter, sent two HNS trainers to St. Louis for flood relief work. One crashed en route at Somerset, Pennsylvania, the "result of pilot error and lack of experience." Nothing came from this experiment.[13]

Arctic Rescue

Some events did occur, however, that helped boost the helicopter's popularity, and they did not come from stratagems contrived by Kossler and Erickson. Serendipity sometimes did a better job. This time the luck came in the form of a complex rescue. A near tragedy, averted only by the unique abilities of the helicopter, again garnered international press coverage for the unlikely little trainer craft.

Late in April, as the sonar tests were concluding, the Army Air Forces and the Coast Guard teamed up to assist in the rescue of the crew of a Royal Canadian Air Force twin-engine PBY-5A Canso (the Canadian name for the Catalina) forced down on 19 April in Labrador, just north of Anticosti Island. On its return to Iceland following an overhaul, one of the plane's engines failed as the PBY flew through clouds that coated its wings with ice. Then the second engine failed. The plane broke out of the overcast about one hundred feet above the snow-covered mountain peaks. The pilot, in the final moments, was able to crash-land in clumps of spruce trees, thus preventing injuries to the nine crew members. But those same trees ripped the aircraft apart. The crew removed equipment for their survival from the wreckage. While they were in the process of evacuating the airplane, leaking gasoline exploded, destroying the Canso and burning two men who were still inside foraging.

The downed airmen then built a survival camp at the crash site, treated the burn victims, and inventoried supplies. They had just eight days' worth of rations. To hasten their rescue, some tramped out the letters "SOS" and "MO" (medical officer) in the snow on a nearby frozen pond. Signal fires were built with green tree limbs.

A massive search began and as quickly stopped, for a blizzard swept the area for the following two days. Eventually, twenty-two aircraft joined in the search, and all airplanes transiting along the route were alerted to report any sign of the downed PBY. The survivors did see several search aircraft, but they themselves were not spotted. Disappointment after three days of these conditions finally drove them to send a party on foot to Goose Bay—ninety miles away—through thawing snow marshes, bogs, and lakes with the likelihood of frequent blizzards sweeping the area. The overland party started with only four days' worth of rations.

The survivors' fortunes changed immediately. Both the wanderers and the main camp were spotted on the first day of the trek by the crew of a Douglas C-47 Skytrain. The rescue seemed assured. Soon, two C-64 Norseman single-engine ski-equipped airplanes arrived to retrieve survivors.[14] One landed on the trail of the hikers but crashed on takeoff after taking aboard the stranded airmen. No injuries resulted. The other plane boarded the burned crewmen at the base camp and departed safely.

Nine men still remained, but they were adequately stocked with survival supplies brought in by the two Norseman aircraft. Again the survivors faced two more days stranded by bad weather before a C-64 could return and extract them. When the skiplane prepared to leave with some of the survivors, however, its skis stuck in the mushy snow, and the plane could not take off. Eventually, the two airplanes and four crewmen did get out by stripping off unnecessary equipment to reduce the weight. This meant, though, that no other survivors could be carried out in the immediate future because the spring thaw prevented any further attempts by ski-equipped airplanes, dog sleds, or snowmobiles.

Rescuers anticipated that the nine men left behind would be stranded for weeks until the lakes completely thawed, thus making it possible for floatplanes to land. An alternative evacuation plan was to wait until the next winter when they could be rescued by ski-equipped airplanes. Even set against a background of wartime news, the story of the survivors' dilemma reached a sympathetic public.

This situation was tailor-made for Erickson and his rescue helicopter. The XHOS, the only aircraft suitable yet still only marginally capable for the task, was loaded with the sonar equipment and dedicated to the dipping program. It was not available. However, Erickson still had with him an operable HNS trainer at Floyd Bennett. Though lacking in range to accomplish the mission—and capable of carrying merely one passenger—this flyable HNS was loaded into an Air Transport Command Douglas C-54 Skymaster at Floyd Bennett Field on 27 April. It left the next day and arrived in Goose Bay on the twenty-ninth after a weather-enforced stop en route. Working continuously, the crews finally got all the helicopter pieces out and reassembled by the morning of the thirtieth.

Lt. August Kleisch, U.S. Coast Guard, flew off with the float-equipped helicopter burdened with seven, five-gallon jerry cans of gasoline that had been lashed to the floats for the 184-mile trip to Lake Mecatina via the survivors' camp. This distance was 30 percent greater than the normal range of the HNS. A Canso, flying lazy circles to keep pace with the slower-moving craft, escorted the helicopter along the wilderness route.

At Lake Twenty, about midway on the flight, Kleisch landed to refuel from the gas cans. Ten feet of snow still covered the lake, but the helicopter did not break through the crust on touchdown. Kleisch did. As he climbed out, he sank to his hips in snow. In the Arctic wilderness, alone, Kleisch remembers, "was a desolate and eerie sight, the heavy silence broken only by the comforting sound of the PBY as it circled overhead. Getting back in the air was a relief."[15]

Soon thereafter the helicopter landed after surveying the survivors' location from the air. The camp was nestled at the edge of a small lake inside a mountain peak; the elevation was twenty-two hundred feet.

Woods surrounded the lake. As Kleisch landed, "the sight of the machine brought cheers." The survivors gathered around the strange new aircraft and invited Kleisch in for coffee. Kleisch noted:

> [D]espite the wretched conditions of the wilderness, the airmen had constructed a fairly comfortable camp. They had received food and equipment by parachute and were living in a snow cave ten feet deep, with a parachute roof. Later, as more supplies and a tent were dropped, the camp expanded until it resembled a trapper's outpost. The men foraged the vicinity daily, resulting in an occasional roast spruce hen or porcupine stew. They were comfortable enough in spite of deep snow and freezing weather.[16]

Kleisch refueled then started his takeoff from the snow. The helicopter would not lift. He struggled with the power and controls, but it remained stuck to the ice. Even at full power, it would not lift off. Finally, Kleisch found, "[I]n order to get off the ground at 2,000 feet, I had to make a jump takeoff, revving the motor, and giving the rotor blades all the pitch I could."[17] This meant Kleisch had to overspeed the engine. Once separated from the snow, he held "level flight to the other end of the lake." Even this "was just sufficient to gain necessary air speed for the climb." Kleisch noted his first passenger, Sgt. G. J. Bunnell, was "tense as we flew across the lake but relaxed as we cleared the jagged tree tops. He continually looked up apprehensively at the rotor blades."[18]

With a helicopter that could fly the trip at barely fifty miles per hour, just one man was evacuated the first day before dark. Kleisch flew Bunnell to the Mecatina radio range station on an island in the middle of Mecatina Lake. This site was about thirty-eight miles east of the crash scene and served as the base camp. Nine Royal Canadian Army enlisted men were spending a year at this isolated station. Kleisch remembers, "[They] welcomed us with such enthusiasm that it almost seemed they were the ones being rescued."[19]

Gasoline drums dropped there earlier by the PBYs from Goose Bay had burst on impact. An existing cache of five hundred gallons, however, was stored in drums under the ice. The men dug it out, strained it through chamois cloths, and used it to refill the helicopter fuel tank and jerry cans.

That first night, the ten-degree temperatures froze the helicopter's engine. Aviation Machinist Mate 1/c Gus Jablonski, U.S. Coast Guard, and Photographer's Mate 1/c Michael Stehney, U.S. Coast Guard, arrived at Mecatina in a C-64 with a heater to thaw the engine. (The Norseman aircraft would later shuttle the survivors back to Goose

Bay.) As a precaution, a large piece of canvas was spread on the ice at Mecatina to serve as a landing pad for the helicopter. Even so, Kleisch feared the floats would freeze to the ice and destroy the fabric. It was noon the following day before the helicopter could take off again to recover some of the remaining eight survivors. Stehney went out with Kleisch on the first trip to the encampment to take photos.

The little helicopter, pushed by its crew, persevered; the last survivor finally came out three days and nine trips later on the afternoon of 2 May. This was the first Arctic rescue by a "Flutter-buggy."[20]

Army Notices the Helicopter's New Capabilities

News of this remarkable feat spread. The acclaim once again attracted a visitor to see Erickson. Within days of the rescue, Lowe returned to Floyd Bennett Field, bringing with him Gen. Jacob L. Devers, U.S. Army, for a helicopter demonstration. Devers had just returned from the European theater of operations and was taking command of the Army Field Forces. Erickson tailored his presentation, using a special helicopter equipped with the rescue hoist, a bull horn mounted in the nose, and a new skid-type landing gear.[21]

A vocal welcome from the bull horn greeted the generals' plane as it stopped on the runway. The helicopter then escorted Devers to the Coast Guard air station parking area by flying slowly ahead, just off the ground. When the generals disembarked, they saw the helicopter land on a small bomb trailer. Devers suddenly exclaimed: "Why the hell didn't we have some of these over in Africa and Europe! With that bull horn, I sure could have raised hell with my battalion commanders!"[22]

The Army Air Forces were moving ahead and already had the first operational seagoing helicopters. They assigned R-4s to specially adapted Liberty ships designated Aircraft Repair Units, Floating, with landing platforms. These units supported the B-29 Superfortresses in the Pacific during the last months of the war by bringing needed aircraft parts rapidly to downed planes scattered among the islands along the bomber routes to Japan.[23]

New Helicopters and a Flying Doctor

On 15 June the Nash-Kelvanator Company in Detroit had ready for delivery the first three Navy-production HOS-1s of the thirty-six allocated to the Coast Guard. Though they had never built aircraft, Nash-Kelvanator nevertheless manufactured the HOS-1 according to Sikorsky designs. This machine suffered the same inadequacies of the first helicopters: not enough power. It was designed when wartime restrictions prevented Sikorsky from obtaining more powerful engines.[24]

The engine for the HOS created still more problems by being unreliable. The 245-horsepower 0-405-9 Franklin engines had so many failures on delivery flights that a circuitous route was chosen from Detroit to New York to avoid having to fly them over water and mountains. On one occasion the pilot landed his HOS in a brickyard on the banks of the Hudson River without even "scratching the paintwork." Only two of five helicopters on one delivery flight reached Floyd Bennett Field without being forced down en route.[25] Lt. Comdr. James L. Baker, a U.S. Public Health Service physician—the first flight surgeon to qualify as a helicopter pilot—flew solo in the first batch of new aircraft from the factory to CGAS Brooklyn in June 1945.

The new HOSs entered into the modification program Erickson had previously arranged with Barnaby at the Naval Aircraft Modification Unit at Johnsville. The facility had already installed "rescue hoists on twelve HNS trainers [when] the HOS-1s were fed into the production line." In addition to those modifications, the Navy required that the HOS-1s be outfitted "with dual controls for training Naval pilots for the Navy's first helicopter squadron." Therefore, only thirty of the HOS-1s could be adapted for rescue work.[26]

War Ends, Helicopters Stored

The modifications did not matter. "Unfortunately," according to Erickson (revealing some of his underlying bitterness), "most of these helicopters were immediately placed in storage, because they did not fit into the air-sea rescue program as it was then envisioned by those in control of Coast Guard Aviation."[27] Some helicopters were stored at Floyd Bennett Field; the balance were sent to the Coast Guard's Aircraft Repair and Supply Base at Elizabeth City, North Carolina, and the air station in Traverse City, Michigan, for storage.

The war's end saw the curtailing of many projects and units. The *Cobb* continued in service for a few months until Rear Adm. Harvey Johnson, then the Coast Guard engineering officer, joined with Admiral Donohue in condemning the vessel. Donohue endorsed its decommissioning with the remark, "The helicopter program will not justify the retention of *Cobb*."[28]

The war's closure further damaged the developing helicopter industry. Most rotary-wing production contracts were canceled. The Coast Guard's allocation of HO2S helicopters was cut from fifty to two. Erickson's spirits were further crushed. He felt that "any hopes of converting the HO2S helicopters for Coast Guard rescue operations went down the drain." Sikorsky, however, did continue to modify the rescue version of approximately twenty R-5s for the Army Air Forces.[29]

First Hoist Rescue

Ironically, it was one of these Army Air Forces aircraft that once more brought public attention to the helicopter's rescue capabilities. An oil barge broke loose in a November 1945 storm off the Connecticut coast. Two men were stranded aboard as it was driven up on Penfield Reef, off Bridgeport, by winds gusting over sixty miles per hour. The barge began sinking, but attempts at rescuing the doomed men by boats failed. The police called the Sikorsky plant asking if they could offer aid.

Sikorsky's chief test pilot, Dmitry Viner, flew a new R-5 modified for the Army Air Forces with Jackson Beighle, one of its captains. He operated the hoist and thus rescued the two crewmen. Although the first rescue using Erickson's hoist design was not a Coast Guard achievement, this fact did not diminish his resolve. Nonetheless, Erickson lamented, "[T]his real life rescue demonstration should have provided convincing proof of what was to come, but many people in the rescue business still closed their eyes to the helicopter's capabilities."[30]

New Powerful Helicopter for Sonar Tests

Work on the dipping sonar project was ready to move ahead. In January 1946 Coop told Erickson the new sonar unit was ready for installation, and within a week of its delivery to New York, the Coast Guard took delivery of a new 450-horsepower HO2S Sikorsky helicopter, BuNo 75690. Installation of the XCF sonar took six weeks. Jamaica Bay, next to the Coast Guard base, was the scene for the initial flight tests.[31] Satisfied with the equipment, "On March 12, after minor adjustments," Graham and his crewman, Martin Westerburg, flew the HO2S to Key West, Florida. There they reported to commander, Anti-Submarine Development Detachment, VX-1, for temporary duty. In mid-April, Ens. William Coffee, U.S. Coast Guard, joined the detachment as the second pilot.[32]

A bizarre fleet was to assist the XCF sonar-test mission: a Landing Ship, Tank (LST), fitted with a platform, served as the helicopter carrier; a destroyer was the project control station; two smaller ships took underwater sound measurements; and several submarines—including a captured German U-boat—from the Key West base served as targets.

Each morning before dawn Graham or Coffee and Westerburg would push the helicopter from the hangar and launch it to rendezvous with the LST. The helicopter would land aboard as the ship motored down the channel to the operating area in the Florida Straits.

Actual testing of the underwater detection equipment began on 22 March 1946, using a U.S. submarine submerged somewhere between Key West and Cuba. Success was almost immediate. "The submarine was located by tracking ranges which were considered to be very good."[33] These exercises continued almost daily, with Coop and Rather alternating as the sonar operators.

The HO2S had a tandem cockpit; the pilot flew from the rear seat. This posed a problem for the 5'-8" Graham. Coop, in the front seat, was "over six and a-half-feet tall thus blocking all forward vision." Furthermore, Graham recounts, "this helicopter was very unstable and hard to fly because of the heavy control stick forces." He rigged a bungee cord to the control stick to help him hold it in position. "Nevertheless," Graham emphasized, "it still took sheer strength and determination to maintain a good hovering position with the sonar sphere lowered at a depth of 60 feet with no reference to hover on."[34]

The advantage of the helicopter sonar was dramatically proven during the concluding tests, as Coop was to report.

> Our last flight [of a series] was conducted against a German U-boat, the streamlined type XXI operating at a speed of 15 knots. . . . This passive listening test was terminated while still in contact at a range of 3600 yards when suddenly I heard Morse Code signals, which I could not read, and soon saw the target surface. We quickly flew back to the LST 506, where we played the tape recording of the signals in the presence of my assistant, who could read Morse Code. He said that the message stated that the submarine had sprung a leak and was surfacing. The surface ship assigned to protect the submarine in case of just such an emergency, as well as to pull us out of the water, did not detect the urgent underwater telephone message from the XXI submarine, the signals we had received and recorded.[35]

Once the final results of the helicopter sonar tests were analyzed, wrote Graham later, "even the most skeptical decision-makers were convinced that the helicopter-mounted sonar was the answer for the anti-submarine warfare program."[36]

A problem that would plague helicopter ASW operations for more than a decade—and further supported the arguments against its use—occurred on the last flight. It was the last flight because the helicopter and the sonar unit were lost. "Unfortunately," said Coffee, "the project ended with the whole helicopter getting dunked."[37] The helicopter did not have sufficient power to stop its descent in the landing approach to the deck of the LST. It settled into the water alongside the ship, and sank.

The Navy Takes Over

Graham returned to Key West in 1950 for fifteen months to complete the helicopter antisubmarine warfare project begun in New York in 1943. Graham experimented and developed tactics for helicopter ASW, and he trained Navy pilots for the first Navy helicopter ASW squadron. "In October 1951 the Navy's Operational Development Force completed the dipping sonar development project, and the first two Helicopter Anti-submarine Squadrons, HS-1 and HS-2, were commissioned at the Naval Air Station, Key West, Florida."[38]

Erickson's developmental work was about over. The Coast Guard ended 1945—"a year of progress"—with the helicopter exhibiting most of the basic systems it carries today. "There have been few new concepts in the helicopter itself."[39]

Beginning on the first day of 1946, the Coast Guard was back under the authority of the Department of the Treasury. The Navy, who until this time depended on the Coast Guard for helicopter services, was forced to organize operational helicopter units of its own. Erickson began a six-week training session to qualify the Navy crew.

In April, Comdr. Charles R. Wood, U.S. Navy, took four HOS helicopters from the Coast Guard, which had stored them at Floyd Bennett Field. They went to the Navy's new task force assigned to "Operation Crossroads." The helicopters left New York for the aircraft carrier, USS *Shangri La,* departing Norfolk for the Pacific to test the effects of atomic bombs on naval targets.[40]

Capt. C. C. Marcy, U.S. Navy, in charge of the helicopter operations at Bikini lagoon, later told Erickson of the important contribution made by the helicopter on its first operational Navy mission, namely, to recover cameras surrounding Bikini lagoon after the bomb test. The waters were "too radioactive to permit boats to approach" the camera towers. Leaving the cameras until it was safe to retrieve them would have "resulted in fogging of the films and possible loss of all or at least part of the photographic records."[41]

The Navy continued to pick up the pieces of Erickson's shattered domain. Just after Wood took the four HOSs, "Comdr. Charles

Huston, USN, and Major Armand DeLalio, USMC, arrived at Floyd Bennett Field with a contingent of officers and enlisted men to establish the Navy's first helicopter squadron." The new Navy squadron, VX-3, took fourteen more helicopters out of Coast Guard storage.[42] VX-3 then took over the responsibility for training all Navy helicopter personnel. They also took from Erickson the radar calibration flights for the New York, Boston, and Philadelphia Navy Yards and the torpedo tracking duties for the torpedo station in Newport, Rhode Island. Helicopters from VX-3 were assigned to Development Squadron VX-1 for the Operational Development Force responsible eventually for antisubmarine development.[43]

The Navy resurrected helicopter operations from the ashes of Erickson's lost cause. Years later he lamented: "[I]t looked like [headquarters] had killed the helo program for good. We no longer had either Bill Kossler or ADM. Waesche to defend the program. . . . It looked pretty hopeless, but it has made a remarkable comeback and instead, all of the 'flying coffins,' those seaplanes that killed so many of our friends as well as the people they were trying to help, are all gone."[44]

NINE

FLYING COFFINS

Captain Mac

He had that clean-cut, nice-boy-next-door look except for the ever present cigar, the tip tilted upward. The image was complete down to the strong jutting dimpled chin. All who knew him describe Donald Bartram MacDiarmid as a true hero. He epitomized in real life the type often portrayed by the movie idol John Wayne. His hubris and the success it achieved led both his admirers and his rivals to elevate "Captain Mac"—if it was a friend speaking to him—or "Mac Dee"—if he was spoken about—to nearly legendary status within the ranks of the Coast Guard in his lifetime.

"Capt. Mac was cool and unflappable. Once, when we were tearing down the runway at Lindbergh Field in a PBY-5A, he dropped his cigar. He let go of the controls and started looking for the cigar under the seat. I completed the takeoff and had the gear up before he assumed command, with the cigar in its proper location."[1]

This exalted image has diminished little since. Capt. John Waters, who flew and served with MacDiarmid, wrote: "Before he was through, Mac was a legend among seaplane pilots everywhere. Like many pioneers, he was not only a dedicated man, but one of single purpose."[2] And that single purpose was the Coast Guard's use of the seaplane.

MacDiarmid, the second son of a Methodist minister, graduated from the Coast Guard Academy "through the Grace of God and somebody's mistake"—two years ahead of Erickson, in 1929, although he was one year younger. Prior to attending the academy he, like Erickson, served as an enlisted man in the Navy. MacDiarmid shipped aboard the battleships USS *Texas* and USS *New York* and in 1925 became the "Fleet Champion Miler." He admitted later that his cadet honors at the Coast Guard Academy were "meager," but he did receive a major letter in football.[3]

Following a year at sea as a junior Coast Guard officer aboard the USS *Erickson*, MacDiarmid went through Navy flight training—almost. He failed his final flight and "washed out." He would have been the Coast Guard's fourteenth designated aviator since Coast Guard officers began flight training in 1915. Speculation among shipmates later was that his belligerence with instructors, rather than his flight performance, returned him once again to sea.

Then, through some undocumented efforts, he once again obtained orders to Navy flight training in the summer of 1937. MacDiarmid successfully completed the Navy's flight training program, a second time, in April 1938.[4] Soon after, he became an air station commanding officer, the only position he held at various air stations for the remainder of his career.

MacDiarmid always insisted on speedy responses to rescue alerts. When the alarm sounded to launch the "ready aircraft," *his* men ran or used bicycles to reach the airplane fast. He expected even the cumbersome seaplanes to be rolled down the ramp, the "beaching gear" removed, and the plane in the air in five minutes. If pilots were a little slow in reaching the airplane, they could expect to find their commanding officer, MacDiarmid, sitting in the pilot's seat. Frequently, he scrambled to the airplane with the crew, taking pleasure in beating a "ready" pilot out of his seat. On one occasion all the crew beat him to the airplane and locked the doors, preventing him from entering. He ran down the launching ramp, pounding on the side of the airplane, abandoning his attempt when he reached the water. Then there was the time he flew into a rage when someone stole *his* bicycle.

His lack of enthusiasm in the areas of administration had staffs moaning over his disrespect for paperwork, and the language he used in those few official communications he did write was often inflammatory. MacDiarmid's files were filled with dunning notices from his superiors regarding late or missing reports.

MacDiarmid was a cockpit man. His mission, as he saw it, was to save lives and, moreover, prove the seaplane capable of that task. Consequently, he held the helicopter in open disdain. To one of his junior officers leaving for helicopter training, for example, he said, "[Y]ou will be no good for the Coast Guard. The only thing you'll be good for is county fairs and hauling Santa Claus."[5]

MacDiarmid fostered an understanding of the sea and its interface conditions that led to safer ways for aircraft to successfully ditch on the oceans. Results of his studies in ocean technology are the foundation of today's SAR manuals.[6]

It was this unwavering pursuit by MacDiarmid that distracted the Coast Guard away from dedicating some attention to developing the helicopter. MacDiarmid's energies reinforced convictions held by seaplane pilots in headquarters then directing the future of Coast Guard aviation in the postwar service. Chief among them were Donahue and Olsen, both successful pilots in early seaplane operations.

The Coast Guard and the Seaplane

Thus, there were two dreamers in the Coast Guard at war's end, each with a vision for the future of Coast Guard aviation. Both were dynamic. Each had an unwavering conviction. Both were indoctrinated simultaneously with the early traditions of seaplane rescues offshore. One had an immediate solution; the other still believed in a dream of a little machine that one day could do the job. The Coast Guard aviation camp divided as it moved into a new era following World War II. Battles ensued with bitter acrimony; most officers, following tradition, accepted the seaplane and its inherent problems of landing in the open sea.

MacDiarmid believed that even open-sea landings could be done successfully. Erickson, with the same intensity, attempted to prove the helicopter's merits. In 1944, just when Erickson was advancing the rescue helicopter through his school and potential orders for great numbers of new aircraft on the books, MacDiarmid started his experiments landing seaplanes offshore.

The traditional seaplane, the workhorse of the Coast Guard, was now available in large numbers as surplus from the Navy. From its very beginning, the air arm of the Coast Guard was composed of seaplanes. As an example, just before the outbreak of World War II, forty-three of the Coast Guard's fifty-six aircraft in service were flying boats or amphibians.[7] By 1947, with the influx of surplus military airplanes, the Coast Guard had 118 amphibians or seaplanes and forty-three land planes.[8]

This devotion to seaplanes started early. The Coast Guard established an aviation section in headquarters in 1928 led by Comdr. Norman B. Hall. This new office created the design requirements for a multi-mission aircraft for the Coast Guard. Their specifications dictated a large seaplane or amphibian or "flying life boat." Until 1930 the Coast Guard acquired aircraft designed for other services, usually as castoffs or obsolete machines. Then Congress appropriated funds for the Coast Guard to acquire its own service aircraft. Hall's office found a new airplane, manufactured as a commercial amphibian and suited for their service.

The Douglas Aircraft Company's Dolphin was purchased in 1931. The military designation, RD, had an all-metal hull and a plywood-covered high wing with twin engines mounted on top. Through the 1930s the Coast Guard purchased four different versions including both seaplanes and amphibians. This rugged little plane, having space for eight people aboard, served in the Coast Guard until nearly 1944.

In 1933 Lt. Richard Burke was awarded the Coast Guard's first Distinguished Flying Cross for landing a Dolphin 160 miles off the coast of Massachusetts and retrieving an injured crewman from a trawler. It was the first open-sea rescue made with a Dolphin. The second attempt at a rescue became newsworthy globally and established the Coast Guard's aerial maritime responsibilities.

The Navy's rigid airship USS *Akron* crashed at sea near Barnegat Light off the coast of New Jersey on 4 April 1933. Aboard with the sixty-three-man crew was Rear Adm. W. A. Moffett, chief of the Bureau of Aeronautics. Lt. Comdr. Elmer Stone, the Coast Guard's first aviator and friend of some of the crew, was in Washington, D.C., when he heard of the crash. He got a Dolphin at the Naval Air Station Anacostia and flew to Cape May, New Jersey, in the same storm that had struck down the airship. The next morning he flew to the crash sight, discovered no survivors, but picked up two victims following an offshore landing in the storm-churned seas.

These rescues lifted the boundaries to the limits of Coast Guard responsibilities. "Stone and Burke's landings at sea in the Dolphins," according to Erickson, "convinced the Coast Guard that this aircraft had the capability of performing offshore rescue missions."[9] The coastal patrols and rescues were extended to the limits of the aircraft's endurance and more airplanes were purchased. The ten Coast Guard air stations planned for in 1916 were finally constructed by the Works Progress Administration as the Depression wound down.

The next aircraft the Coast Guard purchased was a competition winner from designs submitted by eight companies. The Fokker Model AF-15 became the official "Flying Life Boat" (FLB). It was similar in style to the Douglas Dolphin, but its engines were mounted pusher style. The Fokker Company became a division of the General Aviation Company, making the new aircraft, and later became the North American Aviation Company. It was then that the aircraft acquired the military designation PJ. Until that time they were simply known as FLBs.[10] First deliveries began in 1932; some remained in service until early 1941.[11] The FLBs, "which literally flew until they wore themselves out," achieved performance records, according to Kossler, "few planes have equaled." He noted, "[A]s an airplane it was a crate, however, it had some very desirable features such as freedom from spray in taking-off and was very well constructed."[12] Its landing and takeoff speeds were low as was its weight. These were critical positive factors for landing at sea as MacDiarmid was later to prove.

"The Coast Guard," Kossler further pointed out, "accomplished some really fantastic missions with this plane and to [my] knowledge, no one was ever injured in these operations. . . . Considering the time at which these planes were designed and built and lack of much previous knowledge or experience, they were a remarkable development."[13]

These small seaplanes, however, were locked into a time period when airplanes were getting larger and faster. According to Kossler, "That was directly opposite to the Coast Guard requirements for this type of work." He went on to explain, "The cost of developing and building a few ships of this type was very high and its justification was questionable, considering the volume of missions of this character." Kossler, in 1943, summarized the situation that was to confront Coast Guard officers from that time onward when he said, "[It] became necessary for the Coast Guard to attempt to adapt rather obsolete available designs to our needs."[14]

Just before the beginning of the war, with the FLBs going out of service and with no replacements, the Coast Guard relied on the small available amphibian aircraft such as the twin-engine Grumman G-21 Goose. Grumman originally designed this airplane for wealthy "aircraft-owner businessmen." The Coast Guard first purchased seven with 450 hp engines in 1939, using the Navy's JRF designation.[15] Shortly thereafter, the Coast Guard purchased twenty-five Grumman G-44 Widgeons, designed later as a scaled-downed Goose having merely 200 horsepower from each engine. The Widgeons carried the military designation J4F. Deliveries started in 1941. Ironically, this was the Coast Guard's only airplane to locate and sink an enemy submarine during the war. These aircraft were suitable for operating from sheltered waters and could not do the offshore landings of the older FLBs.

To fill this gap in the late 1930s, the Coast Guard went back to a design created for the Navy in the 1920s for a seaplane for offshore work. They purchased twelve Hall-Aluminum PHs: five were PH-2s and seven PH-3s. They duplicated the Navy's PH-1s of 1930 and "typify the seaplanes in service between 1928 and 1936," with stick, wire, and fabric wings.[16] These aircraft were biplane flying boats that emulated a basic design reaching back to the end of World War I. They too went out of service early in World War II. PBYs slowly replaced these for the Coast Guard by mid-war.

With the victory, and a large inventory of modern seaplanes available, the Coast Guard returned to the task of rescuing mariners offshore. The reliable PBY amphibian was giving away to the larger, more rugged Martin Company's twin-engine PBM Mariner seaplane, itself a design of the late 1930s. Eventually, the Navy would transfer twenty-one of them to the Coast Guard for the Air Sea Rescue program.[17]

Testing Seaplanes Offshore

MacDiarmid believed the Mariner offered a far better service "if," using its long-range ability, it could land at sea anywhere to retrieve downed aviators and shipping disaster victims.[18] He set out to prove the possibility.

"There were many aviators who still insisted that the Coast Guard's future in aviation required the operation of seaplanes from the open seas." The modern seaplanes were tough but heavy and required speeds much higher for takeoffs and landings than the Coast Guard's previous aircraft. A rough-water-operations capability was not a design criterion for the Mariner. Martin Company was required solely to demonstrate twelve takeoffs and landings in at least two-and-a-half-foot waves to prove the PBM's worthiness. Erickson postulated "these aircraft were not designed to withstand anything more than a slight sea."[19]

The Coast Guard had no fleet of proven aircraft for their new responsibility of oceanic search and rescue. Even their ability to undertake this SAR role was open to question, at least in the eyes of MacDiarmid. In a memorandum from San Diego after the war ended, which, coincidentally, was the day the Coast Guard began its transition to the Department of the Treasury, MacDiarmid complained: "[W]e [must] maintain our Air Sea Rescue setup here because if we let it drop the Navy is simply going to accept that gesture as an admission that the Coast Guard is unable to adjust itself to solve problems and are consequently unreliable or undependable. There are, as you know, quite a few people in the Navy who are watching Coast Guard operations critically, hoping that we will stumble."[20]

In May 1943, the commanding officer of the CGAS San Diego proposed that his unit test a Navy's PBM offshore "to gain experience in rough water" to pass on "to other units of the Coast Guard [later to be] engaged in Air-Sea rescue." The commandant, in endorsing this letter, added the requirement of developing procedures for rough-water tests and accumulating technical data. Finally, the chief of BuAer approved the tests, appending to them the study of rocket-assisted takeoffs.[21]

The letter approving the special tests arrived in San Diego the same month that MacDiarmid took command of the San Diego air station. The Navy provided MacDiarmid with a modified PBM, instrumented to measure structural loads and assigned to his offshore landing test project.

For the next three years MacDiarmid tested the airplane against the sea. He approached the task first by "studying open sea conditions," not the airplane. MacDiarmid consulted with experts from the University of California at Berkeley and the Scripps Institute.[22] He concluded, after landing and taking off in all directions from a given spot, that "the practice of taking off and landing parallel to the crest of the swells" was the safest course. Further experiments revealed that reversible pitch propellers shortened the landing run and jet-assisted takeoffs (JATOs) reduced the takeoff run. Nevertheless, the airplane still had to endure the impact pressures at speeds above eighty knots on the water. JATO bottles were small rocket motors, both liquid and solid propellant, mounted on the side of the aircraft in multiples.

Even landing in line with wave crests MacDiarmid discovered it was difficult to keep wing tip floats from submerging in a wave before the hull was buoyant and slowed. This condition led to a near disaster and concluded MacDiarmid's program of teaching new pilots his techniques for offshore landings five miles southwest of Point Loma, California. The aircraft being flown by a young copilot skipped back into the air after its first contact with the water, lost airspeed, and the right wing stalled. The plane then hit hard on the nose and right wing tip. The right float submerged, ripping off the entire right wing. The airplane plowed on ahead uncontrollably—still at high speed—with MacDiarmid hanging onto his armrest yelling, "Whoa, whoa, Goddamit, whoa!" as the left wing dropped and dug its float into the swell. This ripped the float off and the aircraft spun around ninety degrees. Extra pilots on board and some of the crew tried to keep the left wing up by climbing out on the stub of what was left of the right wing but the plane slowly rolled over and sank. The crew escaped.[23]

"Some of Capt. Mac's senior officers did not share his enthusiasm for seaplanes and open-sea landings," the latter requiring the approval of an admiral. MacDiarmid once thought in a certain mission that lives were unnecessarily lost. He went to his senior officer with the plea that the admiral consider the hundreds of times he, Captain Mac, had landed in the open sea and therefore leave the decision to land to his own judgment. The admiral grinned easily and said, "Mac, I don't think a man who would take an airplane into the sea hundreds of times has very good judgment."[24]

MacDiarmid, for his research, received the Navy's Distinguished Flying Cross and, immodestly, believed himself "[the] second most experienced rescue pilot in the Coast Guard, after Captain [Richard L.] Burke [Coast Guard aviator number fifteen]."[25]

MacDiarmid conducted a second series of tests with the PBM, the Martin P5M Marlin, and the new Grumman UF (later designated HU-16) Albatross between 1949 and 1951. From these tests he "planned to meet all known ocean conditions up to limits of aircraft strength and sea capability." MacDiarmid tested devices to slow the aircraft rapidly once on the water plus more testing on "rocket assisted take-off in open sea using solid fuel." For this research of correlating the effects of waves on seaplanes, he received the Institute of Aeronautical Sciences' Octave Chanute Award in 1950. He never proved, however, that the modern seaplane could land at sea successfully.

Personnel reductions following the war were a problem for the new Coast Guard that had expanded ten times in five years. At war's end, the Coast Guard had a larger number of many types of new aircraft allotted to it, with no size limitation on the aircraft. This provided a healthy option for planners in headquarters to retain personnel. The large seaplanes required twenty or more crew assigned for each aircraft; helicopters needed far fewer.

Despite the setbacks in proving the offshore capabilities of seaplanes, MacDiarmid still thumped his theses. In a 1951 paper to the Society of Automotive Engineers, he reported, "[The] seaplane excels the surface ship today in speed and search efficiency," but he conceded that it did not have the "ability to do a job on the scene of action." He did point out that the helicopter had one desirable ability: namely, "[to excel] at the scene despite rough seas, or shoals or surf, all conditions unfavorable to seaplanes." MacDiarmid then acceded, "[T]he records show occasional brilliant rescues accomplished under average command competence," but then he pointed out, "Partisans for this or that gear will quote such examples as proof of what the equipment used can do." MacDiarmid ignored the steady accumulation of remarkable rescues by the helicopter, which supported its role in such missions, concluding, "This is not realistic thinking."[26]

No More Seaplanes

The Coast Guard went out of the seaplane business in 1960 and returned its remaining seaplanes to the Navy. The new Grumman amphibian UF-1G was later rebuilt with longer wings and other modifications and redesignated the UF-2G/HU-16E Albatross. Though restricted from offshore operations, it could accomplish most of the intermediate-range search missions more efficiently at a fraction of the cost, both in money and manpower, when compared to the PBMs and

P5Ms.[27] Its amphibious capabilities did not restrict its landing locations like the larger seaplanes. This medium-range aircraft was aided by the Lockheed C-130 Hercules reaching out on the long-range flights.

The seaplane's disadvantages of excessive weight and operational inflexibility contributed to its demise; it was simply too bulky to compete with landplanes. Furthermore, it was never able to meet the conditions for landing out of protected waters, and seadromes were becoming fewer and fewer as the wartime airport building programs placed airfields convenient to land planes virtually everywhere in the world.

MacDiarmid the Helicopter Pilot

MacDiarmid, ever the opportunist, noted that helicopter pilots were getting the SAR action. Whereas the airplanes searched for them, it was the helicopter crews who picked up the survivors. Consequently, the helicopter pilot was becoming the public's hero. In June 1953 MacDiarmid wrote, "So many boys have been busting these mechanized Pogo sticks—and a few killing themselves in the operation—that I decided inasmuch as I have to order people out in these things I'd better learn to fly them myself." Typically, MacDiarmid was overstating the case. At the time he wrote this, only one fatal accident had occurred involving a Coast Guard helicopter; two crewmen died. In a sense to depreciate his acceptance, he continued, facetiously, "I actually employ these monstrosities only to get across the apron to a real flying machine without burning my delicate feet on the hot cement."[28]

MacDiarmid qualified in helicopters on 11 June 1953.[29] As a result, he was also the target of attacks by contemporaries who had endured many years of his scorn over the machine. "I hear via the grapevine," John Waters wrote MacDiarmid in a flippant note, "that you are now a helicrapper (*sic*) pilot, and have conceded that Erickson was right all along. We have heard rumors that the ready spot at the ramp is now occupied by a HO4S instead of a PBM."[30]

Even as a forty-seven-year-old commanding officer, MacDiarmid volunteered to stand the search-and-rescue alert duty with the junior pilots, still racing them to the pilot's seat when the SAR alarm sounded. In the end, it was not the type of plane that mattered to the man.

All-Helicopter Coast Guard Predicted

Erickson retired early from active duty, disappointed at failing to promote his dream and not officially being recognized by the Coast

Guard for his contributions. Years later, he wrote about "a new study out of Headquarters [showing] that six HH3F helicopters can replace eight HU-16 airplanes at a saving of some three and a half million dollars. I told them that twenty-five years ago, so I am glad to see it made official." In that letter to his brother Harold, written in 1969, Erickson once more predicted "Coast Guard Aviation will be an all-helicopter outfit before long except for a few land planes used for logistic purposes."[31]

TURNAROUND

Post-World War II Coast Guard Helicopters

Erickson and his "Helicopter Test and Development Unit" moved to Elizabeth City, where he had his own hangar and a small band of brothers, plus one HNS and two HOS helicopters.[1] On 18 June 1946, the test and development unit was officially established under the command of the Coast Guard air station to conduct projects for the headquarters' Office of Operations. In actuality, however, it came under the technical control of the engineer in chief, U.S. Coast Guard. Thus, Erickson had three bosses—a command structure that caused problems for Erickson, but no more than he was causing the Coast Guard in his persistent pursuit of the helicopter for rescue work at a time when headquarters was concentrating on seaplanes.

The total Coast Guard aircraft inventory was set by law. Helicopters were viewed as nonproducers in a world of Coast Guard missions dominated by seaplanes and amphibians, despite their offshore restrictions. The Coast Guard at that time was operating thirty-one rotary-wing craft, which were scattered among the stations and used indifferently for pilot proficiency. They were not operationally equipped, and Erickson had yet to develop rescue procedures or equipment other than the rudimentary hoist and sling.

This number of helicopters was going to drop significantly over the next two years such that by June 1948, the Coast Guard had just eight helicopters in operation, and that only because, early in 1947, the Coast Guard purchased four used Sikorsky S-51 commercial helicopters that were redesignated HO3S-1G and repossessed by Sikorsky from civilian operators. These were, according to Erickson, the first helicopters "designed specifically for Coast Guard rescue work."[2]

The Coast Guard had no sound aviation plan. Within the following few years, Elizabeth City alone would have up to ten different types of aircraft at one time. Most were hand-me-downs from war service and adapted to their various employments. Missions varied from long-range over-water search and rescue, iceberg patrols, and medical evacuations, to photo mapping of the United States and Alaska for the Coast and Geodetic Service. Some of the airplanes the Coast Guard used were the PBY, PBM, PB1-G, HU-16, Martin P5M-2G Marlin, Douglas R5D-3 Skymaster, and ConVAir PB4Y-2G Privateer (the Navy version of the B-24 Liberator). Coast Guard aviators even flew small former artillery spotters—the ConVAir OY-1 Sentinels, single-engine light planes—in their search for illicit whiskey stills throughout the southeastern United States.[3]

It was difficult in those chaotic times for mission programmers to match crew qualifications to the aircraft on hand and both crew and aircraft to the assignments. Aircrews and mechanics had to be qualified in several types; none (men and airplanes) totally suited the roles they played. Operational commitments robbed crews of training opportunities. As the commanding officer at Elizabeth City during this period wrote:

> For the past quarter, our figures are forty-eight assistance cases, 1732 hours flown, 34,000 square miles searched, three lives saved, ten medical cases transported, nine disabled vessels assisted, four aircraft assisted, two helicopter pickups at sea, seventy stills located, $21,381.00 revenue saved the Federal government. I do not have the figures yet of the areas mapped by the Photo PB-1G in Alaska this summer. We have twenty-five pilots assigned, most of whom fly everything. Last summer we were caught by the inspectors at one stage with four pilots absent with R5D in Japan, two pilots with PB-1G in Alaska, two pilots with the two OYs in Mississippi and Tennessee and three pilots absent on a logistic flight in Bermuda. At times like this, we go to watch and watch and have serious trouble covering our commitments.[4]

Erickson, working as he was at a base with high SAR potential along the middle Atlantic coast, discovered the diversion he sought. He was soon engaging the helicopter in local rescue missions, absorbing some of the responsibilities from the fixed-wing aircraft assigned to Elizabeth City. Erickson continued garnering publicity due to the novelty of the craft and the remarkable human drama it created. He was also generating disharmony within the command.

Erickson was likewise proving the ease with which the helicopter could execute a case without the complex requirements needed for conventional aircraft or amphibians, providing the helicopter flew within its envelope of capabilities: daylight, out of clouds, limited loads, and short range. Erickson's scheme, in a sense, was demeaning for many overworked fixed-winged crews, however. The good (meaning high-recognition) cases were gobbled up by helicopters while the fixed-winged crews spent hours and hours "tooling around the skies" just looking at the water.[5]

Several cases involved injured or ill patients who were living on the isolated coastal regions of Virginia and the Carolinas where landing facilities were often not available for conventional airplanes. Helicopters were also used to search for numerous crashed military airplanes and to recover downed aviators in coastal waters and the region's inaccessible swamps. An informal record—most likely compiled by Erickson—noted forty-two helicopter cases flown out of Elizabeth City from 1946 through 1948.[6] It was one of these cases that proved to a world audience this new machine had a role in human survival.

Helicopters Rescue Plane Crash Victims

A Sabena (Belgian) Airlines DC-4 crashed into a mountain while attempting to land at Gander, Newfoundland, on 18 September 1946. The airliner went undiscovered for two days in the nearly unpenetrable tundra. There were survivors among the casualties, but the terrain prevented any effective rescue efforts to assist them out over land. Airplanes could not land near the crash scene. The only hope for the survivors, several of whom had suffered serious injuries, was to be brought out on the backs of men over the seven miles of snow and muskeg to the nearest lake, where amphibians could fly them out.

Capt. Richard Burke, U.S. Coast Guard, a former seaplane pilot, was now the eastern area rescue officer. He ordered two Coast Guard helicopters to Gander for this mission. Floyd Bennett Field had just two helicopters in commission at that time. The one suitable HOS was not flyable because of a time limit on the rotor blades. The other was rigged for and testing the dipping sonar. Burke had the grounding for high-time blades temporarily lifted for this one mission. Erickson's test and development unit provided the second, backup, rescue aircraft, the HNS from Elizabeth City.

The helicopters were loaded into two Air Transport Command C-54s. The C-54 carrying the HOS from New York arrived at Gander the morning of 21 September. The other, with the HNS from Elizabeth City, arrived twenty minutes later. While the helicopters were being unloaded and reassembled, the four helicopter pilots—Erickson, Graham, Kleisch, and Bolton—rode in a PBY over the scene of the crash and to the lake near the crash site, where the PBY could land.

As Erickson later described: "The entire [land] surface [was] a vast marsh covered with muskeg that could not support the weight of a helicopter. Men walking on this surface would frequently sink to their knees in the muck."[7] Consequently, he had helicopter landing platforms built from lumber dropped from a PBY at a small clearing about a quarter of a mile from the crash site. Still, one witness wrote, "It required able-bodied persons over thirty minutes to travel" the quarter mile from the wreckage to the helicopter landing site, slogging through knee-deep sphagnum mosses and sedge.[8] The Army ground crew that had hiked in to aid the survivors built this and a second platform at the lake. The helicopters would shunt the victims to that second platform, from which they would be moved to the nearby floating PBY for the flight to Gander.

The HOS was reassembled by early afternoon and flown on a short test flight. Kleisch flew to the landing pad at the crash site and evacuated eight stretcher cases to the lake before dark. The HNS was reassembled and test flown but experienced accidental damage on the test flight. This caused the remaining victims "to spend another night in the marsh at the site of the burned-out wreckage of their aircraft [with] the bodies of those who died." The following day both helicopters flew out the remaining survivors, plus the fourteen members of the Army ground rescue crew that had hiked in. Eighteen of the fifty-four on board the airliner survived; the dead were buried where they died.[9] Erickson returned to his projects with one more convincing coup in his battle to create rescue helicopters.

The Coast Guard Accepts the Helicopter

Meanwhile, the helicopter was gaining favor among "the higher Coast Guard administrative officers," according to Erickson, and was supported by "all of the commanding officers of the icebreakers." Furthermore, a firm of efficiency experts known as the EBASCO Group, hired in 1948 to study the Coast Guard and make recommendations to improve its operations, concluded that Coast Guard operations were satisfactory "with the exception of helicopters, which should be replaced as soon as possible by an increased number of more recently developed and highly versatile rotary wing aircraft." The report further recommended that "Research and development in applications of helicopters to Coast Guard rescue work should be materially increased. Additional helicopters of modern type and increased capacity should be authorized and obtained. All Coast Guard air stations should be provided with the helicopters, and be authorized trained complements of personnel to operate and maintain this additional equipment." This recommendation, however, resulted in an order for only five new HO3S helicopters.[10]

Rotary-Wing Development Unit

Erickson received orders on 16 March 1948 to Buffalo, New York. There he was to report on board the Coast Guard icebreaker *Mackinaw* in the HO3S CGNR (Coast Guard Number) 230. The Great Lakes icebreaking season was about to start with the aid of the helicopter for the first time.

According to Erickson's report, opening the Great Lakes navigation season early in 1948 was essential because "steel makers had less than half their normal supply of iron ore on hand, while the demand for steel was greater than ever to meet the post war manufacturing boom."[11] The small task force of Coast Guard vessels—the *Mackinaw* and several buoy tenders fitted with ice-breaking bows—began opening a lane from Buffalo harbor early on the morning of 18 March. The *Mackinaw* led a convoy of ore carriers headed for Cleveland. This little force, guided by a helicopter, achieved the earliest opening of Buffalo harbor in recorded history.

Comdr. Edwin J. Roland, U.S. Coast Guard (commandant of the Coast Guard from 1962 to 1966), task force commander, utilized the helicopter for daily photographic reconnaissance flights. He flew as observer with Erickson, "keeping a constant check on the ice conditions." A change in the wind might suddenly pile up huge windrows of ice that would be difficult for the small ships to break, or it could possibly carry ships ashore in a field of ice. "Advantage was taken of open leads in the ice," Erickson explained, "that could only be spotted from aloft."[12] Erickson went on to quote from an uncited aviation periodical:

Use of helicopters operating with Coast Guard icebreakers in the Great Lakes last winter freed icebound shipping at Buffalo sixty-seven days ahead of schedule and increased the effectiveness of the ice breaking operation by fifty percent. The helicopter scouted as much as one hundred miles ahead of the icebreaker and determined the route of the thinnest ice ahead. It also permitted the icebreaker skipper to perform frequent inspection of icebound groups of ships to determine the most effective route for freeing them.[13]

Emergency Flotation for Helicopters

There was an inherent danger to the helicopter crew when they flew over slush ice. If forced down, the ice might not support the helicopter, and freezing water could quickly entomb the crew. After the mission, when he was back at Elizabeth City, armed with experience flying over ice and endorsements from Roland on the absolute need for helicopters on icebreakers, Erickson urged for and was granted authorization to pursue the HO3S doughnut-float proposal. These flotation bags were concealed in "pants" on the landing gear through which the wheels extended for normal ground operations. When inflated, the bags could float the helicopter on water in an emergency. "This project really paid off," Erickson reported. "A week after these floats had been installed on all of these aircraft an HO3S was forced down in Delaware Bay. . . . The floats prevented the loss of this aircraft, which had been purchased at a cost of $91,977."[14]

On a SAR case that occurred after the floats had been installed, Lt. Gordon MacLane, U.S. Coast Guard, inflated the floats on the HO3S he was flying and landed in flood waters to retrieve trapped children. He and his crewman, William Peyton, an ordanceman, saved thirty-nine lives during the 1950 San Joaquin Valley, California, floods. In the instances when the children were too small to use the "horse collar" sling (a design which resulted from Erickson's experiments) attached to the hoist cable, Peyton waded through chest-deep water, carrying the small victims through the "swift current" to the helicopter.[15]

This case supported two developmental causes for Erickson to pursue. First, a basket was needed to safely pick up and retrieve all size and conditions of victims, conscious or unconscious. Second, MacLane unquestionably demonstrated the need for an amphibious helicopter, the very concept Kossler expounded in 1943 in his call for a flying surfboat.

Erickson's success with the lifesaving capability of the helicopter was causing embarrassments once more for the command where he was principally a tenant. Headquarters could no longer ignore the problem; it interceded on 30 June 1948 by pulling him under their command. The unit's new name became the Rotary Wing Development Unit, and it was to be independent of, but still at, Elizabeth City. This time, however, Erickson was responsible directly to headquarters. His mission was "to develop rotary wing aircraft for use by the Coast Guard in carrying out its assigned functions." This, in part, fulfilled another EBASCO recommendation.[16] A turnaround had finally come for Erickson: a rescue mission for the helicopter was officially recognized four and a half years after the first rescue.

Erickson's Rescue Basket

The Rotary Wing Development Unit continued to work on the rescue sling. A universal, simple, easily donned harness or device was needed to hold survivors securely on their journey via the hoist cable from the ground or water to the hovering helicopter. The sling, or horse collar, they created, though adopted by the military, had shortcomings and eventually proved to be dangerous even to people trained in its use.

For example, the Navy and space science staged a successful mission in 1961, but at a tragic expense. The manned research balloon *Stratolab* was launched from the USS *Antietam* carrying Comdr. Malcom D. Ross, U.S. Navy, and Lt. Comdr. Victor A. Prather, U.S. Navy (Medical Corps), to a new record altitude for manned balloons. During the crew's retrieval after landing at sea, Prather fell from the sling being used by the recovery helicopter, and died.[17] One other tragedy occurred when a woman rescued from California flood waters by a Navy HUP "dropped" from the sling as she was being hoisted to safety and "disappeared in the swirling muddy water."[18]

(Erickson also commented later on the second American astronaut in space, Capt. Virgil I. Grissom, U.S. Air Force. Though extensively trained in the rescue sling's use, he pulled it on backwards when he was retrieved from his capsule. Only his physical strength kept him from falling back into the ocean during the hoist by helicopter.[19])

Erickson cataloged these losses and other near tragedies and used them to motivate others to accept his proposed solution, the rescue basket. As late as the end of 1951, however, he was still trying to convince headquarters of the importance and need for such a basket. In one memorandum, he noted, "In recent years several persons have fallen out of slings rigged for helicopter use." He then emphasized, "[I]n at least two cases persons were killed by falling out of such slings while several other persons lost their lives because they did not have the strength to get into the rescue sling when [it was] lowered to them." Erickson called attention to the dangers of using the horse collar sling by referring to a photograph of a pilot who was being lowered to a carrier deck, hanging head down, unconscious. His life was saved only because his foot caught on the sling as he slipped from it. Erickson concluded his passionate note summarily rejecting any device a person could fall from.[20]

In such cases where the persons being recovered were not conscious or able to assist themselves into a harness, helicopter pilots occasionally had to lower the flight mechanic into the water to put a harness on a survivor, then leave the mechanic behind. Erickson reported at least one instance where the helicopter pilot had difficulty relocating the crewman after safely delivering the survivor to a nearby ship.[21]

The rescue basket, by design, could be lowered into the water and dragged under an inert body by the maneuvering helicopter. Erickson designed his basket to have a spreader or bail with attached floats that permitted the basket to submerge about twenty inches under the surface while the basket remained level. When the helicopter exerted a slightly lateral pull on the bail, the basket would heel over and scoop objects in its path. Erickson claimed, "[W]ith a maneuverable helicopter, it was a simple matter to lower the basket slightly up-wind of a person in the water; pay out slack in the hoisting cable; then drop down wind, placing the man between the basket and the helicopter." In early tests, "pilots had no difficulty scooping up a dummy named 'Oscar.'"[22]

A major drawback in using the basket was that it was a bulky item, too large to fit in the HO3S, which had limited cargo space. "So it was not used in actual rescue operations until larger helicopters became available."[23]

Erickson's designs finally came together in 1949 in a rapid series of diverse rescues that exemplified his preliminary concepts. Two separate cases involved removing ill seamen from ships eighty and ninety-five miles off the Virginia coast, respectively. The seas were too rough for seaplane landings, and in one case the HO3S flown by Lt. David Oliver landed on the fantail of the Coast Guard cutter *Chincoteague,* having only a five-foot clearance for its rotors.

The open-sea test came when a burning Navy F-8F Bearcat forced the pilot to bail out thirty miles offshore. An Elizabeth City Coast Guard PBM flew to the scene, but rough seas kept it from landing. It could merely orbit and direct an HRP, piloted by Lt. James Swanson, U.S. Coast Guard, to the downed pilot. The fighter pilot was scooped into the basket, hoisted by Lt. (jg) H. M. Wills, U.S. Coast Guard, and trundled aboard the helicopter "forty-five minutes after hitting the silk!"[24]

Another example of the versatility of the craft envisioned by Erickson came when Lt. Shirly W. Reese, U.S. Marine Corps, bailed out over a dense North Carolina swamp. He suffered major injuries, including two broken legs. Safe extraction by ground party was improbable. Lt. Fletcher Brown Jr., U.S. Coast Guard, flying an HRP, hoisted Reese to safety. According to Erickson's account: "It was the first time that a litter patient was lifted out of a swamp by a helicopter in flight. It would be repeated many times over the next few years."[25] This act set the precedent for the thousands of helicopter rescues to follow shortly thereafter during the Korean War and, much later, from the jungles of Vietnam.

By early 1950, rescue devices created and developed by Erickson's unit were standard equipment for new *military*, not Coast Guard, helicopters. As Erickson predicted, these devices came "just in time for the Korean War." The helicopters added a new dimension to warfare. Battlefield casualties were whisked away, frequently within moments, to medical facilities. Furthermore, helicopters moved stealthily into enemy territory and recovered downed pilots, returning them to safety. Sergei Sikorsky, in a personal summary of helicopter rescues, noted, "[B]y the end of that [Korean] war well over twenty thousand wounded had been carried by helicopter to MASH hospital units, and over one thousand two hundred have been rescued from behind enemy lines."[26]

The importance of helicopters for warfare was recognized by a wide new audience. Television started bringing war into homes in daily news reports. Interest in this new vehicle was compounded as much from the novelty of the craft as the successes. An early television series even featured the antics of this unique machine. Finally, the Coast Guard received public acknowledgment for its contribution in developing the helicopter's rescue capabilities.

Collier's Publishing Company named the Coast Guard as a recipient of the "Nation's top aviation award" in 1951. The Collier Trophy was presented by President Harry S Truman to "the industry, the Coast Guard and the Military Services for developing and using the craft in air rescue work." The article went on to report, "[T]his year in Korea alone, over 10,000 UN wounded have been evacuated with whirly birds." Colliers singled out the Coast Guard, reporting: "It has pioneered in peace time rescue work. During the eight years it has been using helicopters, it has saved many hundreds of lives in offshore rescues, in floods, fires and other disasters on land."[27]

The End for Erickson

Erickson completed his research and development projects by early 1950 with the few helicopters the Coast Guard had remaining. "We did suffer a terrible set back in the Olsen-MacDiarmid era [1944–1953]," he wrote, "when the Coast Guard program was reduced to six HO3S and two HTL trainers in 1950."[28] When Erickson's unit was decommissioned on 31 March 1950, "the prevailing attitude of the old seaplane drivers, who were in control, was to get rid of those dammed things as quickly as possible."[29] Erickson later reflected on the Coast Guard's loss of helicopters, writing, "It's too bad the CG was in such a hurry to dispose of the old R-4s (HNS-1s) and HOSs when the Rotary Wing Development Unit was decommissioned, but there were a lot of old diehards around who were determined to eliminate all trace of those dammed grasshopper things as soon as possible."[30]

Erickson then moved on to headquarters as assistant to the chief of the Aviation Division. No more command opportunities, as predicted, came his way. He had served as commanding officer only once—the few months he headed up the helicopter school. Olsen, it appears, made good on his promise to Erickson that Erickson would never hold a responsible job in Coast Guard aviation.[31]

Erickson's stay in headquarters was as an "office boy" working for a "'black shoe man' right to the core [who] resented anybody or anything connected with aviation." Erickson then transferred to New York as chief search-and-rescue officer. Both jobs kept him from the cockpit and busy with routine paperwork unrelated to helicopters. Erickson retired on 1 July 1954 after twenty-two years of commissioned service, disappointed that he was unable to create a rescue helicopter for the Coast Guard. There was no traditional farewell party for Erickson; in fact, he "didn't even get a handshake, friendly or otherwise."[32]

Captain Erickson risked his career over a dream, a dream ignited by the lost souls in Pearl Harbor, and he lost.

ELEVEN

SEA LEGS

rickson accepted that the restrictive range of the helicopter could never be solved by improvements in the aircraft. Additional horsepower from a gasoline-powered piston engine came with the cost of weight: more weight for the engine and drive train, more weight for the fuel. Only small gains were made in payload and range with each new helicopter model. He would not be a part of it, but a breakthrough did come after Erickson left the Coast Guard. The helicopters he was seeking arrived with the application of lightweight turboshaft engines to the helicopter airframe. The only way Erickson could establish an effective operating range for the helicopter was to hitch the aircraft to ships.

Helicopters for Icebreakers

For twelve years following the *Cobb*'s decommissioning in 1946, ship/helicopter operations were limited in the Coast Guard to icebreakers. The first such icebreaker to receive a float-equipped HNS was *Northwind*. The ship sailed in December 1946 to take part in the Navy's expedition Operation High Jump. The *Northwind* was the sole ice escort vessel available to traverse the "worst pack in Antarctic history."[1] With the little helicopter flown by Lt. David Gershowitz, U.S. Coast Guard, Lt. James Cornish, U.S. Coast Guard, and aviation pilot Jack Olsen, U.S. Coast Guard, leading the way, the icebreaker battered a track through 650 miles of ice in eighteen days.

A few weeks earlier, in October, Gershowitz was called before his commanding officer, Hesford, at CGAS Brooklyn and offered a job flying "down south." Hesford began, "Gersh, you've been flying helicopters for three years and your 550 hours in them give you the rating of one of the ten leading flyers in the country." Gershowitz (widely known as "O'Hara" because tower operators could never understand his name on the radio, pronounced as it was in his heavy Brooklyn accent) misinterpreted the assignment, thinking, "A jaunt to the 'south' conjured up images of Florida's sandy beaches, palm trees, and calm skies." Instead, he heard Hesford continue, "You have been picked to be one of three helicopter pilots on the expedition to the Antarctic and Little America."[2]

Adm. R. H. Cruzen, U.S. Navy, led the expedition of four thousand men. As Gershowitz remembers, he "went up with us" in the HNS "on every suitable occasion." The sky was light twenty-four hours each day, and the helicopter was ready for flight within an hour when called for. The airplane, a Grumman JF-2, also on board, took much longer to get ready. "We took off and flew slowly ahead of the little caravan of vessels, looking for iceleads—those cracks in the pack which would make it possible for our ships to penetrate." When seeking iceleads, the helicopter crew did so without slowing the van, "[w]hereas in the three operational flights made by the JF-2 Grumman Duck—valuable time was consumed lowering it over the side. Of course the Duck had a greater range, but the slow-moving ships created a situation where range wasn't too important a factor."[3]

The *Northwind*'s commanding officer, Capt. Charles W. Thomas, U.S. Coast Guard, recognized that this feat would not have been possible without helicopter reconnaissance. "Had the Task Group penetrated the pack without 'eyes' it would have arrived too late in the season to establish a base." Thomas concluded his remarks by noting he had sent a dispatch of this success to the commandant. "HELICOPTER BEST PIECE OF EQUIPMENT EVER CARRIED IN ICE VESSELS." His emphatic message was provoked by personnel at headquarters having previously denied his previous efforts to obtain a helicopter for the icebreaker *Eastwind* "more than a year earlier."[4]

In 1949 Erickson went to Canada to assist the Department of Transport in designing a helicopter deck for their new icebreaker, *D'Iberville*. He took plans with him of helicopter decks that had been installed on the *Cobb* and the icebreaker *Northwind,* as well as of a ship's helicopter-deck model built by Graham. Canadians forged ahead in shipboard/helicopter accommodations. The unique telescoping hangar later installed on Coast Guard icebreakers came from plans developed in Canada after Erickson's visit.[5] It was not until the spring of 1963, however, that the Coast Guard began installing telescopic helicopter hangars, purchased from Canada, on its own icebreakers.

The Coast Guard got its start in icebreaking years earlier. President Roosevelt's executive order of 21 December 1936 directed the service to assist in keeping channels and harbors open to navigation by breaking ice-choked routes. Icebreaking in American navigational waters, by this act, became a new duty for the Coast Guard. Following World War II, the Navy and Coast Guard shared icebreaking roles through an informal arrangement formally agreed upon in March 1963. The Coast Guard operated two icebreakers in the Arctic and Antarctic in support of naval missions. The Navy, however, owned the larger icebreaker fleet. In its move to reduce noncombatant ships, the Navy transferred five icebreakers to the Coast Guard in October 1965. The last ship arrived under the Coast Guard ensign in November 1966.[6] But the Coast Guard did not have enough helicopters and aviators for the five newly acquired vessels plus the two already in their fleet. The Navy had to provide both.[7]

The few Coast Guard helicopter pilots and mechanics assigned to icebreakers prior to 1966 had no special Arctic survival training or cold-weather-operating experience. A major program soon emerged requiring large numbers of skilled aviators and crews to be deployed to the Arctic and Antarctic. Once more the standardized approach developed for the introduction of the HH-52A was pursued. All aircrew and mechanics were trained, aircraft were maintained, and ships were manned by helicopter detachments from a single unit.

A helicopter Icebreaker Support Section was established and added to the Coast Guard Aviation Training Center, Mobile, on 1 January 1969. It was composed of thirty officers, ninety-one enlisted men, and fourteen HH-52A helicopters. Each icebreaker detachment consisted of two HH-52A helicopters with four aviators and eleven enlisted flight support personnel. When the HH-65A replaced the HH-52A, crew requirements were dropped to nine, ten if a rescue swimmer deployed. The unit is now named Polar Operations Division and currently supplies crews to only two remaining polar icebreakers.

The first detachment (AvDet1) from the new command at Mobile to supply helicopter support to polar icebreakers began in the summer of 1969. Its crew operated the HH-52A. Detachment number fifty-seven (AvDet 57) was the first to operate off the new *Polar*-class icebreakers seven years later in the summer of 1976. In the summer of 1988, AvDet 120 was the first detachment that deployed with the HH-65As. A special event occurred on 22 August 1994 when Mark Mobley, an aviation electrician's mate first class, "became the first active duty Coast Guard member to set foot on the geographic North Pole."

Mobley, flying with AvDet 134, stepped from HH-65A CGNR 6564 after the Dauphin landed squarely on the pole. This same helicopter flew in Antarctica in December 1989.[8]

Flight crews on board icebreakers on the early deployments to the "ice" discovered that the standard paint scheme on helicopter fuselages proved to be effective camouflage in the polar regions. If one was down on the ice, spotters had difficulty finding it. Aircraft were soon painted with a Coast Guard red fuselage to aid searchers in spotting them against the predominately white background. Aircraft in both fleets of helicopters—the HH-52A and later its replacement, the HH-65A—were painted with both white (commonly used in domestic SAR) and red fuselages. Scheduling of red-only airframes for icebreakers became difficult so, to simplify matters, the entire HH-65A fleet— whether the ship will be used in the ice or not—has red hulls.

Coast Guard Cutters Get Helicopters

Through the 1950s the Coast Guard deployed helicopters from icebreakers, the only ships then designed to accommodate these aircraft. As the decade closed, a few helicopter aviators with shipboard operating experience were promoted to headquarters staff positions, thus enabling them to exert a feeble but positive influence. They encouraged the Coast Guard to adopt ship/helicopter designs and operations.

A major advance in helicopter operations occurred in 1956. The commandant, Vice Adm. A. C. Richmond, convened a board to examine the needs of Coast Guard aviation and to propose recommendations for future aircraft procurement. The board was headed by an aviator, Capt. S. C. Linholm, and was composed of four nonaviation officers and six aviators. Three of the latter were qualified helicopter aviators. Erickson noted a strange dichotomy:

> Some senior aviators, who had dictated Coast Guard Aviation policy for many years, were strongly opposed to any increase in the number of helicopters. . . . [I]n contrast, many line officers, particularly the icebreaker skippers, were very well aware of the need for helicopters on board icebreakers. . . . The fact that it had been necessary to ask the Navy to supply helicopters and flight crews for Coast Guard icebreakers used in Polar operations was an example of the failure of the officers, who had directed Coast Guard Aviation, to recognize the helicopter's importance.[9]

The board, in a striking turnaround, did not recommend increasing the number of fixed-wing aircraft, but it did recommend the purchase of ninety-nine helicopters: seventy-nine of the new Sikorsky HUS-1 for search and rescue, and twenty Bell HUL-1 for icebreakers. "This action by the board," Erickson predicted, "started the swing toward the development of an all-helicopter air rescue fleet in the Coast Guard."[10]

While the board had taken a bold initial step, the Coast Guard nevertheless moved with cautious reservations. It was not until the early 1960s before the Coast Guard began adding new cutters to the postwar fleet designed specifically for the helicopter. The 210-foot *Reliance* was the first medium endurance cutter—at 930 tons—intentionally designed from the keel up to support helicopter operations. Sixteen of the thirty cutters originally planned were built. The *Hamilton* followed as the first of a new class of high endurance cutters designed to accommodate helicopters. It had an overall length of 378 feet and displaced 2,748 tons. The Coast Guard intended to purchase thirty-six of this class cutter, but with the curtailment of the ocean station vessel program, just twelve were built.

Both designs originated as a preliminary design project by a graduate student in 1945.[11] Later, the "270 footer" *Famous* class (named for earlier famous Coast Guard cutters) was designed with "special emphasis on ability to conduct helicopter operations throughout a two-week patrol." The first, *Bear,* was commissioned in February 1983.[12]

The concept of designing ships to carry helicopters was possibly sown by Erickson in 1945 when he flew his friend Capt. John P. Lattimer, U.S. Coast Guard, in the HNS to demonstrate the ship/helicopter potential.[13] From this early indoctrination, Lattimer "plugged away for better helo accommodations on ships" during his tour of duty in headquarters from 1947 to 1952.

In the summer of 1962, the construction of the first three ships in the *Reliance* class was in progress, and the bid package was nearly completed for the larger *Hamilton* class. The single person responsible for putting helicopter platforms on those ships was undiscovered. However, the ships were designed principally by "Gil Schumacher, Chief of ENE in 1960–1962, and Sam Lank." Lattimer recalled, "[B]ased upon some memory of the design history, and knowledge of personalities, it would be my guess that Gil and Sam evolved the design and that Gil pushed it through with practically no changes."[14]

Lattimer served a second tour of duty in headquarters from 1962 to 1968. He observed, "[Naval engineering] lost no ground on helo facilities" for *Wind, Hamilton,* and *Reliance* classes and "made improvements in some areas. There were other substantial improvements that could have been made but we ran into honest differences of opinion from working level budgeteers and non-aviation operations."[15]

The *Reliance* was scheduled for simultaneous acceptance sea trials and helicopter compatibility evaluation. The ship was delayed at the shipyard because of main propulsion plant problems, so the "first helicopter recovery was made on 6 July 1964 with the vessel tied at the dock alongside an old abandoned shed." The helicopter was a Sikorsky HH-52A Seaguard, CGNR 1356. Comdr. Frank L. Shelley, at headquarters, emphatically implored Comdr. John Redfield, in charge of the evaluation, "Don't prang one!" A crash on the ship during the test would end the project and any promise of a ship/helicopter scheme. Redfield was convinced all future ships would be built *without* helicopter landing decks if *anything* bad happened.[16]

Tugbird

When the sea trials finally commenced the next day, the *Reliance* lost all power. With the ship "laying dead in the water about 4 miles off Galveston, [Redfield] half-heartedly suggested" to the captain that he use the helicopter to tow the ship back to the dock. The commanding officer, Comdr. Frank Fisher, "in a good-natured jesting way, said he would tow it back by pulling boat or scuttle it before he would permit a helicopter to tow her back to port."[17] Underlying the humor was an attitude toward the helicopter still prevalent twenty years after Erickson introduced its abilities to the Coast Guard. Towing the ship, however, was not an idle boast of Redfield's. He had conducted helicopter towing tests for the Coast Guard with the Sikorsky HO4S-3G in St. Petersburg during the fall of 1957.[18] The HO4S and HH-52A were nearly equal in towing power.

Redfield's results were successful, and the "Tugbird" was created. But because of required advanced rigging, calls for its use were essentially nonexistent.[19] Side tows were practiced whereby the crewman would hold a towline for pulling small craft from immediate danger, but the helicopter pilot could use the down-wash from the rotor system to blow boats more easily. The tugbird procedure was never put into practice, however. The largest vessel towed then by the helicopter was the 177-foot buoy tender *Juniper,* at 794 tons displacement. During that event the ship, secured at the end of a quarter-inch steel cable, was dragged along behind the helicopter tug at three knots.[20]

The calm-water test with the HH-52A aboard the *Reliance* proved that the helicopter could work with a ship during both day and night operations. A later rough-water test in October confirmed what Graham demonstrated twenty years before: the ship/helicopter combination could work.

The Next Helicopter "Is Gonna Float!"

The HO4S helicopters were reaching an expected lifetime limit after an average of ten years in service when a fatal helicopter crash caused by mechanical failure of rotor head linkage nudged the Coast Guard into seeking a replacement helicopter. In 1960 the Coast Guard acquired six Sikorsky HUS-1Gs, "the Cadillac of the piston engine 'copters,'" with its 1525-horsepower engine.[21] It had automatic stabilizing equipment that permitted safer flight over water at night and instrument flying in helicopters for the first time. Additional radio equipment was included since the pilots were freed momentarily from the controls to use radios.

The lack of an all-weather capability in previous helicopters was the Coast Guard's argument for not procuring more of these aircraft. "This argument was completely dispelled when one of the new HUS-1G helicopters, piloted by LCDR James L. Sigman, USCGR, flew through torrential rains and hurricane force winds to come to the aid of the crew of the fishing vessel . . . directly in the eye of Hurricane Ethel."[22]

Their popularity was short-lived, however. Two crashed in Tampa Bay—within the same hour and at the same spot—after their engines lost power in hovers. The first one fell into the water attempting to rescue a B-47 crew that had ditched. The second one ditched trying to rescue the crew of the first helicopter. A third HUS-1G was stricken soon after in the Gulf of Mexico after its rotors struck a ship's rigging. The remaining three were out of service within two years.[23]

By 1962, then, the Coast Guard had to find the seventy-nine helicopters they had determined earlier that were needed for their aviation plan. The HUS was not the aircraft. Rear Adm. Charles Tighe, a seaplane pilot and then-Aviation Division chief, reportedly said, "The next goddam helicopter we buy is gonna float!"[24]

TWELVE

"GOLD-PLATED CADILLACS"

A Short-Range Recovery Helicopter

Sikorsky provided the answer. They built a new amphibian: a free-turbine, turboshaft-powered helicopter. The new S-62 was designed for the commercial market using various parts already manufactured for earlier production aircraft. The S-62 was a smaller, single-engine version of the S-61/SH-3 series Navy ASW helicopter first flown in 1959. The automatic stabilization system (ASE) used on the new model was a 60-percent scaled version of the larger S-61s. The rotor system came from the S-55/HO4S, as did most of the drive system already proven through nearly ten years of service. This dynamic assemblage (rotors, gearboxes, and controls) would absorb, through design, only 730 horsepower. Small jet engines in a variety of horsepowers suitable for helicopters were rare, however, and not available in this size.[1]

So Sikorsky simply used the General Electric T58 turboshaft power plant already used in pairs for the S-61 though it had nearly twice the output needed. This compromise of over-design because the equipment existed, like other "tried and true" features adapted to this helicopter, quite likely contributed to the successful twenty-five-year life span of the new HH-52A. According to Comdr. Frank Shelley: "The result was that while there was always the unknown synergy of the combination, there was nothing new or cutting edge about ol' rusty-trusty. It was in reality a helicopter comfortably behind the cutting edge."[2]

The civilian market did not buy the S-62 in great enough numbers for it to be a profitable venture for Sikorsky. The engine was too big and too expensive. None of the branches in the Defense Department

had use for it either. The Navy was already committed to another manufacturer for a similar sized helicopter. Problems with the HUS made
the Sikorsky Company unpopular at headquarters.[3] But Sikorsky desperately needed to sell a helicopter, and the Coast Guard desperately
needed one, so they reluctantly agreed to a test *at* the manufacturer's
expense. After all, the S-62 did have two desirable features: it floated
on its amphibian hull, and it had turbine power.

It passed. Twenty-eight were ordered for the Coast Guard's Short
Range Recovery (SRR) helicopters; the first of this order was delivered
in January 1963. The HH-52A's mission responsibility was to reach
out 150 miles, do a rescue in twenty minutes, and return. The aircraft
was successful at the start.[4]

The HH-52A, or "Seaguard," a name even crew members could
never remember (most called it simply the "52"), was originally designated the HU2S-1G. It was an extremely flexible rescue aircraft that
could fully perform missions with just one pilot and one crew member
in the cabin aft. Night and all-weather flight was possible with a pilot
and copilot. The 52 had a hydraulic hoist and normally carried a rescue basket. It had space in the cabin to haul a litter and a de-watering
pump routinely. The cabin could accommodate up to ten passengers
or six litters and three troop seats. A special feature was a removable
foldout rescue platform, looking like a large extended step. This platform was a rectangular grid, and when installed, it sloped slightly
downward beneath the water's surface out from the main entrance
door when the helicopter was afloat. Inert bodies could be scooped or
dragged onto it for ease of hauling them into the cabin.[5]

The amphibious design proved itself a month after the first
"machine" was received by a station for operational use.[6] On 22 March
1963 an HH-52A was airborne on a search for missing fishermen off
Newport, Rhode Island, when a Navy ship nearby lost a man overboard. "It was a bitter cold day, and a man could not survive long in
the freezing water." The search began astern the ship. Precious time
passed without a sighting when "suddenly, Jim Webber, [the] hoist
operator, yelled, 'There he is, close aboard at three o'clock!'" The victim sank. The pilot, Comdr. John Waters, landed the helicopter at the
spot on the water just as the sailor's head reemerged.[7]

"Quickly rigging out the rescue platform, Webber grabbed him by
the shoulder, but he was a big man, and semiconscious." Waters then
demonstrated the flexibility of crew positions by quickly unstrapping
himself, twisting out of his seat in the cockpit, and stepping back into
the cabin to help Webber drag the victim aboard, all the while yelling to
the copilot, Bob Russell, to "Take off!" The pickup took less than one
minute; ten minutes later the comatose sailor was in an ambulance.[8]

A Navy pilot landed his helicopter near the HH-52A to "look at our new amphibian." He had been flying overhead, able merely to watch the rescue. He remarked, "It's a good thing you were there." The Navy helicopter had only a horse collar sling with which to retrieve the victim, who, unconscious, couldn't have been hoisted. Waters noted that the Navy pilot "looked at the boat-hulled chopper again with admiration," then followed with the question, "You wouldn't like to trade, would you?" "Not for a lot full of gold-plated Cadillacs," Waters thought.[9]

A standing joke among early HH-52A pilots was the dispensability of copilots; as crews sometimes quipped, "the copilot can walk home." At times when an aircraft was overloaded, the copilot was left behind. On other occasions, he or she might leave the cockpit in flight to assist the crew members in the cabin administering first aid or CPR.

Lt. (jg) Terry Sinclair, U.S. Coast Guard, as copilot of Seaguard number 1386, was lowered in the rescue basket into twelve-foot waves in the Pacific Ocean off the California coast to retrieve victims of a plane crash. He reached one unconscious man "with remarkable effort" and got him into the rescue basket. Then Sinclair was left behind to tread water in the ocean alone while the helicopter rushed the "critically injured man" to safety. "Sinclair was later retrieved by the helicopter."[10]

Helicopter Air Stations Are Assigned

More HH-52As were ordered, bringing the total number purchased to ninety-seven. These could be used on icebreakers in place of the Bell helicopters. The Coast Guard was getting the aircraft Erickson dreamed of, but it did not have the number of pilots or stations spread along the coast that could utilize this new rescue vehicle. HH-52A test pilot Shelley was later assigned to headquarters where he undertook to establish air stations in a geographical pattern that suited the number of new helicopters, their operating parameters, and regional needs. This was a revitalization of Erickson's plan: the extension of the earlier lifeboat station concept of Coast Guard stations rimming the continent's coasts.

Determining needs in specific areas was impossible, however. No statistical base existed to determine helicopter SAR caseloads. The only figures that were available recorded cases already handled in places where the few helicopters were located and available for missions. Shelley discovered, as predicted, that "the closer to the facility, the more cases there were. Clearly, that wasn't going to be any help, so Dick [Commander Penn], working with [Shelley] took out . . . dividers and started striking arcs" based on the HH-52A operational range. They even chose the base names, traditionally named for the nearest community, from the Atlas, based on the geographic location.

Shelley "was absolutely amazed to find ten years later that we got exactly that, place for place, name for name."[11]

Quarter-Century Workhorse

"The first of the amphibious choppers designed specifically for SAR," wrote Waters, "the HH-52A was the most successful life-saving vehicle of all time, with over 15,000 lives saved in its twenty-five years of service before being replaced by the HH-65 twin-engine light helicopter."[12] This figure does not begin to disclose the unrecorded numbers of people, animals, and property helped by this venerable aircraft.

For example, a deer fell on the frozen Detroit River, but the ice was too thin to support rescuers. The sheriff's department requested a Coast Guard helicopter to carry a sharpshooter to destroy the apparently injured animal. The air station's commanding officer, Comdr. James Leskinovitch, refused to kill the deer, however, choosing instead to have his crew lasso the animal from a Seaguard, then gently tow "Bambi" across the ice by air taxiing the helicopter to the beach. The deer was found to be uninjured and released.[13]

Pilot training became a new problem after the introduction of the HH-52A. Traditionally, all aviators for the Coast Guard were trained at the operating units once they received their qualifications from Navy flight training because the Coast Guard had not had a formal helicopter school for nearly twenty years. A few aviators with experience were recruited directly from other military services, but none of these normally came with the skills for flying the SAR helicopters employed by the Coast Guard. The largest group of SAR-skilled helicopter aviators, therefore, came from experienced Coast Guard fixed-winged aircraft commanders trained to fly or transitioned to helicopters.

When hurricane Betsy struck the New Orleans area in 1965, "HH-52As hovered over buildings, boats, levees—with too-near trees, structures, wires and water a constant threat, with wind and flood still strong. They rescued nearly 1,200 people."[14] The dangers were all too evident: a Navy helicopter crashed in the vicinity of the Lawless School, and when a Coast Guard 52 landed lightly on the school's roof, a surge of people all tried climbing in the cabin at once. The aircraft was immediately overloaded and unable to remain airborne with the weight. One landing gear crashed through the roof, lowering the main rotor path. The rotor tips—traveling nearly 420 miles per hour—struck a raised air-conditioner housing. The sudden shock to the rotor system tore the transmission loose; the entire dynamic system ripped apart, hurling aircraft pieces all over the rooftop. The tail rotor drive shaft, like a whirling spear, flew off and penetrated a concrete block wall about 175 feet away. Miraculously, no one was struck by parts ripped and flung from the disintegrating helicopter.[15]

Lt. Comdr. M. T. Tilghman at CGAS Corpus Christi, Texas, rescued ninety-one persons, eighty-nine of whom were hoisted aboard, during a thirty-day period after hurricane Fern struck the Texas coast on 10 September 1971. On the first day following the hurricane, Tilghman, flying an HH-52A with Ross Longmiere, an aviation electronic technician first class, as hoist operator, pulled aboard a family of eight, including a mother with a baby, who had been trapped on the roof of their home by the swift flood waters. Before the day was over Tilghman and Longmiere picked up forty-three more people trapped by the flood. Tilghman and Mike Oliver, an aviation machinist mate third class, picked up four persons from a flooded fishing shack where they had spent the night after their boat capsized. Later in the month, Tilghman, together with copilot Lt. Mike Wade and crewman AD1/c Douglas Barker, made an emergency night pickup of a fisherman with appendicitis from his shrimp boat in the Gulf of Mexico. Finally, on the thirtieth day, Tilghman and Longmiere once more rescued thirty-five people trapped by flood waters in Mexico.[16]

Helicopters not only aid the distressed at sea. Survivors have been plucked from mountain slopes, rivers, and rooftops. People scaling or falling from cliffs have introduced another dimension to helicopter rescue. Perhaps typical of a cliff rescue was one performed with a Seaguard in 1974 with just a pilot and one crewman aboard. Three people were hiking along a Washington wilderness beach at the base of a 250-foot near-vertical oceanside headland. The tide came up, trapping them in a miniature cul-de-sac at the cliff's base which soon became an ocean-filled caldera. Two hikers climbed in one direction, arriving safely on top in time to seek help for the third hiker trapped atop a large egg-shaped boulder at the base of the cliff, already an island surrounded by the heaving ocean. He stood precariously just feet above the rising tide and crashing waves. The rock would soon be swept by waves at high tide.

Ground rescuers could not reach him from the top of the cliff with climbing ropes, nor could the HH-52A reach him with its 100-foot hoist cable. However, about eighty to ninety feet above the beach, the sheer bluff had a small ledge with a narrow cavelike opening cut back into it. This was the only spot where the helicopter could get close enough to lower the rescue basket to the victim.

The pilot did so by inserting the main rotor into the slotted opening inches at a time, directed by the crewman who calmly called out verbal commands. The rotor whirled away, cutting tufts of weeds from among the rocks and sweeping hummingbirds away in the rotor tips' wake. A ten-knot breeze was blowing the helicopter on to the cliff. The stranded hiker grabbed the basket as it swung toward him, tumbled in, and was retrieved as the helicopter flew away from the wall. A few seconds later he was set down on a clear, safe beach area one-quarter mile away where he rejoined his companions to continue their hike.[17]

The helicopter served in still more dramatic rescues. To illustrate: the *Ocean Express* was an offshore oil drilling rig 166 feet long and 109 feet wide. It had three legs—steel tubes twelve feet in diameter. With the legs jacked down in the rig's working position, the legs and lower platform rested on the seabed. The lower platform was raised to eighty feet below the surface and the main platform floated on it, becoming a barge. In this configuration, the legs stuck up 232 feet above the sea's surface. Centered between them was the towering drilling derrick.[18]

"What happened that night in April 1976 wrote a new chapter in offshore rescue—a chapter so complex" it was years before a "Coast Guard Board of inquiry pieced together the story." Lt. Comdr. John Lewis lifted a 52 off CGAS Corpus Christi, Texas, into a storm and flew out into the Gulf of Mexico, "pleased to hear from the barge master that the entire crew had gotten away in capsules." It was a bad night for flying. The unexpected storm was driven by winds gusting to hurricane force. A Navy helicopter following Lewis turned back when its pilots saw the state of the seas and experienced the wind's strength.[19]

Earlier, three tugs were pulling this elevated rig along the Texas coast at three knots against the building southerly winds when one tug "blew its starboard engine's clutch." Sixty-knot winds twisted the rig around; the crippled tug was unable to hold. Next, the tow cable from a second tug snapped with a "sound like a cannon shot." Night fell. The storm increased in intensity. Waves began sweeping the barge as it wobbled in rolling seas. Then it began to lean. Drill pipes broke loose; the 363-ton derrick came "unpinned" and began sliding, these elements shifting the critical center of gravity. Most of the twenty-nine crew feared the entire barge would capsize. They abandoned ship immediately after calling for help. The captain, however, remained on board, and with the lifeboats gone, he had no way to escape. Lewis discovered this when he arrived on scene. He was no longer a witness to a maritime casualty, as he expected to be, but the only element available to save a man's life.[20]

The sight of the floundering rig as he approached "was nightmarish." Seas were rolling over the barge. The *Ocean Express*'s helicopter landing platform was upwind and tilting upwards at an unusable angle. If it were usable, Lewis would have to back his tail into the wavering towers to land. Impossible. His only course was to hover alongside the towers, flying crosswind and hoisting the captain from the outer edge of the landing platform.

Lewis briefed his crew and started his first approach. Turbulence from wind bounding over the platform made control of the helicopter impossible. Huge waves were crashing into the bottom of the platform and washing over the helicopter. The single jet engine mounted over the cockpit ingested large gulps of seawater. The turbine surged, the rpms dropping with each surge. Lewis waved off with an instrument departure. By the time he started his second approach, the towers were listing thirty degrees. The rig was beginning to capsize. The aircrewman, AD1/c Harold J. Thomas, was hanging out in the slipstream, attached to the aircraft only by a gunner's belt about his waist, the other end attached to a ring in the cabin floor. He verbally directed Lewis into position; Lewis could not hold it. Work lights glowed over the entire rig, creating a strange illusion. There were no references other than the rolling and swaying giant spaceship. But it appeared stationary, unmoving against the black night. The helicopter, in contrast, seemed to jump and roll about unmanageable against this false backdrop. Lewis experienced vertigo. His instruments read correctly but the stage was wandering.[21]

Then the entire rig suddenly lit up in a glaring bluish light. The helicopter crew "clearly saw the tangle of pipe on deck, the shifted derrick." In this new light they saw the barge "rearing up backward like a horse and falling off to its right side." Capt. Howard Thorsen, the Corpus Christi air station's commanding officer, followed Lewis's 52 out several minutes later in a second HH-52A, this one fitted with a "Night Sun" flood light. He lit the scene.[22]

Lewis backed away and planned for one more attempt with this new aide. The tower tips were now halfway to the water, leaning at forty-five degrees. He thought, "It's now or never for that poor guy." He moved in for his expected last attempt. His only reference was pitching over backwards. The platform rose suddenly. Thomas yelled, "Up! Up!" Lewis pulled away abruptly, water cascading over his windscreen.[23]

Lewis wanted to try once more. He told his copilot, Ens. John DiLeonardo, "See if you can monitor a seventy-five foot hover on the radar altimeter and keep us there." Then he told Thomas to start the basket down so it would be in position when the helicopter arrived over the platform. DiLeonardo called the altitudes and Thomas directed Lewis into position with words spoken in a monotone, devoid of emotion—"forward, back, left, right, up, down"—and repeated until he got the desired response.[24]

Only Thomas could see the rig's captain. Just at the critical point, DiLeonardo barked: "You're losing altitude *too fast*. We're going down!" Thomas yelled, "Pull up, pull up, we're going down fast." The barge was rolling further; its helicopter pad with the stranded captain rose suddenly. It was not the helicopter going down but the platform rising. Lewis once again pulled away, flying on instruments, waves blinding his view to the outside and battering the helicopter as they crashed completely over it. At that very same moment, the basket which was on the platform but downslope from the captain started sliding toward him with the rising helicopter. He caught it as it scooted by and dropped in. Lewis, just trying to avoid the rising deck, did not know it until Thomas exclaimed, "We got him—he's in the basket!"[25]

Thorsen, watching from astern, saw an awesome sight. "Five seconds after John pulled away, the rig rolled over." The crew in the second helicopter did not see Lewis's helicopter at first. It was beneath the shower of waves passing over the capsizing barge. Then it emerged, seemingly coming up from beneath the sea, in flight.[26]

The barge sank suddenly in 167 feet of water. Thirteen men in an escape capsule drowned when it capsized.

Thomas, after returning to base that evening feeling tired, suffered a heart attack.[27]

About seventy HH-52As, flying from seventeen air stations during one three-year period, accounted for an average of 3,920 SAR cases, saving 913 lives, and preventing property loss at a value of more than 83 million dollars *each year*.[28] Rear Adm. Richard Appelbaum noted: "[F]or every dollar spent to purchase these ninety-nine helicopters, the Coast Guard saved $10 in property. This doesn't include the thousands of lives saved during the past twenty-five years. Not a bad return on our investment."[29]

But there was a price in lives—Coast Guard crew members. One accident was noteworthy because it involved the Coast Guard's third woman aviator, who responded to a distress call from a sinking fishing boat. Lt. Colleen A. Cain earned her private pilot's license on her own time while working as a young Coast Guard officer in headquarters. She was later selected for flight training and earned her Wings of Gold in June 1979. She earned a Coast Guard achievement medal in 1980 for saving the life of a three-year-old child.

She lost hers two years later, on 7 January 1982, when the helicopter in which she was copilot, flying in instrument conditions under the guidance and control of ground radar, flew into the near-sheer walls along the rugged north coast of Molokai. She was twenty-nine years old and reportedly the first woman aviator on active duty to lose her life in an aircraft crash since World War II.[30]

Forty years after Erickson's emotional pleas for the Coast Guard to use helicopters, the Seaguard's performance records finally provided the service with the foundation on which to establish future aircraft needs. The HH-52A's quarter-century life ended in June 1989 and will be remembered for its astounding feats in thousands of recorded and unrecorded stories. This little helicopter, manufactured figuratively from parts off the shop floor, became an international icon for rescue and the catalyst for Coast Guard aviation. The helicopter, a craft adapted to many missions, is best known today as a vehicle of mercy largely based on the exploits of the 52.

A New Training Command

The Navy did helicopter transition instruction for Coast Guard fixed-winged aviators but not in the aircraft types flown by the Coast Guard. Therefore, further training was necessary to qualify aviators in the Coast Guard aircraft. A compounding problem came when the Navy stopped this helicopter transition training for the Coast Guard at the end of 1965 to meet their own requirements for aviators for the new Vietnam War. This happened just when the Coast Guard needed many experienced helicopter aviators for the HH-52As assigned to the new stations and icebreakers.

A solution—about the only option available under the existing organization—was to continue the pilots' training at operating units as time permitted. Two problems emerged with this scheme. It did not offer enough training time for the large group of pilots needed. Time devoted to training frequently meant riding as copilot during actual missions. Second, standard practices typically did not apply from one station to the next or, indeed, from one senior aviator to the next. Even MacDiarmid, notorious for setting rules in his aircraft, recognized "standards and procedures vary widely in nearly all spheres of Coast Guard aviation such as plane qualifications, instrument checks, readiness standards, intercept and escort procedures, night illumination for ditching, offshore rescue, minimum proficiency flying, maintenance, etc."[31]

Ambivalent attitudes toward standard aircraft operating procedures were carried forward from the postwar fixed-winged community where a pilot might be qualified to fly several different types of aircraft. Procedures were often what was developed by individuals to meet a broad set of circumstances, aircraft, and personal preferences or weaknesses. Commonly, standard procedures were whatever the senior aviator determined on flights. The "keeping book" by copilots on their seniors was no joke. Each successful junior aviator kept a notebook or a good memory on how every aircraft commander flew for his own professional survival.

The Coast Guard, now committed to a large fleet of helicopters, with no other option open, was forced to return to a formal school for helicopter training and transitioning. A Basic Operational Training Unit (BOTU) was established at the air station in Savannah, Georgia. Standardized procedures were adopted and taught. Because of the uniqueness of the HH-52A, carryover practices from earlier aircraft did not always apply. A bootstrap effort began to get all aviators to conform to procedures taught in BOTU as newly trained aviators returned to their stations from Savannah. Soon, with the large number of aviators needing training in the HH-52A, this small station could not support both operational missions and the school.

The Coast Guard finally was pushed to create their own training command. A search for a location began in 1965 and resulted in obtaining an abandoned Air Force Reserve base at the commercial airport—Bates Field—in Mobile, Alabama. It was commissioned the Coast Guard's new BOTU on 17 December 1966 and operated as a unit under the command of the Eighth Coast Guard District. In 1969 the base was designated a headquarters unit and renamed United States Coast Guard Aviation Training Center (AVTRACEN, or ATC).

The helicopter BOTU unit moved to Mobile along with the decommissioned fixed-winged SAR units from Bermuda and Biloxi, Mississippi. The new command had facilities to conduct qualifications and transition full time, for both helicopter and the fixed-winged aircraft. The unit also met SAR responses for the Gulf Coast region.

New Coast Guard aviators just graduating from the Navy's flight training, along with experienced Coast Guard aviators from operating units, were taught standardized procedures in the aircraft they would fly at their assigned Coast Guard air station. Aviators could now go from ATC to any Coast Guard air station already qualified in that unit's aircraft. As standardization progressed, pilots transferring between units could begin operational flights without further retraining. The program to develop pilot proficiency brought about additional features that are still performed at Mobile. Aviators are brought to ATC on an annual basis for proficiency and instrument checks and crew resources management. The same instructor pilots that teach these courses at Mobile form teams and routinely visit air stations, flying with each aviator and examining local operating procedures.[32]

One other advanced feature of the Coast Guard's school was the reintroduction of flight simulators, a computerized version of Erickson's mechanical trainer that was suspended in the hangar at

Floyd Bennett. A building complete with computerized cockpit trainers became operational in 1972. The Variable Cockpit Training System (VCTS) reduced the amount of time required in aircraft for qualifying trainees. With this device, aviators can practice dangerous operational procedures too costly in actual aircraft. "Students can now respond to simulated emergencies which could only be discussed in the past." The VCTS has "been acknowledged as the finest example of synthetic rotary-wing flight in the world."[33] The facility was named Erickson Hall to honor Capt. Frank Erickson. He attended the dedication ceremonies on 4 August 1972, six years before his death.

A Long-Range Rescue Helicopter

The immediate success of the HH-52A along the coastal regions revealed the need for helicopter coverage farther out to sea. Though the HH-52A's theoretical range was 150 miles, prudence and a lack of sophisticated navigation equipment dictated a need for a fixed-winged aircraft escort beyond twenty-five miles from the coastline. In 1965 the Coast Guard determined that its helicopter coverage responsibilities offshore should extend to three hundred miles; this required adding a second type (long-range) of helicopter to its fleet.

Sikorsky had the right aircraft. It was a modified version of the H-3 series developed earlier for the Navy for their ASW program as the HSS-2/H-3 and from the S-61 for the civilian market. The first model HSS-2 flew its first test flight on 11 March 1959 and was delivered to the Navy in September 1961. (In February of that same year the twin-engine amphibian established a new helicopter world speed record of 210.6 miles per hour.[34]) This aircraft represented a "quantum jump in helicopter capability . . . [and] soon became a staple product of Sikorsky Aircraft." More than a thousand were built. "The Naval observers were especially impressed by the boat hull and single engine performance, which would eliminate much of the danger associated with the antisubmarine helicopters in use up until that time."[35]

In 1965 the Coast Guard determined that the Sikorsky H-3 series fulfilled their requirement and ordered the HH-3F version. It was equipped with the most sophisticated "rotary wing avionics platform in the U.S., quite possibly in the world."[36] A navigational computer system was capable of direct and continuous readouts of the aircraft position based on combining inputs from TACAN, LORAN, and Doppler navigation receivers. It carried search/weather radar, and HF, UHF, VHF, and FM communications. The HH-3F began service in New Orleans on 1 November 1967. During its career of nearly seventeen years, the forty-aircraft fleet saved 23,169 lives while helping 65,377 more people, and it provided assistance to property valued at 3.7 billion dollars.[37]

The value of this long-range helicopter was dramatically demonstrated in the Gulf of Alaska on 4 October 1980. The largest peacetime maritime rescue in history happened when fire swept the cruise ship SS *Prinsendam*. Four Coast Guard HH-3Fs from CGAS Sitka and Kodiak, Alaska, one U.S. Air Force HH-3E, and two Canadian Forces HH-46A Labradors battled sixty-knot winds, rain, fog, and forty-foot seas to hoist 329 passengers and 190 crew members from pitching lifeboats. "In the end we were praying because we didn't think we would be picked up that night," lifeboat passenger, Roger Ray, said. "I don't think we would have survived."[38]

Lt. Bruce Melnick, who later became the Coast Guard's first astronaut, and his crew flew for twelve hours, and in one two-hour period alone they hoisted 109 ship's passengers. On one trip they even loaded twenty-four survivors aboard.[39] Lt. Terry Sinclair, U.S. Coast Guard, said he had never seen more than six passengers before in the HH-3F he flew. "Eighteen was a sight, and they were huddled so close together I think five more would have fit. But we were up to maximum power due to the added weight and so moved off." Passengers had rushed from their beds to the lifeboats and so were clothed in what they could find at hand. "Few were dressed warmly. . . . blankets, curtains, and pajamas were the fashion of the day." Not one person was lost and only one woman was accidentally dunked during the helicopter hoists. "The remarkable outcome took the dedication and efforts of hundreds of men and women, and the quest and zest for life from the survivors."[40]

When Lt. (jg) John P. Currier was awakened at 3:40 A.M. and told a fishing boat was sinking east of the Nantucket Lightship, to him it was just another "duty night" launch, this time into a New England October storm. He could not anticipate that this case, which involved saving ten lives, would lead to two awards and recognition from outside the Coast Guard.

Winds were forty knots, with higher gusts as the crew towed the HH-3F CGNR 1484 from its hangar at CGAS Cape Cod. The fishing vessel *Terry T* was taking on water and unable to control flooding. Its master wanted pumps. The weather varied, as did the visibility, which went from three-quarters of a mile in rain to ceilings ranging from four hundred to a thousand feet en route. Currier contacted the vessel's master as the helicopter passed Nantucket Island and was told the fishing boat had now lost steering and was at the mercy of the thirty-foot seas and fifty-knot winds. Moments later the master reported the vessel was on fire and wanted all crew members taken off immediately. Then radio contact was lost.

Ten minutes later the Pelican arrived, hovering over the 110-foot scalloper, which was rolling up to sixty degrees. Attempts to pass weighted trail lines to guide the rescue basket failed twice before the boat's crew captured it. The trail line is a 110-foot long, 3/8-inch diameter orange-colored polypropylene rope carried aboard all Coast Guard helicopters. The line is fitted with a small ring at one end for attaching two or more lines together or attaching small shot-filled sacks ("weight bags") for ballast. A snap hook at the other end is connected to a "weak link" set to break at three hundred pounds. In use, the line is snapped to the basket at the weak-link end, and the ring end with weight bags is dropped to a boat for its crew to guide the basket down to a spot. When the helicopter pulls in the basket, remaining crew members can steady the basket, further allowing the helicopter to back off at an angle that provides the pilot a visual reference on the boat. By holding on to the line, they can expedite the return of the basket for the next load.

The hoists began from the *Terry T,* two men coming up in the basket each time. The boat crew lost the trail line on the second hoist and a "no reference" hoist was tried, unsuccessfully.

The trail line was doubled in length and the helicopter's anchor was attached for weight. Two more hoists were made; the pilot now used the vessel's radio antenna for a visual reference. But before the second hoist was complete, a thunderstorm moved in, reducing the visibility to zero. Lightning bolts began striking nearby.

As the basket went down for the last hoist, a wave rolled over the stern, already awash, flushing the last two crewmen into the seas immediately downwind of the hulk. The flight mechanic guided the pilot with voice commands to a spot over the men and dropped the basket next to them. Quickness was required; the fishing boat was drifting down on them. Then, the trail line dangling from the rescue basket snagged on the vessel, which prevented the basket, now containing the survivors, from reaching the helicopter.

With two men in the basket already, Currier could not pull hard enough to pop the weak link without exceeding the load limit of 600 pounds. Pulling harder could pop the basket loose and drop the two men back into the sea, unrecoverable. Currier had to fly back over the scalloper with the basket dangling some distance below to allow enough slack in the trail line for the basket to reach the helicopter so the crewman could reach out and cut the line as the basket neared the door. The flight mechanic and avionics man administered first aid to the injured crew on the return flight. Four of the survivors were from the same family.[41]

For this rescue, Currier received the American Helicopter Society's Frederick L. Feinberg Award in March 1981. This award is given to the helicopter pilot who accomplished the most outstanding contribution during the preceding calendar year. Currier was also awarded the Harmon International Aviation Award in 1980, presented by Vice President Dan Quayle on 21 June 1991.[42] The Harmon trophy "recognizes outstanding international achievements in the art and/or science of aeronautics." Previous U.S. recipients include Amelia Earhart, Gen. Jimmy Doolittle, aviatrix Jackie Cochran, Chuck Yeager, and astronauts Neil Armstrong and Michael Collins.[43]

The last HH-3F retired from Clearwater, Florida, on 6 May 1994. The ceremony officially noted "the close of the amphibious chapter of Coast Guard aviation,"[44] a chapter the Coast Guard started seventy-four years earlier, in 1920, by borrowing "old" Navy surplus "Curtiss HS-2L flying boats."[45] The Golden Age of Coast Guard aviation began with the HH-52As and HH-3Fs flying from twenty-five stations located along the coasts of the United States. With their replacements, a new era began, using aircraft that no longer required a traditional landing surface, the sea.

A Short-Range Rescue Helicopter

In November 1973 the Coast Guard began developing specifications for a short-range recovery aircraft (SRR) to replace the HH-52A. A study released on 17 June 1975 determined that the extension of the service life of the HH-52A beyond fifteen years was not economical. The study further recommended that the Coast Guard purchase new aircraft to "minimize the exposure to the rapidly escalating HH-52A ownership costs." Funding was approved for only ten SRR helicopters in 1978. The overage HH-52A fleet of "eighty HH-52A helicopters, assigned to seventeen Coast Guard Air Stations, was expected to meet SAR responses presently numbering over 70,000 per year [and increasing] at no less than the historic rate of six percent per year over the next ten years."[46]

When it came time to replace the HH-52A no production military aircraft was suitable, though if one were available, it would have been preferred for the contract breaks and support logistics already in place. The Coast Guard, however, not bound by Defense Department regulations for purchasing aircraft, went to the civilian market. Three manufacturers had helicopters that met Coast Guard requirements, but Sikorsky withdrew its aircraft after completing the flight test and all phases of the evaluation. On the day for "best and final offers," Sikorsky retracted its bid from the competition for unexplained reasons, even though "it was by all measures superior to either of the other two machines."[47] The resulting "fly before buy" contest between

Bell-Textron and Aerospatiale was won by Aerospatiale's Dauphin. The first of ninety-six HH-65As entered service in 1984.[48] The HH-65A's advanced cockpit management systems make this helicopter a formidable rescue aircraft. "It still is the most sophisticated helicopter for its size in the world."[49]

The HH-65A has a mission control unit, flight director system, and automatic flight control system that relieve pilots of flying duties. The aircraft can fly by autopilot to a predetermined location, then conduct a planned search pattern. More of the pilots' time, consequently, can be spent on mission duties. When needed, the aircraft will fly an approach generated by the mission computer. The computer-controlled autopilot will lower the helicopter to fifty feet and establish a hover into the wind, holding zero ground speed—all without the pilots ever touching the controls. The pilot can fly the aircraft in a hover while the autopilot maintains a fixed altitude based on information from the radar altimeter. The Dauphin carries search radar, a two-thousand-pound capacity cargo hook, and a 3.5-million-candlepower controllable searchlight. It also features advanced communications and navigation equipment.

Over the operational history of the amphibious helicopters, few rescues involved pulling survivors from the open sea from a helicopter floating on the water's surface. Conclusions drawn from data on SAR cases using the HH-52A did not support this mission. A Coast Guard Aircraft Characteristics Board met first in the summer of 1974 and reviewed requirements for new helicopters based on needs developed from the experience gained in operating HH-52A and HH-3Fs. Seventeen requirements were proposed, but amphibious abilities was not included. Thorsen, the project's manager, emphasized, "There were few rescues made using the platform, and essentially no records of rescues effected which could not have been done if the helo couldn't have landed on the water." Tradition was still strong, however; as Thorsen disclosed, "It WAS an *emotional* issue, but not an *operational* one." Because it is not an amphibious aircraft, a rescue swimmer was added to the HH-65As' crew on search-and-rescue missions.[50] This compensation for the lack of a water-landing capability changed the complexion of rescues somewhat.

Rescue Swimmers

The amphibian helicopters, along with the nonamphibious HH-65As and HH-60Js, could not always land at sea to recover victims unable to help themselves. When this occurred, crew members or pilots sometimes volunteered in the capacity of rescue swimmers. The added weight of a fourth crew member and associated equipment, however,

reduced the mission capability of the HH-65A to the point of insti-
tuting a program to upgrade the aircraft to a higher gross weight limit.

Perhaps the most vivid case to illustrate this shortcoming and to
bring political pressure for a solution was the loss of the freighter
Marine Electric during a January 1982 storm off Cape Hatteras,
North Carolina. A Coast Guard HH-3F arrived on scene to find the
ship's crew scattered, floating and swimming in chilling heavy seas.
The waves were too high to allow the amphibian helicopter to alight.
The ship's crew, all suffering from exposure, were no longer able to
assist themselves into the rescue basket. The Coast Guard did not at
that time have rescue swimmers. The HH-3F called a Navy SH-3, with
a rescue swimmer on board, but it arrived too late. Three survivors
were rescued; thirty-three people died. It was just one more tragedy
where crews in a powerful rescue machine could only watch as victims
died just a few feet below them, each beyond the grasp of the other.

It was evident from accumulated experience by helicopter crews
that a trained Coast Guard person at the scene of trouble with communications was more valuable than a crew in a hovering helicopter
standing by as a helpless witness. For example, in addition to assisting
survivors, helicopters can deliver de-watering pumps, survival equipment, or needed parts to distress vessels. On occasion, panicking or
terrified crews cannot operate the pumps, use survival devices, or ratio-
nally fend for themselves. The rescue crew member whose job it is to
maintain the emergency equipment can. A rescue swimmer aboard a
distressed vessel sometimes can even solve mechanical problems, thus
preventing abandonment of that vessel. They are also prepared to
administer emergency medical assistance and CPR as trained EMT
technicians. Their presence often has a calming, reassuring effect, providing "the human link . . . between exhausted, terrified, and often
injured sailors and their only ride to survival."[51]

The Coast Guard developed its own rescue swimmer program following the *Marine Electric* inquiry. Lt. Comdr. Kenneth Coffland and
Lawrence Farmer, an aviation survivalman master chief, reviewed several
military and civil rescue services.[52] They decided to design a program
specific to Coast Guard requirements. Because Coast Guard personnel
manning levels prohibited adding more people, one choice was to add
the swimmer requirement to selected members from all the aviation
ratings. Thorsen, at the time chief of the Aeronautical Engineering
Division, rejected this proposal outright, fearing that "the rigorous
training—both initial and recurring—would have a very serious neg-
ative affect on any individual's ability to compete for promotion"
within his or her rating.

Furthermore, only one or two billets would be added to a typical small helicopter station, not enough to provide a rescue swimmer to each duty section. In a compromise, personnel were drawn from the aviation survival man (ASM) rate, a combination of the aviation ordanceman (AO) and parachute rigger (PR) only. The ASMs are the mechanics that maintain all safety and survival equipment associated with and on the aircraft. All members of the ASM rate at the time of the program's inception were required to train as rescue swimmers; however, they still maintain the aircraft's safety and survival equipment used by the Coast Guard.

In March 1985 CGAS Elizabeth City became the first unit to go operational with rescue swimmers. The rescue swimmer program was completely implemented at all twenty-four Coast Guard helicopter air stations by December 1991, adding a vital link in the helicopter rescue capabilities.[53] Seldom today is a significant case executed without one. For instance, a Coast Guard rescue swimmer dropped fifteen feet from an HH-65A into the Pacific Ocean off the Oregon coast to rescue two Air National Guard crew from a F-4 Phantom who had ejected from their disabled fighter and parachuted into the wintertime waters. The pilot, suffering from hypothermia and several broken bones, was hanging on to his survival raft, entangled in his snarled parachute and shroud lines. He could no longer assist himself and was in danger of being dragged beneath the waves by the sinking parachute.

The rescue swimmer, Kelly Mogk, an aviation survivalman third class, swam over and, recalled later, "[T]he first thing I did when I got to the raft was talk to him. His lips were moving but I couldn't hear him because of the noise from the helicopter . . . all he could do was follow me with his eyes as I moved about trying to untangle and unhook him from his parachute harness."[54]

At one point while clearing the entangled parachute and lines Mogk squeezed the hand of the pilot. "He squeezed back. That was a good sign." It took twenty-seven minutes for the 115-pound Coast Guard swimmer to free the 240-pound pilot and get him into the rescue sling. Alone, Mogk began suffering hypothermia from water seeping into her torn dry suit; her hands and fingers lost feeling and she had injured her back. The helicopter left her floating in the ocean to rush the injured pilot to medical attention. A second helicopter, searching for the other crewman, recovered Mogk shortly thereafter. The missing Phantom's weapons officer was later discovered tangled in his parachute twelve feet below his raft. He could not be revived. Mogk was one of three women qualified and working as Coast Guard rescue swimmers.[55]

In another dramatic case, two brothers were hiking along a rocky ledge just above the water's edge in a large cavern below the cliffs of Cape Lookout on the Oregon coast. Waves were surging in the water-filled cavern on the early April 1993 afternoon. Moments later a wave crashed into the chamber, sweeping the hikers from the rocks. One was sucked under; his body was never found. The other, struggling against the swirling eddies, regained temporary refuge on rocks well back in the cave while the tide slowly rose in the chamber. He could not be seen from outside.

An HH-65A flown by Lt. Edward J. Gibbons dropped rescue swimmer, ASM2/c Tristan P. Heaton off near the cave's mouth. Heaton then crawled in along the rocky ledge and finally locating the survivor. Building waves crashed along the northern wall and washed both the rescue swimmer and the victim into the water.

Heaton did not call and did not emerge. He could not explain his situation with his PRC-90 hand-held radio, and the helicopter crew waited "what seemed like forever." The two in the cave could not; they were being bashed into the rocks by the surging seas, trapped by an "eddy line." Heaton could not swim against the rip. Furthermore, they were near exhaustion. They suffered more injuries with each wave.[56]

Impatient in the helicopter hovering outside the cave, Gibbons could wait no longer. He nosed the Dauphin into the hole in the cliff, slowly moving into the cave that looked like the "Pasadena Bowl," leaving just enough altitude so waves approaching from his rear did not strike the aircraft's tail, his "major concern." Clearance for the main rotor was minimal. Then, an unexpected hazard occurred. Rotor down-wash whipped up the water's surface and blew water onto the cave's ceiling. The helicopter then came under a dousing in a strange saltwater rain shower.[57]

The aircrewman floated both the rescue basket and a rescue sling line out to the two struggling in the water. "They were bracketed." The rescue swimmer grabbed the basket and dragged the victim along with him to the helicopter. Both were hoisted into the helicopter outside the cave and flown immediately to the nearest hospital to be treated for injuries and salt water ingestion.[58]

Rescue swimmers are not always carried as a crew member on helicopter flights if missions do not require one. On 5 March 1994, Lt. Alda L. Siebrands, a former Army and commercial helicopter pilot and one of Coast Guard's twenty-six women aviators, was conducting a maritime pollution patrol and instructional flight for copilot Lt. (jg) Erik C. Langenbacher, who was sitting in the right-hand, or pilot's, seat.[59] He had only about 350 total hours flight time, 130 of which were in the

HH-65A. They received a call alerting them to an overturned skiff fifteen minutes from their position. Two men were in the forty-five degree ocean water off the Washington coast. A third had swum ashore.

Langenbacher flew the HH-65A to the scene and controlled the aircraft through his first "live" hoist, assisted by aircrewman Kevin T. Parkinson. The second victim, suffering hypothermia, was unable to get into the rescue basket. Siebrands, not dressed for survival in the cold water, unstrapped and crawled from her seat, leaving Langenbacher to fly the aircraft alone. She leaped from the helicopter, then hovering at ten feet, into the sea to help the seventy-three-year-old man. She got into the basket and held on to the victim, but he slipped from her grasp on two attempts as they ascended.

Parkinson's microphone failed during the second hoist. He had to shout positioning commands to Langenbacher. "Despite this complication, Parkinson expertly guided the pilot perilously close to the rocky shore, relocated the drifting survivor," who had been blown about 150 feet away by the seventy-knot rotor downwash. He was face down in the water when Siebrands finally grabbed him. She held on this time and was hoisted with the victim to the helicopter's doorway. Parkinson was unable to bring the "bulky load" into the aircraft unassisted. Siebrands, unable to communicate with the pilot and direct his actions, dangled outside the aircraft, holding onto the victim, as Langenbacher flew to a nearby sandbar. The crewman lowered the basket to the beach, leaped from the aircraft after it landed, and assisted Siebrands in performing CPR on the man, who showed no vital signs. About fifteen minutes later, Langenbacher saw the ambulance arrive at a beach about one mile away, its access blocked. He flew over, picked up the emergency medical technicians and their equipment, and delivered them to the sandbar where the victim lay.[60]

With the critical victim stabilized, Siebrands resumed her position as aircraft commander and took the three survivors to the nearest hospital. The elder victim arrived at the hospital in critical condition and was later airlifted to a trauma center.[61]

Another Long-Range Rescue Helicopter

The helicopter that replaced the HH-3F was another Sikorsky aircraft created at company expense. It started as the Sikorsky S-67 Blackhawk, again utilizing proven components of earlier successful aircraft, in this case, the H-3 series.[62] The Coast Guard purchased forty-two HH-60J versions and named it the Jayhawk. "The power provided by the HH-60Js' two T700-GE-401C engines [1,543 horsepower each] gives the Jayhawk a great lift capability." In addition to its ability to reach out three hundred miles, execute a rescue, and return, it also "transports navigational aid structures weighing up to 4,000 pounds to remote locations." It, like the Dauphin, has advanced avionics and "can communicate in crypto or clear modes on HF, VHF and UHF bands." Navigating with its Global Positioning System (GPS) receiver and tactical navigation system give the Jayhawk the ability to fly different search-and-rescue patterns generated by the on-board computer with accuracy measured in feet anywhere on the earth's surface.[63]

Whereas the operational range of the HH-60J is fixed at about three hundred miles, one case in particular dramatically stretched that limit. In December 1993, a Jayhawk departed North Carolina and flew out to a sailboat "battered by a severe storm" four hundred miles east of Cape Hatteras. Three men on board the ketch, the *Malachite,* feared for their lives. After reviewing the winds, Lt. Bruce Jones determined he could fly the HH-60J to the boat, rescue the sailors, and proceed to Bermuda, 275 miles beyond.

A Coast Guard Hercules led the way, flying "cover." It located the boat whose crew had reported their position using their own GPS. The helicopter arrived after dark and "came to a hover next to the *Malachite*." The official Coast Guard report then noted, "*Malachite* was surfing up and down seas in excess of thirty feet, with rogue waves in excess of seventy-five feet." The winds were thirty to forty knots. "Her one sail was in ribbons, and six [of eight] of her mast stays were broken." These wire cables were whipping in circles or trailing in the water astern, thus preventing any close approach by the helicopter. Recovery of the men directly from the boat was impossible.[64]

"Despite having her sea-anchor deployed, she was making eleven knots. Lightning flashed regularly around the aircraft. Although ten life rafts had been expertly dropped to *Malachite* by the C-130, *Malachite* was unable to retain them as the lines holding them snapped in the heavy seas." The helicopter crew determined it was "highly improbable that *Malachite* would remain afloat much longer." Sea conditions would make a transfer from the sailboat to a ship impossible "in the unlikely event that *Malachite* lasted another nine hours" until the nearest ship would arrive. Furthermore, it had a fire in the engine room. "*Malachite*'s captain was advised that the only way to evacuate his crew was to have them jump overboard and be recovered by CG 6008's rescue swimmer."[65]

The helicopter crew plucked the three sailors out of the water in twenty-nine minutes. Wires in the hoist cable started breaking as the rescue swimmer was pulled up after the sailors were safely in the helicopter.

He was recovered; the hoist was no longer usable. The Jayhawk landed in Bermuda after a nonstop flight of five hours and six minutes and nearly 650 miles, with fifty minutes of fuel remaining.[66]

The shaky machine that took Graham "all the legs of a spider" to control, that had no range, nor the capacity to lift little more than itself, is today—with its current jet turbine engine and computers—so sophisticated it can meet new challenges even Erickson could not have dreamed of. Searches, as conducted in the past by fixed-winged patrol airplanes, are a declining function with the introduction of GPS, emergency locator beacons, and reliable long-range communications. Even the smallest boat can have an inexpensive hand-held navigation device telling the navigator, within yards, where he or she is located— anywhere on the earth.

Many offshore vessels and yachts now also carry moderately priced high frequency, single-sideband transmitters with the ability to call from half a world away. Emergency locator beacons can transmit automatically via satellite not only a beacon indicating distress and *where* but also *who* is in danger. All Coast Guard helicopters have the ability to home in on radio beacons from most any radio source—AM, VHF-AM and FM, and UHF. The helicopter's range is no longer restricted just to coastal waters. Naval and Coast Guard ships equipped with helicopter landing decks are now available as emergency landing and refueling platforms at sea.

THIRTEEN

TEAMWORK

The helicopter envisioned by Erickson as a vehicle for rescue also became a weapon of war. But its fame in battle as a life-saver all but eclipsed that of its warrior cousin. The Army and Marines found it useful as a tactical weapon, but the Air Force and Navy, losing aviators shot down behind enemy lines, revived a use developed during the Korean War and the Coast Guard got involved.

Coast Guard Helicopter Aviators in Vietnam

In March 1968 three Coast Guard helicopter aviators entered the Vietnam War as combat rescue pilots. They joined the U.S. Air Force's 37th Aerospace Rescue and Recovery Squadron at Da Nang. Lt. Comdr. Lonnie L. Mixon, Lt. Jack C. Rittichier, and Lt. Lance Eagan were assigned under a Memorandum of Agreement between the U.S. Air Force and the U.S. Coast Guard which provided for the exchange of rescue qualified helicopter aviators. Seven more Coast Guard helicopter aviators followed this first group for one-year tours in the exchange program. They flew the Air Force versions of the H-3 and the HH-53B. One did not return.[1]

Lieutenant Rittichier had formerly been an Air Force B-47 pilot who joined the Coast Guard under the Direct Commission Program. Eleven days after arriving in Vietnam in April 1968, he received his first Distinguished Flying Cross (DFC) for rescuing four crewmen of a downed Army helicopter gunship "in the face of hostile ground fire." A month later, as "Rescue Commander of an HH-3E" Jolly Green

Giant, Rittichier twice entered an "extremely hostile" zone to rescue nine survivors in another downed helicopter. "The survivors were located in an extremely small landing zone surrounded by trees on the side of a steep mountain slope." He made the rescue by flying the approach and departure with the route illuminated by flare light because his "sight was obscured by smoke clouds." For this, Rittichier received his second DFC.[2]

Less than a month later he went to the aid of a Marine jet attack pilot who had been downed in a North Vietnamese Army (NVA) bivouac area and was severely injured. Rittichier flew the backup helicopter. The downed Marine in this instance was used by the NVA as "bait to lure Jolly Green Giant rescue helicopters within killing range." Rittichier made one pass with his helicopter after the primary HH-3E failed—following three passes—and had cleared out, "severely damaged" from heavy ground fire and low on fuel. "Sandy" fixed-winged attack aircraft (A-1E Sky Raiders) then swept the area suppressing enemy opposition.

Rittichier returned a second time for the pickup after receiving heavy fire on the first pass. Just as he reached a hover and started to lower the forest penetrater (a folding seat attached to the hoist cable), gunfire was commenced by enemy forces. He started to move off the hover when an orbiting forward air control aircraft called Jolly Green and told him his left side was on fire. The helicopter was observed to fly approximately two hundred yards toward an open area in the jungle where it burst into flames and contacted the ground.

Many low flybys were conducted by fixed-wing aircraft, and their stories were unanimous: the helicopter was scattered over a large area, no survivors in sight. Three times later the same day, helicopters tried to go into the area, but they were denied by enemy gunfire.[3] Rittichier was officially listed as missing in action; his remains were never recovered. The lieutenant and the members of his crew were posthumously awarded Silver Stars for gallantry in action.[4]

On another mission, Jolly Greens went out to rescue an Air Force crewman lying in dense jungle, suffering from a back injury. The rescue helicopter was driven off by heavy gunfire. A flight of Sandys strafed and bombed the gun positions in an attempt to "sterilize" the area. They missed one. The next Jolly Green team moved in, and the "low bird," piloted by Mixon, was hit several times. Mixon withdrew temporarily while Sandys again worked over the area. Mixon and his crew found that no vital components of their helicopter were knocked out, so they returned for another attempt. They aborted once more in a hail of fire. Several bullets hit the bottom of the aircraft. Darkness fell; the rescue aircraft were recalled.

The first helicopter had to move off during the first attempt the next morning because it met such intense fire. A B-40 rocket lodged in the belly of this HH-3, penetrating a fuel cell. The rocket failed to explode. At the same time, an A-1E was downed and the pilot killed. Hours later, after a B-52 bomber strike close to the scene, another attempt was made to recover the injured pilot.

The next Jolly Green crew in was led by Lieutenant Eagan with A1/c Joel Talley, U.S. Air Force, a para-rescueman. During the slow approach over the jungle canopy, bursts of 37- and 57-millimeter anti-aircraft artillery fire shook the aircraft. Eagan jinked with violent maneuvers to evade the fusillade as he moved to the spot where the signal smoke from the downed pilot was rising through the trees. Eagan brought the aircraft to a hover. Talley rode the three-pronged forest penetrater down through the jungle canopy. The helicopter waited motionless, vulnerable, as Talley took sixteen critical minutes to thrash his way through the jungle undergrowth to the pilot. Then Eagan, directed by Talley on the radio, slid the helicopter over to within a few meters of the victim, slicing off limbs and branches in the jungle canopy with the rotor blades. Talley carried the injured pilot to the penetrater and, strapping both to it, started up.

As the hoist began, NVA troops, waiting for this moment of vulnerability, sprang the trap. Automatic fire from a tight circle below struck the helicopter's bottom and sides. Bullets holed four of the five main rotor blades. Eagan started forward as a shell smashed the windshield with Talley and the injured airman still dangling exposed on the slender cable below the helicopter. Eagan flew on, safely recovering Talley and the pilot. After landing at a Marine base, they discovered the helicopter had taken many hits, including nine in the fuel tanks, and was too badly damaged to fly.[5]

By 1971, Lt. Comdr. Joseph L. Crowe Jr., among the last of ten Coast Guard aviators to arrive in Vietnam to serve in the 37th Aerospace Rescue and Recovery Squadron, flew the new giant S-56A/HH-53C Super Jolly. This Sikorsky helicopter was built from the dynamic components of their largest helicopter, the S-64/CH-54A Skycrane, and was powered with two 3,925-horsepower engines. Vital areas were protected from antiaircraft fire with titanium plating. The Super Jolly carried an in-flight refueling probe plus jettisonable auxiliary fuel tanks. The Coast Guard would not get or use such sophisticated equipment, but its exchange pilots (who later assumed Coast Guard management positions) gained experience in these technologically advanced helicopters which was useful in the Coast Guard's own planning and training.

Crowe piloted a Super Jolly in June 1971 to recover two crewmen from a downed OV-10 Bronco in the jungle at the bottom of a box canyon.[6] He waited at fifteen thousand feet above the small arms fire, watching the area after it was cleared first of AA guns and SAMs by "fast movers" (attack jets). Sandys then flew by the area slowly, "trolling" purposely to draw fire. They did. One source was too far away from the downed pilots to be a problem, but the second was too active for Sandys to "sanitize," so they planned to "smoke it off," obscuring the helicopter from the gunners' view during the Jolly's run-in with smoke. The Jollys, to further conceal themselves, planned to fly at maximum speed below treetop level along the canyon rim. They began the run-in; escort Sandys joined Covey 504 (the HH-53C's call sign) when Crowe entered an autorotative descent from his holding position.

Dropping at a seven-thousand-feet-per-minute rate, he noted about halfway down, "how heart stopping this business could get." Crowe rolled out at 170 knots on the inbound-heading for the downed pilots. He noted how "watching fighters lay smoke, and Sandys swirl around in rockets, machine gun, and CBU passes, will really get the adrenaline flowing. By the time you can discern their tracers from yours, it's too busy to do anything but trust in God and the Sandys and jink like hell."[7]

Crowe's crew located the first survivor and hoisted him without difficulty. The second was different. "He was on a jungle-covered ridge within the canyon." Trees were taller than the 250-foot rescue cable, so they eased the helicopter down into the tree canopy, mowing a vertical path with the seventy-two-foot-diameter main rotor blades the "five or six feet needed" into the treetops. Clearing away from the area and climbing to the tanker for in-flight refueling was "uneventful." But, "I can not describe the sensation of victory I had as we rode wing on *King* [HC-130P on-scene control aircraft and tanker], taking fuel with fighters making aileron roll passes and loops around us; the sky was never quite so blue or the clouds so puffy and white."[8]

A report prepared by the Life Sciences Division, Air Force Inspection and Safety Center, summarizing helicopter use in combat rescues, noted that during the Vietnam War, between 1963 and 1971, helicopters were involved in 645 combat rescue operations involving downed aircraft. Crews were rescued in six hundred, or 93 percent, of these cases. The hoist was used on 363 rescues, or just over 60 percent. The use of the hoist limited exposure of the rescue helicopter to hostile fire. It was also essential where victims were inaccessible, for instance, trapped under a jungle canopy, in terrain inaccessible for landings, or in the water. Nearly one-third of these rescues were accomplished within a half hour. Downed airmen, in some instances, were actually snatched from the enemy.[9]

Engaged in the Drug War

One role for the helicopter that utilizes all the elements accumulated over the past half century by the Coast Guard is its use in law enforcement, specifically, in the pursuit of drug smugglers. The illegal drugs smuggled into the United States by aircraft were estimated in 1987 at 142,000 pounds of cocaine and more than two and a half million pounds of marijuana.[10] In the summer of 1986, the new commandant, Adm. Paul A. Yost, instructed his staffs to review the Coast Guard's abilities at air interdiction. Their conclusion: the Coast Guard, with the largest fleet of fixed-wing aircraft and helicopters outside the Department of Defense, with its experience of maritime search, and with its capability to stand seven-day, twenty-four-hour ready alerts, had an excellent potential.

On 27 October the president signed the Anti-Drug Abuse Act of 1986. It provided additional funding for the Coast Guard to establish a Drug Interdiction Task Force and to upgrade aircraft with special communications equipment and search radars. Then, on 14 November 1986, a memorandum authorized the establishment of the Coast Guard Air Interdiction Implementation Team.[11]

The helicopter became a formidable weapon in a team of interceptors when operations began just a month and a half later, in January 1987. The helicopter portion of intercepts continues at this writing, while other segments of the program were stricken or reduced due to federal budgetary considerations and changes in smugglers' tactics.

Helicopters have teamed up with fixed-winged airplanes in the Coast Guard's anti-drug warfare in the Caribbean. The operations, called OPBAT for Operation Bahamas, Turks, and Caicos, deploy Coast Guard, Army, U.S. Customs, and Drug Enforcement Administration (DEA) helicopters, carrying teams of armed agents, to fly from the Caribbean Islands and Florida, working with local enforcement officers. The area covered by these operations throughout the Caribbean is approximately the size of California. It encircles more than seven hundred islands and two thousand cays, including the Bahamas, Turks, and Caicos Islands. Seventy-five airstrips or airports and 115 harbors dot this region.

OPBAT missions aim to intercept smugglers at transshipment points in the islands. These comprise locations where airplanes drop or deliver drugs from South America to waiting speed boats scattered throughout the islands or where they off-load the drugs at remote sites and airfields for waiting airplanes. Helicopters carry or direct DEA agents, Bahamian drug enforcement units, and the Turk and Caicos police to suspect drop points to interrupt the process, apprehend smugglers, and recover drugs.

During 1993, "[A]ircrews from Clearwater seized over 12,900 pounds of cocaine and over 3,700 pounds of marijuana destined for the U.S. Since this operation [OPBAT] kicked off in 1987 [the air station crews] netted more that 36 tons of cocaine alone."[12]

An HH-3F crew was alerted in Nassau about "midnight" to prepare for a drug drop by smuggling aircraft east of Georgetown, Exuma. The helicopter arrived after the drop occurred and found another Pelican chasing a "go-fast" boat with a second boat racing away followed by the "high bird." The HH-3F took over the fixed-wing jet's pursuit and tried to stop the boat. "During the chase [the helicopter] closed within five to ten feet of the boat in an attempt to stop it. When the boat made a severe turn at thirty knots one of the crewmen fell out." The pilot immediately spun the Pelican back in an attempt to pick up the person, however, "the boat was able to get to the guy first with (the HH-3F) right on top of them."[13]

The helicopter continued chasing the boat right into the Georgetown harbor where it hurriedly tied to a dock at a waterfront bar called the Blue Hole, an alleged hangout of drug smugglers in Georgetown. The helicopter, without benefit of lights, landed in the bar's parking lot. The approach and landing were done with the pilots using night vision goggles.[14]

The helicopter crew saw the suspects run into the bar. The drug enforcement agents jumped from the HH-3F chasing after them. "All of a sudden we heard automatic weapons going off." The suspects successfully evaded capture by "hiding in a secret room." The orbiting C-130 controlling the case then instructed the HH-3F pilot to search the woods for the suspects from the other boat with its FLIR (forward looking infrared) scanner that might spot fugitives hiding in the darkened forest. This time, all suspects eluded capture, but the boats were confiscated. One HH-3F returned to the drop scene, landed on the water, and loaded aboard two thousand pounds of cocaine.[15]

Few cases are typical. Lt. Mark Feldman, U.S. Coast Guard, remembers one. He was flying a Pelican from Nassau to Andros Island in the Bahamas on patrol when he heard the pilot of a commercial jet on the runway at Nassau International Airport asking for airport security because a passenger had smuggled a gym bag on board, which, the pilot suspected, contained contraband. "I contacted the [airliner's] pilot directly and told him who I was and asked if I could be of assistance." The airline captain replied he was getting no help from airport security, so Feldman flew back to the airport and landed directly in front of the airliner, blocking it. He then sent agents from the helicopter into the airliner to arrest the Miami-bound passenger who was trying to smuggle twenty pounds of cocaine.[16]

Coast Guard crews currently work from the OPBAT Operations Center in Nassau with two Jayhawks: HH-60Js replaced the HH-3Fs in 1993. One aircraft and crew is on duty twenty-four hours a day every day of the year. In addition to their active intercepts, they conduct daylight and nighttime patrols and are on standby for search and rescue. Other HH-60Js from CGAS Clearwater might be deployed to Freeport and Matthewtown in the Bahamas.[17] The U.S. Army flies H-60 Blackhawks out of a base in the Grand Turks.

Additionally, the Coast Guard deploys both HH-65As and HH-60Js aboard its larger cutters, the 270-footer *Famous* class and the 378-footer *Hamilton* class. These vessels typically range farther down the Caribbean chain of islands, working east of the Dominican Republic. The Jayhawk is popular aboard the "270s" for its range and endurance. It can stay out for about five hours, thus giving the ship/helicopter combination a formidable search-area coverage.[18]

In the past, before the realignment of drug interdiction resources that began around 1994, the cat-and-mouse game usually began when U.S. Defense Department radar units detected an unidentifiable aircraft flying north, and alerted interceptors. Those radar units, typically, were either a Navy ship or Coast Guard cutter, Air Force E-3 Sentrys, Navy or Customs' P-3C Orions, Navy or Coast Guard E-2C Hawkeyes operating in the southern Caribbean off the South American coast, or Aerostats (balloons supporting airborne radars) tethered to Florida land bases or Seastats (radar balloons) raised high above Coast Guard ships moving about the Caribbean.[19]

The interceptors, Coast Guard twin-jet HU-25C Falcons equipped with the intercept radar—the type installed on F-16 fighters (AN/APG-66)—and FLIR (Westinghouse WF-360) homed in and began the tracking after picking up and closing in on the suspect airplanes. The aptly named Falcons locked on the smuggler's aircraft with the active radar, shutting it down miles away on their pursuit, switching to the passive infrared stealth tracking—not disclosing their position with radar emissions. At night, when most operations occurred, the Falcon, or "high bird" (radar airplane), with its FLIR, can "monitor heat emissions sensitive enough to read identification numbers from airborne aircraft." Crews on board these tracking airplanes extinguish

all lights and wear night-vision goggles as they fly, invisible and unde-
tected, in a loose formation behind the smugglers' aircraft.

The intercept forces, with tracking information and intelligence
resources, normally attempt to determine a rendezvous point. Helicopters are then moved into the suspected drop area to wait. Typically
at this point, the chase plane photographs the drug-carrying aircraft
dropping cargo, also videotaping the on-board infrared screen image
for evidence.[20] At the moment of rendezvous by the smugglers, the
helicopters move in to chase away the awaiting "go-fast" boats, recover the drugs, and attempt to capture the boat operators.

Though the helicopter crews are armed, the policy was and remains
that no weapons can be fired from the aircraft except in the defense of
the crew. The nonamphibious HH-60J must use the rescue swimmer
to load floating contraband into the rescue basket while the helicopter
hovers overhead.[21]

Capt. William J. Kossler, U.S. Coast Guard, inscribed this portrait, "To Erick the C.G.'s #1 Windmiller—Bill." Almost no photographs exist of the "shy" Kossler. *(Official U.S. Coast Guard Photograph)*

A Grumman JF-2 is taken under tow near the seaplane ramp at CGAS Port Angeles circa 1938. *(U.S. Naval Institute Collection)*

This PH-2 Hall Boat seaplane, mounted on "beaching gear," rolls down the launch ramp. Wheels were removed before the takeoff from the water. *(U.S. Naval Institute Collection)*

Dr. Igor Sikorsky and Col. H. F. Gregory, U.S. Army, stand before the YR-4A after one of its first landings aboard the SS *Bunker Hill*. *(U.S. Coast Guard)*

On the deck of the *Daghestan,* rotor blades are installed on a British YR-4A Hoverfly behind the protection of a temporary wind fence. The deck's turntable is clearly seen, as is the permanent list of the ship because of cargo shift. *(U.S. Coast Guard)*

An HNS-1 practices a landing on the movable platform "USS *Mal de Mer.*" The platform simulated the conditions of landing aboard a ship at sea by rolling five to ten degrees. The deck was built by the Special Devices Division of BuAer at CGAS Brooklyn in March 1944. *(U.S. Coast Guard)*

Erickson *(left)* explains the benefits of using a helicopter for OSS missions behind enemy lines to Gen. William "Wild Bill" Donovan, U.S. Army *(center)*, as Gen. Frank Lowe, U.S. Army, looks on. *(Naval Historical Foundation)*

A PBM "Mariner" takes off during MacDiarmid's open-sea tests. *(U.S. Naval Institute Collection)*

Dr. Sikorsky volunteers to be hoisted by Erickson during tests conducted in July 1944. *(U.S. Coast Guard)*

An HOS is equipped with hat-shaped blisters on each side to allow space for carrying a stretcher athwartships. Uninflated emergency flotation bags are shown attached to the landing wheels. Two HTLs are flying formation in the background. *(Naval Historical Center)*

Capt. Donald B. MacDiarmid, U.S. Coast Guard, as most everybody remembered him—with the ever-present cigar. *(Courtesy of Edith MacDiarmid)*

An HO3S is photographed at CGAS Elisabeth City in October 1946. Equipped as it was with external fuel tank, emergency flotation bags on landing wheels, and a hoist, the helicopter cost $91,977. *(John Redfield Collection)*

Lt. Stewart Graham, U.S. Coast Guard, transports a survivor of the Sabena airliner crash in Gander, Newfoundland, on 18 September 1946. *(U.S. Coast Guard)*

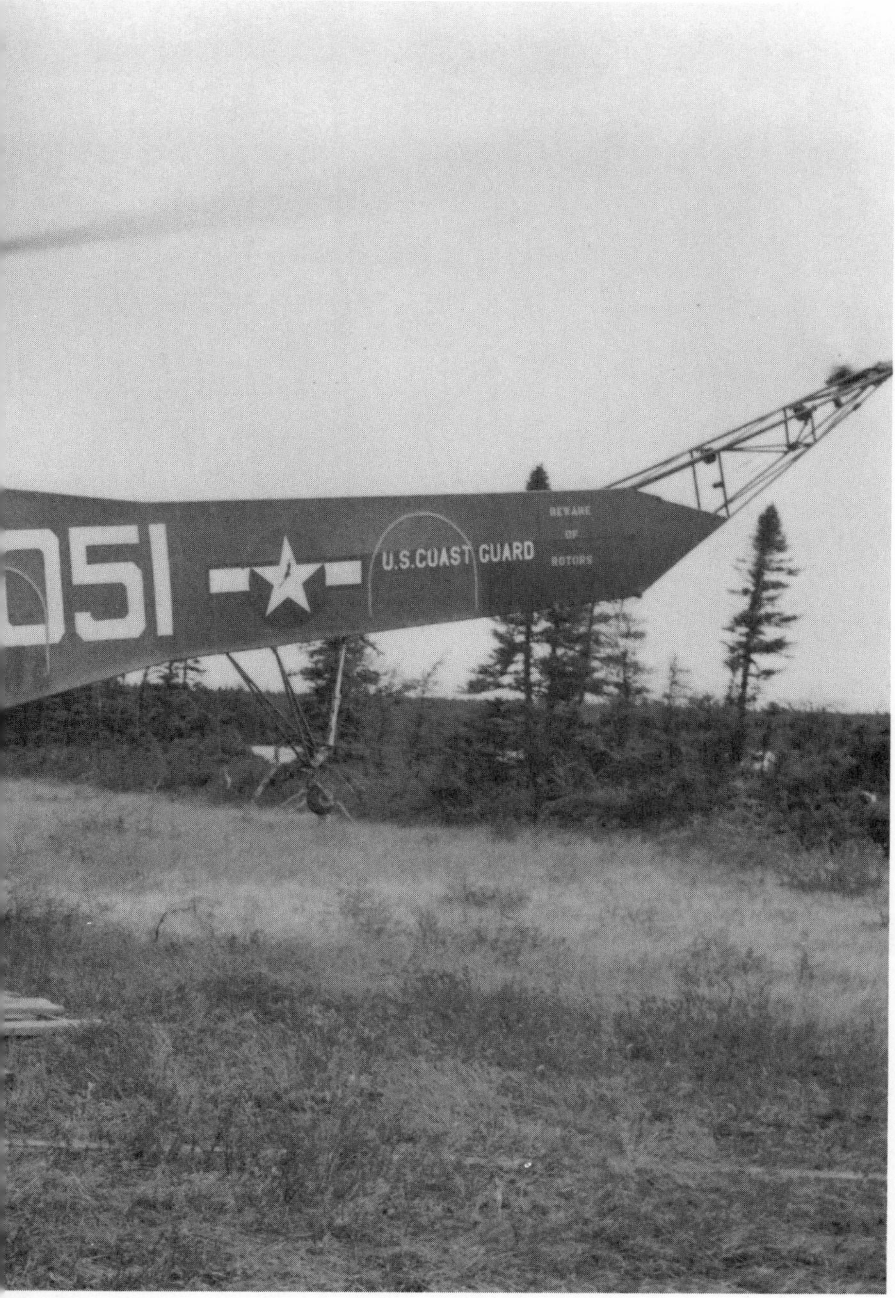
051
U.S.COAST GUARD
BEWARE
OF
ROTORS

A Kaman HK-225 "mixmaster" comes in for a landing at Elisabeth City in January 1951. The HRP-1 in the background contrasts the two twin-rotor concepts. The Sikorsky single-rotor system eventually predominated helicopter designs. *(U.S. Coast Guard)*

This photograph of Erickson in the pilot's seat of an HNS was possibly taken in Labrador during the rescue of downed Sabena airliner passengers. *(U.S. Coast Guard)*

An HO4S experiments with a rescue basket designed by Erickson to "scoop" survivors out of the sea. *(U.S. Coast Guard)*

A hoist-equipped Coast Guard HRP-1 descends for a water landing using inflated emergency flotation bags. *(U.S. Coast Guard)*

An HNS-1 lifts off the Coast Guard icebreaker *Northwind* during Operation Highjump in the Antarctic in January 1947. Trailing in the icebreaker's wake are the USS *Merrick, Yancey,* and *Mt. Olympus.* *(U.S. Coast Guard)*

One of only six such helicopters owned by the Coast Guard, this HUS-1G lowers an "Erickson basket" on its hoist to a victim in the water. *(John Redfield Collection)*

The crew of an HH52-A lifts a stranded hurricane victim from his rooftop in the Louisiana marshlands. *(John Redfield Collection)*

An HH-52A passes just ahead of the bow of the Coast Guard icebreaker *Polar Star*. The helicopter crew is seeking leads through the ice so the ship can strike an Antarctic navigation route. *(U.S. Coast Guard)*

An HO4S-3G "Tugbird," flown by Comdr. John Redfield, U.S. Coast Guard, tows the seventy-five-ton cutter *Birch* at eight knots in Tampa Bay, Florida. The Tugbird flew with a nose-down angle of nearly fifteen degrees because of the average strain of two thousand pounds on the cable. *(U.S. Naval Institute Collection)*

The U.S. Air Force developed inflight refueling from HC130-Ps for their HH-3Es and HH-53Bs for Vietnam War–era rescue work. *(U.S. Naval Institute Collection)*

A Sikorsky HH-60J Jayhawk lowers a rescue basket while its estimated seventy-knot rotor blade downwash whips the water's surface. *(U.S. Coast Guard)*

FOURTEEN

SUM OF ALL DREAMS

U.S. Coast Guard rescue swimmer Michael Odom, dropped earlier from a helicopter, knows he is going to die. Alone, tossed by a winter storm in the Atlantic Ocean 350 miles east of Savannah, Georgia, he lies on a raft exhausted after struggling to save three lives. Waves buffet him repeatedly, cartwheeling him from the raft; ingested saltwater empties his stomach; his body is cramping after violent retching; his core temperature is approaching a fatal low level.

For fifty minutes Odom had struggled, pulling panicked sailors to the rescue basket from seas cresting as high as three-story buildings, driven by forty-knot winds. One by one, Odom watched the sailors soar to safety and disappear inside Coast Guard helicopter number 6019 above him. Suddenly, as the third man reached the rescue helicopter, the hoist cable—Odom's lifeline—broke. Minutes later, he could only watch, bewildered, as the helicopter vanished into the storm-filled night. There will be no rescue for the rescuer. Odom knows it. All he can do is wait, and prepare for his death.[1]

On 23 January 1995, Odom completed his checklist for the rescue of survivors from the sailboat *Mirage*. The sailors were briefed on the radio by Lt. Matt Reid, the pilot of a circling Coast Guard HC-130H Hercules, and Lt. Jay Balda, the pilot of the HH-60J Jayhawk, twin-turbine helicopter. Odom had intended to be in the water just aft of the sinking sailboat and to grab each sailor as he jumped. However, just before the five sailors began their leaps into the sea, the sailboat's captain radioed that he would not leave. The unexpected radio call was relayed to the Coast Guard SAR coordinator in Miami by the C-130. Immediately, the SAR coordinator responded: "The helo will rescue all of them or none." The SAR coordinator's conclusion from the sailboat's radio message was that conditions were stable, since the storm had passed, and the risk of pulling five men from the sea was greater than having them stay with the boat.[2]

Odom waited for the *Mirage* crew's next response. He sat in the crew entrance door of the hovering helicopter, his legs and feet adorned with frog-like flippers, dangling in space. He watched the *Mirage* churn in the waves, illuminated by the helicopter's searchlight. The situation had assumed the appearance of a non-event. Hours earlier, terror had numbed the crew of the forty-foot racing sailboat on its third day out from St. Augustine, Florida, en route to the Virgin Islands. A strong winter front was sweeping down the Atlantic coast, and the men had little experience for coping with its effects. On the second day out the engine failed, the batteries could not be charged, and their food supply was thawing. *Mirage* crewman Mark Cole thought—and hoped—that the storm would pass quickly, but it did not stop.[3]

Three days elapsed, and it just got worse. The electric autopilot did not work because of corrosion in the boat's electrical system. More insidious effects erupted from neglected maintenance. Each man took turns steering the wildly surging boat, and this routine took its toll. First, they steered in two-hour shifts, but fatigue later drove them to their bunks more frequently. Appetites abated, and rest was impossible. Then the savagery of the storm "just started picking up and picking up and picking up, and the waves kept getting bigger and the skies darker," Cole said. Down in the cabin where three crewmen cowered, Cole says the noise was "just incredible . . . you just can't imagine being on a boat and having these kinds of sounds."[4]

The winds reached fifty knots when the front passed, then instantly shifted direction from their southwesterly course to the west-northwest. A confused wave pattern surged from the new, Arctic-driven winds, whose galloping waves imposed themselves on the diminishing rollers from the steady tropical winds of the past three days. This created a confusing tumble of dangerous peaks among already mountainous waves. Allen Brugger, the sailboat's captain, took the helm and steered for about three hours until a confluence of waves that towered fifty feet broke over the small fiberglass shell and plunged it beneath tons of roiling water. The boat rolled to about 120 degrees as the wave tumbled over it, shoving it beneath the surface. The wave passed, and white water boiled in its wake. Slowly, the white hull struggled upright as it popped back to the surface; everything lashed to the deck had been swept away.[5]

Cole, trying to sleep, was thrown across the cabin when the wave rolled over them. Two to three feet of water sloshed throughout the bottom of the nearly upright boat, and cabin lights started going out, shorted by saltwater in the electrical system. Cole burst out of the cabin and into the cockpit, expecting to find it empty, Brugger and his friend Fred Neilson having been washed away. But Brugger was still at the wheel, holding on, staring ahead; Neilson had been washed overboard and was being dragged along behind the boat, hooked on by his safety harness. Cole watched their life raft disappear into the darkness, tumbling with the winds across the spume-washed waves. Brugger and Cole pulled a panic-stricken Neilson back aboard.

Sometime after eight o'clock in the evening, crew member Dave Denman, a private pilot, figured out how to operate the single-sideband high-frequency radio transmitter. Half an hour later, the Coast Guard radio stations at Hampton Roads and Cape May copied a MAYDAY from the *Mirage* and alerted Coast Guard units from Miami to Norfolk, but that offered no solace to the crew. The boat was sinking; their life raft was gone; and in the storm, they believed that no one could offer any aid, even if they could have arrived in time.

Three hours later, the sight of a HC-130H (CGNR No. 1502) from Coast Guard Air Station Elizabeth City, North Carolina, brought the first relief. Lieutenant Reid guided Lieutenant Balda of the H-60, trudging along the track at half the C-130's three-hundred-knot pace, to the sailboat. The Jayhawk (CGNR No. 6019) arrived over the *Mirage* at 1:10 P.M., watching the boat being whipped by the storm. The helicopter had enough fuel to remain on station for about fifty minutes. Reid reported to Balda that the "master of vessel declined pumps and survival kits . . . (and) requested to be removed from vessel" because of flooding from an unknown source.[6]

Balda could not hover over the boat to retrieve its occupants, and lowering the rescue basket to the deck of the sailboat was impossible. The wildly whipping mast was like a rapier thrusting skyward as the boat lunged violently in the twenty-five-foot waves and forty-knot winds. The helicopter crew's sole option for recovering the distressed sailors was to have them jump into the water one at a time, to be grasped by a waiting rescue swimmer and loaded into the rescue basket.[7]

Reid told the sailboat crew, "[If] you don't come off now, you will be beyond the range of helicopter rescue." Then came the unexpected reply from the boat: the captain refused to jump overboard. The other crew members, however, were unaware of Brugger's decision. They were already assembled on deck, preparing to leap, having strung a line, as instructed, about fifty feet long, trailing aft with a boat fender tied to its free end. Odom planned to hold onto this line and grab each man as he went overboard. This procedure meant three hoists for each man lifted. The first hoist would place the rescue swimmer in the water; the second would pull the survivor into the helicopter; and the third would recover the rescue swimmer for the move back to the boat for the next cycle. Confounding this recovery plan was Brugger's decision to keep the sail up; the sailboat barreled along with the teth- ered float skipping off the water like an abandoned water-ski rope towed behind a speedboat.[8]

With the captain refusing to jump, the helicopter crew had to abort their plans. The Coast Guard's official response from Miami was transmitted to the *Mirage:* "All are to remain on board if one intends to stay." Balda moved the helicopter away from the sailboat to wait, consuming critical fuel. Watching the sailboat in the heli- copter's light, the Coast Guard crew was stunned to see the next unexpected scene: Cole jumped into the water. He struggled to hold onto the line, but the boat was going too fast. Odom was not in the water, as planned; no rescue basket was waiting for the survivor. As dark waters enveloped Cole, Odom was still sitting in the cabin door, watching with the same disbelief of his crew.[9]

Balda quickly pushed the helicopter forward and pressed on the left rudder peddle, spinning the nose into the wind, holding a hover to keep Cole in sight. Odom was lowered hurriedly into the water with the cable end snapped to his harness. The cable was retrieved, the basket attached, then lowered for him to catch after he swam to Cole. The boat sailed away and was out of Cole's sight almost immediately. The fifty-three- degree water was shockingly cold, with the air temperature falling to forty degrees. Before he could add new fears to his already terrified mind, Cole felt Odom's touch. "It was a great feeling when that fellow put his arm around me," he remembered. His new world was one of flooding light from above, noise, the blast of air and spray from the heli- copter's downwash, and a comforting voice saying that he was okay.[10]

But these moments were not easy for Odom. He swam hard for the basket swinging below the helicopter while holding onto Cole. Balda had no visual reference to hold a position, and the plunging waves conveyed a false sense of movement to him even when the helicopter was motionless. The thirty-five-to-forty-knot winds were also trying to blow the basket away from that tiny spot on the water where Odom's arm was reaching, grasping. Balda's guidance came from Mark Bafetti, the Coast Guard flight mechanic and hoist operator. He was viewing

Cole and sighting down the cable from the helicopter's open doorway aft of the cockpit on the starboard side. Bafetti was leaning in space and kneeling on the cabin floor, restrained from pitching out only by a strap around his waist which was clipped to the helicopter. He called out in steady, calm tones through the internal communications system, "back ten—right; back, back—hold; hold, hold—left five—hold." Balda applied slight pressures on his control stick, almost wishing the helicopter into the positions called for by Bafetti.

Bafetti tried swinging the basket to Odom while at the same moment controlling its up-and-down movement, matching the wave heights with a push-button controller. Loose slack can be fatal to those in the water if the cable should make a loop and wrap around body parts and then suddenly go tight. Odom just managed to get the basket at his fingertips when a wave dropped him several feet and the basket was jerked away. After several more attempts, Odom captured the basket and got Cole into it. But Cole would not sit down; he froze and stopped responding to instructions. Cole wrapped his arms around the bail, placing his head, arms, and torso next to the whipping cable. The basket was jerked out of the water violently as a wave passed. Odom feared the motion had broken Cole's neck, but he miraculously was still in the basket, uninjured.

After a twenty-minute struggle, Cole was recovered safely. However, four other *Mirage* crewmen still had to be retrieved. Only thirty minutes' worth of fuel remained for the helicopter to stay on station. Odom was hoisted aboard, and the helicopter did a quick turn and chased after the sailboat, which was nearly a mile away downwind. *Mirage* crewman Thomas Steier was the next to jump, but at one point, he nearly refused. "Not that I'd want to go down with the boat," he later explained, "but jumping off the boat into that black water was the most difficult thing to do." Odom, back in the water, grabbed him and said, "Hey, as long as I got you nothing's going to happen to you." Steier had difficulty squeezing his six-foot two-inch frame into the rescue basket in the tumbling seas. When Odom released the hoist and the basket got up about ten feet, a huge wave overwhelmed Steier. "All of a sudden, I was under water being jolted and jerked, and I had a snap when I came out of the water." Coming up in the air, he swung in circles, banging the bottom of the helicopter and fuel tank before he was pulled to safety.[11]

"Here is where a weird thing happened," explained Odom. The wave that swallowed Steier "scared me to the point where I was swimming like heck to get out of the way of the aircraft. I've never seen water so close to a helicopter. It was a good twenty-five-to-thirty-five-footer."

Odom, back on board the aircraft, recommended a higher hover altitude for the next hoist; Balda needed no encouragement.[12]

Backup rescue swimmer Mario Vittone observed Odom during their short passage together in the back of the helicopter and saw that he was fatigued. He asked, "Are you ready for me to go, Mike?" Odom responded with the portentous words: "One more. Let me have just one more."[13]

Time and fuel were becoming critical. Nearly forty minutes had elapsed during the recovery of the first two survivors. Less than ten minutes' fuel remained, with three more survivors on the disabled sailboat. Helicopter 6019 moved about half a mile to the next survivor and climbed to a hundred-foot hover to keep away from any more rogue waves. Denman, the third crewman from the *Mirage,* was in the water. As Odom went down this time, swinging at the end of the long cable, he hit the water hard, gasped for air, and sucked seawater. He coughed and vomited while struggling to reach Denman and work him into the basket. Bafetti, the hoist operator, worked hard to keep dangerous slack from forming loops in the cable, while at the same time allowing enough slack to keep the basket from being jerked from Odom's hands.

As Denman finally was hoisted in the basket, Vittone assisted the hoist operator to control the cable and keep it away from the aircraft. Cable strands started popping. Vittone yelled to Bafetti as he felt sharp spurs of small wires peeling off the cable. Denman was sixty to seventy feet above the churning seas, dangling in the basket. Bafetti reacted and ran the hoist at full speed, winding in the snarled cable to recover Denman before the cable could snap and drop him to his death. Denman was trundled safely aboard as the copilot, Lt. (jg) Guy Pearce, announced "Six minutes 'til bingo." Only six minutes' fuel remained until the helicopter must leave.

Broken cable strands jammed the hoist mechanism; the hoist no longer worked. Odom was still in the water and could not be recovered. Bafetti attempted to signal Odom by flashlight to call back on his radio, but Odom did not respond. The pilot then flashed hover lights—a signal meaning that the aircraft crew no longer sees the rescue swimmer. It is their only signal to indicate to the man in the water that a problem exists. Odom, confused and believing the crew had lost sight of him, fired a flare and attached his strobe light to the top of his head. The copilot called "Bingo."

Next, Odom saw the rescue basket drop into the sea. The Jayhawk was drifting around in a hover about two hundred yards away. Its crew dropped a datum marker buoy, a floating radio transmitter used to track the drift of objects in the vicinity. "I looked at that, and it didn't look right," Odom recalled. Fear gripped him. He did not know what was happening. With a sinking heart, he muttered a choked, "Oh, no." The Jayhawk moved back over him. Through the glare of lights overhead, Odom could not see the faces looking back from twenty-five feet away. Helicopter 6019's crew tried to figure a method to recover Odom, but they had run out of time. At seven minutes past bingo, they had to leave for their own survival; Odom had to be left behind. Vittone, Odom's best friend, kicked out a life raft and closed the cabin door.

Odom inflated the raft and climbed aboard. Darkness surrounded him as the lights vanished with the helicopter. "There's a lot of stress at this point," Odom says. Emotion etches his voice. "I knew how far offshore I was, and I knew there were no other rescue resources backing them up. I saw them disappear into the night. At that point, I got on my radio and began screaming, 'Nineteen—talk to me! What's going on? Nineteen—talk to me!' I was talking to them on the radio, but wasn't hearing back from them." Both were trying to talk at the same time, blocking each other's transmissions.[14]

The rescued passengers knew their two crew mates remained on the sailboat and that Odom was in the water, but "had no idea what was going on," said Steier. "I looked over at one of the Coast Guard lieutenants (*sic*[15]) in the back, and he had tears in his eyes."[16]

Odom, alone except for the seemingly impotent Hercules circling overhead, sat in his raft, one he had recently repacked for use in saving other lives. A large swell hurled him back into the sea—now he was the survivor. Odom grabbed the raft before the winds and seas could snatch it away forever. He clambered aboard and was trying again to find the lanyard to attach himself to the raft when it was struck violently once more, tossing him back into the tumbling water. Recapturing the raft once more, he slithered aboard, exhausted, physically ill, unable to talk to the helo, having no idea what had happened, and knowing that he was three hundred miles offshore. Another helo couldn't reach him for at least four hours.

Reid, piloting the C-130 (CGNR No. 1502), had been out just a little more than four hours, and low fuel state was a concern. A relief Coast Guard C-130 was being readied to fly out from Clearwater, Florida, but it could not arrive in time. Reid was ordered to return to base, but, instead, he shut down two of his four engines to conserve fuel and continued to circle Odom for as long as he could. Odom finally attached himself to the raft as seasickness and depression consumed him. He knew the only two Jayhawks that might reach him were both out of commission in the hangar at Elizabeth City. The Marines at Marine Corps Air Station Cherry Point had nothing that could come this far to sea.[17]

The guided-missile cruiser *Ticonderoga* (CG-47) had an SH-60B Seahawk on board, but since it was out of range, it began steaming toward Odom's position to close the gap. Meanwhile, crew members from the cruiser pushed the helicopter from the ship's hangar and readied it for flight. The task was onerous, because the *Ticonderoga* was being buffeted by the same storm. Also in the vicinity, the merchant ship *Diletta F* was alerted by the Coast Guard through the Automated Merchant Vessel Reporting System. It also turned and began steaming toward the lone swimmer.

The copilot of the C-130, Lt. Mark Russell, radioed Odom that another helicopter at that time was on the way, but that was not true. "You can make it," Russell asserted with unfounded boldness before asking if Odom wanted any equipment dropped and then saying they would drop flares. Together on the radio, they recalled a rumored incident months earlier whereby a Coast Guard aircraft dropped a flare that accidentally fell into a raft full of Cubans. "Remember, I'm not a Cuban," Odom reminded Russell. But the reverie ended suddenly when another wave knocked Odom back into the water. This time he did not have to swim for the raft; he was attached by the lanyard. But Odom was much weaker, and it was harder for him to clamber back into the raft. The seas were wearing him down, and he wondered how much longer he could fight them.[18]

Odom was reaching a critical stage in survival. The numbing coldness overwhelmed him. He passed through the shivering stage, a cause for alarm. He knew the signs from his training as an emergency medical technician; he had little time left. Berry Freeman, an aviation machinist's mate first class, stayed on the radio and kept a spark of life going during this critical period. But that fragile electronic link soon was severed. Odom's limbs were numb, and his hands were drawing up so that he could no longer lift the small hand-held radio to his mouth. He tried to focus on the low-flying C-130 as it swept toward him in its racetrack pattern low overhead, but he was losing his vision. Seeing the lights, he thought for a time that the helicopter had finally come, but when the plane rolled out and he saw the lights at the wingtips spread wide apart, he lost any hope of rescue.

Odom did not want to be thrown from the raft when he died, so he tied himself in, face up. He did not want the Coast Guard to have to waste days searching for his body.

The relief Hercules, CGNR No. 1504, arrived from Elizabeth City at 4:36 A.M. Lt. (jg) Dan Rocco, Odom's boss, was the copilot. The Clearwater Hercules, CGNR No. 1714, diverted north to intercept the Elizabeth City Jayhawk, CGNR No. 6034, piloted by Lt. Comdr.

Bruce Jones. Station policy required a fixed-wing aircraft cover when helicopters ventured beyond fifty miles offshore at night. The Clearwater C-130 escorted the H-60 for thirty minutes, passing its covering responsibility to the Elizabeth City Hercules and diverting to search for the *Mirage* at 5:45 A.M.[19]

After relocating the sailboat, the 1504 took up its vigil there, orbiting until the *Mirage* distress case could be resolved. The crew of the 1504 looked closely to see whether Odom was still with the raft and if he might respond by waving or moving as the aircraft flew low overhead. He had been off the radio for too long. In the glare of their landing lights they saw an apparently lifeless body. The helicopter was still fifty minutes away. Lt. Comdr. Dan Osborn, pilot of the relief Hercules overhead, directed Commander Jones's helicopter to the raft. The merchant vessel *Diletta F* also arrived at the scene as the storm-filled eastern sky began to lighten with the dawn. Although it could not pick up Odom, the merchant vessel acted as a wind and sea break to assist the hovering helicopter in Odom's retrieval.

The Jayhawk settled in a hover above the drifting life raft four hours and fifty minutes after Odom first went into the water, and more than an hour since he transmitted his last words: "I'm cold. I'm cold."[20]

Rescue swimmer Jim Peterson dropped down from the hovering 6034 into the raft. Straddling Odom he shouted in Odom's face and rubbed his chest vigorously. Odom remained motionless, his head rigid, twisted to one side. Next, Peterson inserted his hand beneath Odom's hood to check the carotid pulse. At that moment, Odom's arm came up in an unconscious effort, reaching out to his rescuer. He was alive! Quickly, Peterson snapped Odom's harness to his own and the two were lifted together. As they started up, the life raft's webbing tangled and snagged Peterson's arm. The raft, loaded with water, added a critical load to the helicopter's hoist and cable. After several sharp tugs, Peterson freed them from the deadly trap, and the two were hauled into the hovering helicopter, Odom still unconscious.

Meanwhile, miles away, the two *Mirage* crewmen still awaited evacuation from the sailboat in distress. Jones, with Odom safely in the helicopter, was ordered to pick up these two. When he reported Odom's condition and the urgent need for medical attention, the orders changed, and he was directed to take Odom to a hospital more than two hours away. He proceeded instead to the *Ticonderoga*—150 miles away—to drop Odom off for more immediate medical attention, refueling at the same time. After this mid-ocean stop, Jones was able to return to the *Mirage* with his escort, the 1504, make the pickup, and get back to an airport.

Odom's body temperature was 92.5 degrees Fahrenheit when he was pulled aboard the helicopter. The crew members cut off his survival suit and clothing, wrapped him tightly in blankets, and started him breathing oxygen. The copilot in 6034, Lt. (jg) Dan Molthen, ran the cabin temperature controller up to maximum heat, "which was just smoking those fellows in survival suits." Odom later remarked, "It must have been a hundred-plus degrees inside the cabin." During the seventy-minute flight to the cruiser, Odom recovered consciousness, and his temperature climbed to 97.1 degrees. Navy corpsmen on board the *Ticonderoga* treated Odom for his exposure. His recovery was rapid, but he remained on board for the next twenty-four hours.[21]

Meanwhile, Jones—unaware of the sailboat captain's earlier refusal to jump from the vessel—proceeded to retrieve the two remaining crew. Neilson, suffering from having been tossed overboard thirteen hours earlier, was eager to leave the boat, but Brugger again refused to be evacuated when the helicopter arrived. (*Mirage* crew member Cole speculated later that Brugger's reluctance centered on the personal belongings he had on board, some of which were family heirlooms.) After recovering Neilson, Jones told Brugger that no other assistance would be provided, and he left the scene.[22]

The following day, the Navy's SH-60B Seahawk from the *Ticonderoga* returned Odom to MCAS Cherry Point. His unit's aircraft picked him up and brought him home to a welcome by all hands and a cup of hot chocolate from Captain Walz. Odom returned to work the next day; three days later, he was flying on another rescue mission. Captain Brugger sailed on and arrived safely at St. Thomas, Virgin Islands, after a seventeen-day passage. He then began readying his boat to haul passengers for hire in the popular winter charter service.

Coast Guard rescue swimmer Michael Odom received the Distinguished Flying Cross before Congress on 4 May 1995 for his heroic actions in the rescue of the crew members of the *Mirage*. Senator Mark Hatfield, the Senate Appropriations Committee chairman, and Coast Guard Commandant Adm. Robert E. Kramek presented the award.

EPILOGUE

The helicopter, after fifty years' evolution and a shaky start, is an accepted vehicle for a wide variety of missions. A sign of its significance today is how it is coveted among the armed services. The Army, which inaugurated the rotary-wing project in the 1930s and first accepted the helicopter in 1942, has designs on all future helicopter developments. The Navy, as Capt. Floyd D. Kennedy Jr., U.S. Naval Reserve, Naval Doctrine Command, reported:

> as of September 1994 . . . had 1,349 rotary-wing and 1,646 fixed-wing aircraft; the numbers are almost equal but the fixed-wing aircraft get far more visibility. As if to emphasize the major programmatic plum that naval rotary-wing aviation is, the Army put in a bid to the roles and missions commission to take over the lead in all Department of Defense rotary-wing research and development, test and evaluation, acquisition, depot maintenance, flight training, enlisted skills training, air traffic controller training, and doctrine.[1]

It is now apparent that the value and strength of this rotary-wing force is erupting as a power tool within the defense community similar to the quest by each of the armed services for control of atomic weapons following World War II.

The Coast Guard created the helicopter envisioned by Sikorsky, Kossler, and Erickson. The other military services, U.S. and foreign alike, reaped the benefits of this early development and expanded on it.

175

Helicopter maturation took many years of trial and error, and it left the few who fought for it early unrecognized, tainted with disgrace, or dead.

Coast Guard planners must soon decide on the future of the service's fixed-winged fleet and the strength of its continued helicopter force. Evidence piling up daily from the remarkable missions conducted with Coast Guard helicopters cannot but justify Erickson's 1943 prediction of an "all helicopter Coast Guard."

One element stands undisputed as a prime force in all future forecasts. This is the essential role in rescue missions the helicopter plays. Its reputation is further garnished by the vast number of people who have lived because they were snatched from life-and-death crises by Coast Guard helicopter crews. These deeds cannot be refuted or ignored. "None of this would have been possible without the genius of Dr. Igor Sikorsky and the dedicated group of helicopter designers that followed him," wrote Erickson in the dedication of his unpublished book. He continued:

Captain William J. Kossler of the United States Coast Guard . . . initiated the program which led to the development of the seagoing helicopters. This program was beset by very stiff opposition, but Kossler persisted and overcame the obstacles. It is therefore my pleasure to dedicate this work to the memory of Dr. Sikorsky, Captain Kossler and the helicopter pilots and crewmen, who gave their lives to save the lives of others.[2]

The helicopter was the product of a few men with visions for the future who were not overwhelmed by the realities of mere mechanical boundaries and limits to their knowledge. They lacked neither courage nor a willingness to risk their lives. The genius of these visionaries enabled them to see a valuable rescue vehicle when they looked at a multifaceted machine with its whirling rotors and staccato movements. Today, the vehicle once described by Erickson as a "wonderful new flying machine" does all that Kossler and Erickson envisioned.

What are the parameters for "Igor's nightmare" into the next century? Are there future visionaries dreaming of new devices to revolutionize *history*, not just aviation, as the helicopter did? Is there now a place for new men and women of the Coast Guard, or of any military service, to assume the roles of a Kossler or an Erickson and create a contribution to society as significant as the helicopter? Will managers of today or the future recognize and support this type of genius? Or, on the other hand, did the times and circumstances just happen to coincide for Sikorsky, Kossler, and Erickson to make the helicopter just a product of its time?

The Coast Guard has taken a wild ride on a feisty little beast and contributed something more to the history of humankind than just years or lives saved. The creation of the helicopter took the strange combination of genius and incompetence. The helicopter itself, seen from every angle, is the ultimate visual oxymoron as it lifts from the ground into a hover, motionless, standing on an invisible pedestal.

APPENDIX A

Foreword to Frank Erickson's unpublished **Fishers of Men**

In 1862 a brochure entitled *"L'Aeronef, Appareil de Sauvetage"* ("Aircraft, a Device for Saving Lives") was published in Paris. The pamphlet presented a reasonable description of a helicopter and ended with this prophetic statement: "And then I, a modest narrator . . . will have the happiness to see people rescued at sea, and victims of fires and floods saved by this apparatus."

To my mind, one of the leading pioneers in making that prophesy become a reality is Captain Frank A. Erickson, the U.S. Coast Guard's first helicopter pilot. Captain Erickson was one of the earliest to foresee the life-saving potential of the helicopter, especially for use in situations where anything else but a vertical lift aircraft would be too little or too late. But he was more than a visionary; he was an activist who, after learning to fly a helicopter in 1942, devoted the remainder of his Coast Guard career to promoting, recommending and demonstrating the life-saving capabilities of the helicopter.

As commanding officer of the Coast Guard's first helicopter unit, Captain Erickson personally flew the first helicopter mercy mission on record and then directed the efforts of the little squadron as it began the long list of helicopter life-saving missions for which the Coast Guard has since become famous. [That] these missions continue to this day, now number many thousands, and, despite the many dramatic emergencies involved, have become the Coast Guard's chief aerial vehicle has long since proved correct. His aggressive insistence that

179

helicopters be fully utilized in this way was one of the major reasons why the prediction came true and may be said to be directly responsible for the saving of countless lives.

This book, FISHERS OF MEN, presents a valuable chronicle of the whole development of sea-going helicopters not only by the Coast Guard but by the Navy and Marines, and even the Army and Air Force.

I am most pleased that Captain Erickson, in his retirement, has put this story on the record because as far as my own part in helicopter development is concerned, it has been the life-saving aspect of the helicopter accomplishments that has given me the greatest personal satisfaction. For this I extend my deepest thanks and warmest wishes to Captain Erickson and all the other brave men who have flown these machines for so many years on so many missions of mercy.

Igor I. Sikorsky
Stratford, Connecticut
1972

APPENDIX B

Those Who Died in Service

13 November 1952
Comdr. J. F. McCue
AD1 H. J. White

21 January 1954
Lt. J. W. Day
AD3 R. A. Chauvin
AD3 D. R. Littleford
AD3 P. A. Palombini
AD3 W. J. Goodman

26 June 1954
Comdr. P. A. Ortman

24 June 1956
HM1 J. J. Kohan

25 April 1961
Lt. J. H. Levey

29 June 1961
Lt. Comdr. S. T. Scharfenstein
Lt. Comdr. C. E. Mueller
AL1 J. R. Doherty

22 December 1964
Lt. Comdr. D. L. Prince
AE2 J. A. Nininger Jr.

9 June 1968
Lt. J. C. Rittichier

26 November 1969
Lt. (jg) J. D. Voss
Lt. (jg) R. K. Clark
AD3 R. A. Lumsden

16 December 1972
Lt. Comdr. P. R. Lewis
AD1 E. J. Nemetz
AT3 C. E. Edwards

20 January 1977
Lt. (jg) J. F. Taylor
AT2 J. B. Johnson

17 January 1979
Lt. R. G. Ausness
Lt. R. C. Shearer Jr.
AM1 R. E. McClain
AD3 J. B. Case

29 January 1979
Lt. (jg) D. C. Sproat
AD3 R. W. Stephenson

18 February 1979
Lt. Comdr. J. D. Stiles
AT2 J. B. Tait
HM2 B. A. Kaehler

7 August 1981
 Lt. E. P. Rivas
 Lt. J. G. Spoja
 AD1 S. E. Finfrock
 AT3 J. H. Snyder
22 October 1981
 Lt. R. T. Brooks
 Lt. (jg) R. E. Winter
 AD3 M. C. Johnson
 AD3 J. A. Hinton
14 November 1981
 Capt. F. W. Olson
7 January 1982
 Lt. Comdr. H. W. Johnson
 Lt. C. A. Cain
 AD2 D. L. Thompson

2 November 1986
 Lt. M. C. Dollahite
 Lt. R. T. Carson
 Comdr. D. M. Rockmore
 ASM2 K. M. McCraken
 AT3 W. G. Kemp
 HS3 R. D. King
31 August 1993
 Lt. M. C. Perkins
 Lt. (jg) M. S. Fisher
12 July 1994
 Lt. L. B. Williams
 Lt. M. E. Koteet
 AM1 M. R. Gill
 ASMCS P. A. Leeman

APPENDIX C

Those Who Studied at Erickson's School

One hundred and two pilots and one nonpilot entered training at CGAS Brooklyn between December 1943 and February 1945. That total broke down as follows: Coast Guard, 71; Navy, 8; Army Air Forces, 3; Army nonpilot, 1; Royal Army, Royal Navy, and Royal Air Force, 13; CAA, 4; NACA, 1; P-V Corporation, 1; McDonnell Aircraft, 1. The number who did not complete the training was eight; the total number who qualified, therefore, was ninety-five.

Listed below are the names of students of the Coast Guard's and U.S. military's first helicopter school. The names appear in the approximate order of completion that can be compiled from existing records of the school and other sources. Instructor names are given where known, and the Coast Guard helicopter qualification numbers are shown as determined from training records of the period. In cases where the pilot did not complete the training, the date the class completed the program will still be given. The completion dates on the students through class two are the dates of their final check flights.

Erickson, Coast Guard helicopter pilot number one, was trained by test pilot Morris at the Sikorsky factory and soloed on 10 June, 1943. Lt. (jg) Stewart R. Graham, helicopter pilot number two, was trained by Erickson at the Sikorsky factory as well; he soloed on 20 October, 1943, with approximately three and a half hours of flight time. He completed training and qualified as a helicopter instructor on 20 November, 1943. Graham recalled in a letter he sent me on 16 January 1995 that once he soloed, he was on his own. "There was no one else to teach us anything more."

Name & Rank	Service	Instructor	Date Training Completed	Pilot Number
Miller, John M., Lt. Comdr.	USNR	Erickson	12/5/43	
Klopp, J. W., Lt. Comdr.	USN	Erickson		
reported for training 12/17/43, soloed 12/19/43; no completion date				
Bolton, Walter C., Ens.	USCG	Graham/Erickson	12/30/43	CG #3
Gregg, E. S., Capt.	USAAF	Graham/Erickson	12/31/43	
Miller, C. P., Lt.	USAAF	Graham/Erickson	12/31/43	
Gough, W. V., Lt.	USNR	Erickson	1/15/44	
Lawrence, William J., Lt. Comdr.	USCG	Erickson	1/22/44	CG #4
Kleisch, August, Lt. (jg)	USCG		3/10/44	CG #5
Perry, Loren V., Lt. (jg)	USCG		3/12/44	CG #6
Knapp, W. G., Lt.	USNR		3/15/44	
Richardson, J., Maj.	Royal Army		3/15/44	
Reader, J. P., civilian	NACA incomplete		3/31/44	
Toomey, H. M., civilian	CAA incomplete		3/31/44	
Lindsay, A. M., civilian	CAA incomplete		3/31/44	
Bearcroft, P., S/Lt. A	RNVR dropped		3/31/44	
Gershowitz, David, AP/1c	USCG		4/17/44	CG #7
Curwin, Walter, Lt. (jg)	USCG		4/25/44	CG #8
Welsh, T., F/Lt.	RAF		5/3/44	
Bradbury, F/Lt.	RAF		5/3/44	
Girdler, George W., Lt.	USCG		5/15/44	CG #9
Lawrence, Joe G., Lt. Comdr.	USCG	Perry	5/15/44	CG #10

Name & Rank	Service	Instructor	Date Training Completed	Pilot Number
Mattaliano, F. F., AP1c	USCG		5/15/44	CG #11
Jeffery, J.J.M., S/Lt.	RNVR	Bolton	5/15/44	
Sharpe, W. C., Lt. A	RNVR	Kleisch	5/15/44	
Arkell, B. H., F/L	RAFO	Bradbury	5/19/44	
Mueller, C. E., CAP	USCG	Bolton	5/29/44	CG #12.
First official GG student assigned by orders from Headquarters				CG #12.
Allbeurg, C. R., Lt. A	RNVR	Knapp	5/29/44	
Whittle, A. F., F/O	RAF	Bradbury	5/29/44	
Hosegood, C.T.D., Lt. A	RNVR	Kleisch	5/29/44	
White, C., Lt. A	RNVR	Bolton incomplete	6/1/44	
"not recommended for instructional duties"				
Cayley, F., S/Lt.	RNVR	Perry	6/14/44	
Smeder, Orvan R., Lt. Comdr.	USCG	Graham	6/15/44	CG #13
Mazonson, Barney P., Lt. (jg)	USCG	Gershowitz	6/22/44	CG #14
Redfield, John C., CAP	USCG	Gershowitz	6/22/44	CG #15
Gwynn, Oliver H.J.P., CAP	USCG		6/22/44	CG #16
Causley, Clyde M., CAP	USCG	Girdler	7/20/44	CG #17
		first formal student class 1		
Smith, Paul S., CAP	USCG	Bolton class 1	7/20/44	CG #18
Tremper, Henry S., Lt. (jg)	USCG	Graham class 1	7/20/44	CG #19
Broadhurst	British	Knapp		
started 6/5 no record dropped				

Name & Rank	Service	Instructor	Date Training Completed	Pilot Number
Hughes, Phillip W., AP/1c	USCG	Kleisch class 1	7/21/44	CG #20
Davison, Arthur M., Lt. Comdr.	USCGR	Girdler class 1	7/21/44	CG #21
Lamping, J. J., Ens.	USCG	Perry class 1	7/21/44	CG #22
Townsend, George, *civilian test pilot with P-V Eng Co.*		Gershowitz class 1	7/22/44	
Hilsee, David W., Lt. (jg)	USCGR	Mueller class 1	7/24/44	CG #23
Prindle, William E., Lt.	USCGR	Girdler class 1	7/29/44	CG #24
Kossler, William J., Capt.	USCG	Erickson class 1	7/29/44	CG #25
Burke, Woodward, *civilian test pilot with McDonnell Corp.*		Graham class 2	8/5/44	
Reed, D. O., Comdr.	USCG	Lawrence class 2	8/19/44	CG #26
Ballard, Walter L., AP/1c	USCG	Kleisch class 2	8/22/44	CG #27
Guidroz, H. F., Ens.	USCG	Kleisch class 2	8/22/44	CG #28
Morrill, W. E., Lt. (jg)	USCGR	Mueller class 2	8/24/44	CG #29
Constantino, S. A., Lt. (jg)	USCGR	Mazonson class 2	8/28/44	CG #30
Lockwood, Charles W., CAP	USCG	Bolton class 2	8/28/44	CG #31
Briggs, G. L., Lt. (jg)	USCGR	Perry class 2	8/28/44	CG #32
Thomas, James, Lt. (jg)	USCGR	Smeder class 2	8/28/44	CG #33
Mathisen, E. P., Lt. (jg)	USCGR	Gershowitz class 2	8/28/44	CG #34
Kolyer, Robert J., AP/1c	USCGR	Graham class 2	8/28/44	CG #35
MacLane, G. H., Lt.	USCGR	Gershowitz class 2	8/28/44	CG #36
DuBordieu, R. J., Lt. (jg)	USCGR	Bolton class 2	8/30/44	CG #37
Schuh, Charles W., Lt. Comdr.	USCG	Prindle class 3	9/27/44	CG #38
Hammond, R. E., Lt. Comdr.	USCG	Tremper class 3	9/29/44	CG #39

Name & Rank	Service	Instructor	Date Training Completed	Pilot Number
Solari, W. J., Lt. (jg)	USCG	Graham class 3	9/29/44	CG #40
Lyford, H.R.W., Lt. (jg)	USCGR	Mazonson class 3	9/29/44	CG #41
Felt, Leland G., AP/1c	USCG	Constantino class 3	9/29/44	CG #42
Ethridge, Ralph L., Ens.	USCR	Bolton class 3	9/29/44	CG #43
Wilson, Fred E., AP/1c	USCG	Kleisch class 3	9/29/44	CG #44
Britt, M. G., Lt. (jg)	USCGR	Perry class 3	9/29/44	CG #45
Vukic, John, Ens.	USCG	Mueller class 3	9/29/44	CG #46
Schmidt, V.A.G., Lt.	USCG	Gershowitz class 3	9/29/44	CG #47
Smith, Stanley S., AP/1c	USCG	Kleisch class 3	9/29/44	CG #48
Wood, C. R., Lt. Comdr.	USNR	Knapp class 3	10/26/44	
Doll, R. E., Comdr.	USN	Graham class 3	10/31/44	
Lowe, Frank E., Brig. Gen.	USA	Erickson	11/10/44	
		special training completed		
Bigelow, P. W., AP/1c	USCGR	class 4	11/10/44	
Bracken, R. E., AP/1c	USCG	class 4	11/10/44	
DeFreest, D. W., Ens.	USCG	class 4	11/10/44	
Goldhammer, W. R., CAP	USCG	class 4	11/10/44	
Gould, R. C., Lt.	USCG	class 4	11/10/44	
Jenkins, W. A., Lt.	USCG	class 4	11/10/44	
Macrate, A. N., Lt. (jg)	USCGR	class 4	11/10/44	
Raumer, F. H., Ens.	USCG	class 4	11/10/44	
Sansbury, L. C., Lt. (jg)	USCGR	class 4	11/10/44	

Name & Rank	Service	Instructor	Date Training Completed	Pilot Number
Sharp, C. E., Lt. Comdr.	USCG	class 4	11/10/44	
Vennel, W. W., Lt. Comdr.	USCG	class 4	11/10/44	
West, J. R., CAP	USCGR	class 4	11/10/44	
Chase, W. M. Jr., Ens.	USCG	class 5	12/19/44	
Colmer, C. C., Ens.	USCG	class 5	12/19/44	
Cornish, James, Lt. Comdr.	USCG	class 5	12/19/44	
Evans, J. P., Ens.	USCG	class 5	12/19/44	
Immerman, J. W., Lt.	USCGR	class 5	12/19/44	
Kephart, G. O., Lt.	USCG	class 5	12/19/44	
Palmer, J. A., Lt. (jg)	USCG	class 5	12/19/44	
Woodson, R. E., Lt. (jg)	USCGR	class 5 dropped		
Brown, Percy Jr., Lt.	USNR	class 6	2/6/45	
Douglas, R. O., Ens.	USCG	class 6	2/6/45	
Engel, B. L., Lt. Comdr.	USCGR	class 6	2/6/45	
Flint, K. W., Capt.	USAAF	class 6	2/6/45	
Greathouse, John P., Ens.	USCG	class 6	2/6/45	
Mackey, J. R., Ens.	USCG	class 6	2/6/45	
McCormack, J. T., Ens.	USCG	class 6	2/6/45	
Tygart, B. F., Ens.	USCGR	class 6	2/6/45	
Beardslee, D. C., civilian	CAA	class 6	2/6/45	
Probst, L. S., civilian	CAA	class 6	2/6/45	

APPENDIX D

The Stump Jumper's Lament

Beneath the spreading rotor head
the helicopter stands.
With an underpowered engine
and blades like rubber bands.

The fuselage looks silly,
the whole idea's absurd.
Why anyone would fly it
I really haven't heard.
There's an anti-torque propeller
sticking out the tail.
It looks for all the world
like a highly pregnant quail.

One doesn't need a parachute.
One doesn't need a brain.
In fact, to fly this monster,
it helps to be insane.

Oh, how I hate DeVinci,
and Sikorsky's on my list.
If they had kept their traps shut,
this mess I would have missed.

But I am brave and I am strong
and greatly in demand.
For I'm a helicopter pilot
in the Purple Heart Command.

Anonymous, 1944

APPENDIX E

Ten Commandments for Helicopter Flying

ᴏ 1 ᴏ
Thou shalt not become airborne
without first ascertaining the level of the propellant.

ᴏ 2 ᴏ
Thy rotor RPM is thy staff of life. Without it thou shall surely perish.

ᴏ 3 ᴏ
Let infinite discretion govern thy movement near the ground
for thine area of destruction is vast.

ᴏ 4 ᴏ
Thou shalt not let thy confidence exceed thy ability
for broad is thy way to destruction.

ᴏ 5 ᴏ
He who allows his tail rotor to catch the thorns
curseth children and his children's children.

o 6 o

Thou shalt maintain thy airspeed between 10 and 420 feet
lest the earth rise up and smite thee.

o 7 o

Thou shalt not make a trial of thy center of gravity
lest thou dash thy foot against a stone.

o 8 o

He that doeth his approach and alloweth the wind to gather
behind him shall surely make restitution.

o 9 o

He who inspecteth not his aircraft provideth his Angels cause
for great concern.

o 10 o

Observeth thou this parable lest on the morrow
thy friends mourn thee.

*(From AVSAF NATRACOM and CGAS Mobile HH-52A
Qualification Training Manual, 1972.)*

NOTES

Erickson wrote at least two books and parts of a third. For reference purposes in this book, I will refer to them in the apparent order in which he wrote them, and each will be noted with a Roman numeral. No manuscript is dated. Therefore, the assignment of the order I use is based on clues discovered in his correspondence and is my somewhat arbitrary assignment.

Manuscript number one (I) is incomplete and was titled *The Coast Guard's Flying Life Boats: A History of Coast Guard Aviation*. Though the title is similar to book two, chapter titles and subject matter differ completely. Portions of one additional manuscript exist that seem to predate this one; however, since it is just random pages and otherwise unidentified, all references to it will be in the notes.

Manuscript number two (II) was titled *A Proposed History of U.S. Coast Guard Aviation,* and also *The Coast Guard's Flying Life Boats,* subtitled *Fifty-Five Years of Coast Guard Aviation.*

Fishers of Men, book three (III), originally had the title *The Story of the Development of Seagoing Helicopters.* The *Fishers of Men* title appears to have been added after the manuscript was written and sections widely distributed. This was Erickson's last attempt at creating a book on helicopter development. Portions of this book, since it was microfilmed and is a part of the public record, are found quoted in other publications.

The chronology of Erickson's three manuscripts is approximately as follows: Number one was written in 1969. His next effort was written in 1970 by changing the subject matter at the suggestion of the publishing house editor who encouraged Erickson to write the first book.

Neither draft was accepted for publication. Erickson once more changed the book's subject and wrote his third manuscript starting late in 1970. Erickson completed *Fishers of Men* on 27 July 1972. This manuscript was never accepted for publication, however. He continued working on it nevertheless, revising and circulating chapters nearly to the time of his death in 1978. Because of this, chapters marked with the same title exhibit minor variations.

Preface
1. Erickson, letter to Thomas F. Epley, 26 February 1969 (Bohs).
2. Ibid.; Howard E. Bloomfield, *Compact History of the U.S. Coast Guard* (New York: Hawthorn Books, Inc., 1966).
3. Erickson, letter to Thomas F. Epley, ibid.
4. Ibid.
5. Erickson, letter to Igor Sikorsky, 17 August 1972. Sikorsky died shortly thereafter, on 26 October (Bohs).
6. Graham, unpublished manuscript (Graham); author interviews.
7. Erickson, letter to Capt. James A. Dillian, USCG, 25 June 1972 (Bohs).
8. William P. Wishar, letter to Erickson, 28 September 1969 (Bohs).

Prologue
1. Frank A. Erickson Papers (hereafter Papers); a personal account of the Pearl Harbor attack, possibly delivered as a speech to workers at the Sikorsky plant about 2 July 1943 (Naples, Maine: Stewart A. Graham). See also Robert J. Cressman, J. Michael Wenger, "Infamous Day: Marines at Pearl Harbor, 7 December 1941," *Marines In World War II Commemorative Series* (Washington, D.C.: History and Museums Division, Headquarters, U.S. Marine Corps, 1992), 3.
2. Papers, ibid.
3. Erickson, II-6-6.
4. Erickson, II-8-1. *The Coast Guard's Flying Lifeboats,* chapter eight, unpublished (Edmonds, Wash.: Erickson Papers, Betty Erickson Bohs, [hereafter, Bohs]).

Chapter One
1. H. Frank Gregory, *Anything a Horse Can Do* (New York: Reynal & Hitchcock, 1944), 88.
2. Dorothy Cochrane, Von Hardesty, Russell Lee, *The Aviation Careers of Igor Sikorsky* (Seattle: Univ. of Washington Press, 1989), 120.
3. Ibid., p. 130.
4. Ibid.
5. HR8143, 30 June 1938, Frank J. G. Dorsey, Pennsylvania. This act authorized an appropriation of $2 million to carry out studies and research in the development of rotary-wing aircraft of other aircraft. Initially intended for development of the autogyro, its wording was all

inclusive. Fighters and bombers could be funded. The Army Air Corps was designated the coordinating agency. However, when only $300,000 was actually appropriated a year later by Public Act #61 by the Seventy-sixth Congress, the Army decided to restrict the aircraft selection to the helicopter exclusively. Other members were: the Department of Agriculture's Bureau of Entomology and Plant Quarantine, Bureau of Biological Survey, and the Forest Service; the Department of Interior's National Park Service; the Department of Commerce's Bureau of Air Commerce; the Navy Department's Office of the Chief of Naval Operations, Bureau of Aeronautics and Commandant of the Marine Corps; the National Advisory Committee for Aeronautics; and the Post Office Department.

6. Cochrane, et al., *The Aviation Careers,* 126, 132. The VS-300 first flew 14 September 1939. Sikorsky established a helicopter endurance record in May 1940 by hovering for one hour, thirty-two minutes, and twenty-six seconds.

7. The XR-4 was the experimental version of the later production model of the Army Air Corps designation R-4 and the Navy/Coast Guard designation HNS.

8. Erickson, III-1-11. Gregory, *Anything,* 93, 112. The XR-1 by Platt-LePage started first and received the most attention because it followed on the successful German-designed Focke Achgelis FW-61, with its two large rotors at each side where wings would be on conventional aircraft. "The XR-2 and the XR-3 were a jump-off Autogiro and a cyclic pitch-control Autogiro respectively, both built by the Kellett Autogiro Corporation. Actually they were modified YG-B's." They were never developed further because of the apparent success of the XR-4.

9. Erickson, III-1-11. Those in attendance included: Maj. Leslie B. Cooper, USAAC; Mr. Mandel Lenkowsky, AAC Material Division; Capt. H. F. Gregory, USAAC; Allen W. Morris, CAA; Comdr. W. J. Kossler, USCG; Mr. L. M. Nesbitt; F. J. Bailey, NACA; Wing Comdr. R.A.C. Brie, British Air Commission; Comdr. J. H. Millar, RAN; Col. George L. King, USA; Lt. Col. P. E. Gabel, USA; and Sikorsky employees who worked on the project, along with Igor Sikorsky.

10. Charles L. "Les" Morris, *Pioneering the Helicopter* (New York: McGraw-Hill, 1945), 89.

11. Gregory, *Anything,* 118.

12. Erickson and A. L. Lonsdale, "The Birth of the Sea-Going Helicopter." Unpublished, 5 (Bohs).

13. Gregory, *Anything,* 120.

14. Erickson, II-6-6.

15. USCG Flight Manual, Model HH-52A Helicopters (Washington, D.C.: Coast Guard, 1972), 6-3. "Power settling is the uncontrollable settling of the helicopter when the main rotor is operating in the 'vortex ring state.' In the vortex ring state, air flowing upward near the center of the rotor (due to the descent) and downward through the outer portion (as

lift is produced) generates a giant recirculation of air around the rotor, resulting in near zero total lift. Application of power which normally stops the descent is ineffective. Instead, the rate of descent increases, vibration increases, and the controls become ineffective as the vortex ring state is established."

16. Erickson, II-6-6.
17. Morris, *Pioneering,* 91.
18. Gregory, *Anything,* 119.
19. *The Coast Guard at War, Aviation XXI* (Washington, D.C.: U.S. Coast Guard, 1945), 26. "The national Air-Sea Rescue Agency was officially established at Washington, D.C., by the secretary of the Navy in March, 1944. Commander Burton, USCG, became the New Air-Sea Rescue Operations Officer," a result of the early work he did in the development for the national air-sea rescue plan that incorporated all military and civilian rescue agencies. As a result of this work he might be considered the father of modern search and rescue.
20. R. C. Nalty, Dennis L. Noble, and Truman R. Strobridge, eds., *Wrecks, Rescues, and Investigations: Selected Documents of the U.S. Coast Guard and Its Predecessors* (Wilmington, De.: Scholarly Resources, 1978), 286.
21. Gregory, *Anything,* 90. Attendees were: J. P. Godwin, Department of Agriculture; Frederick C. Lincoln, U.S. Biological Survey; Charles M. Kieobee, Division of Air Military Service; Capt. Lloyd. T. Chalker, USCG; John Easton, Civil Aeronautics Authority; Lt. Comdr. C. L. Helber, BuAer; Roy Knabensheue, Department of the Interior; C. S. Helds and C. W. Crowley Jr., NACA; Maj. W. C. Carter, Maj. D. G. Lingle, and Capt. B. W. Chidlaw, Office of the Chief of the Air Corps; Capt. Paul H. Kemmer, Matériel Division, Wright Field; Lt. Col. W. D. Crittenberger, Army Cavalry; Maj. R. W. Beasley, Army Field Artillery; Lt. Col. E. W. Fales, Army Infantry.
22. Erickson, letter to Arlo Livingston, 27 February 1973 (Bohs).
23. James C. Fahey, *The Ships and Aircraft of the United States Fleet,* Two-Ocean Fleet edition (New York: Ships and Aircraft, 1941), 31.
24. Erickson, "A Brief History of Coast Guard Aviation," United States Coast Guard Academy Alumni Association *Bulletin,* (vol. XXVIII, no. 6), 420.
25. Erickson, I-2-23.
26. Fahey, *Ships and Aircraft,* 31. Hall-Aluminum Aircraft Corp., a subsidiary of Consolidated Aircraft Corp.
27. Erickson, I-2-23. Pilots were Lt. William L. Clemmer, Coast Guard aviator #23, and AP1/C John Radan (II-6-2). On Labor Day 1935, Clemmer recovered eighteen survivors in a Florida Keys hurricane that killed 375 people. He flew them to safety in an FLB, the largest number of survivors ever carried on a rescue mission by a Coast Guard aircraft.
28. Erickson, II-6-1.
29. Erickson, "A Brief History," 420 (Bohs).

30. Erickson, "Early History of Coast Guard Aviation," rough draft, 8 (Bohs).
31. Erickson, "Early History," 8.
32. Betty Erickson, telephone interview, 23 April 1989.
33. Erickson, "The First Coast Guard Helicopters," U.S. Naval Institute *Proceedings* (July 1981), 65.
34. Erickson, III-1-13.
35. Fahey, *Ships and Aircraft*, eighth edition, 27. The "Y" prefix in the model designation meant development model, the "X" stood for experimental.
36. Bill Gunston, *An Illustrated Guide to Military Helicopters* (New York: Arco Publishing Co.), 106. *Pilots Flight Operating Instructions for Army: R-4B Helicopters, Navy: HNS-1 Helicopters*, AN 01-230HA-1, 1 June 1944, and *Handbook of Erection and Maintenance for Army Model YR-4A and YR-4B Helicopters*, 5 April 1944 (John C. Redfield collection, Emil Buehler Naval Aviation Library, National Museum of Naval Aviation, Pensacola, hereafter, Redfield). The single XR-4 had the same Warner Super Scarab seven-cylinder engine at 165 horsepower. Three YR-4As and twenty-seven YR-4Bs had 180 horsepower. Later, the one hundred R-4B/HNS-1s were boosted to 200 horsepower with the same engine. Typically, where modern helicopters have controls for two pilots, it includes two complete sets of controls: cyclic or control stick for attitude control in the right hand, rudder peddles or anti-torque controls pushed by the feet, and collective lever raised and lowered by the left hand control. The throttle is a twist-grip handle located on the end of the collective lever. The collective lever was connected to the throttle linkage so that moving the lever up or down would change power settings. However, the pilot still had to add or subtract additional amounts by twisting the hand grip.

    The XR-4 and subsequent R-4/HNS models had only one collective lever. It was located between the pilots. In modern helicopters, a pilot normally flies from the right seat in the side-by-side seating plan—a convention established by Sikorsky with the XR-4. Regardless of which seat a pilot is flying, the controls are identical. In the XR-4, however, when pilots changed seats they had to learn to switch the controls to opposite hands. One real problem could occur. The pilot flying normally from the right seat adds power with the throttle by twisting the motorcycle type control with the left hand counterclockwise, away from the body. Shifting seats and hands might cause the inexperienced pilot to decrease power when intending to add power.
37. Erickson, III-1-13.
38. Possibly Comdr. Harold Brow, USN: from a roster of attendees scheduled for the 7 May 1943 ten o'clock shipboard helicopter landing demonstration (Bohs).
39. By war's end, the Vought-Sikorsky plant produced more than 6,400 F4Us.
40. Erickson, II-6-8.

41. Morris, *Pioneering,* 111; Gregory, *Anything,* 121.
42. Gregory, *Anything,* 155.
43. Morris, *Pioneering,* 115.
44. Gregory, ibid.
45. Morris, ibid.
46. Gregory, ibid., 158.
47. Ibid., 161.
48. Ibid.
49. Betty Erickson, interview.
50. Erickson, II-6-8.
51. Erickson, II-6-9.
52. Erickson, letter to commandant, 29 June 1942 (Bohs).
53. Erickson, II-6-11.
54. Ibid.
55. W. A. Burton, 30 June 1942, endorsement to Erickson's letter of 29 June 1942 (Washington, D.C.: Coast Guard Headquarters, Office of the Coast Guard Historian, [hereafter, CG Historian]).
56. Stanley V. Parker, 2 July 1942, second endorsement to Erickson's letter of 29 June 1942 (CG Historian).
57. Ibid.
58. William J. Kossler, 6 July 1942, fourth endorsement to Erickson's letter of 29 June 1942 (CG Historian).

Chapter Two

1. John M. Waters, "Finally the Twain Did Meet," *Foundation* (vol. 12, no. 1, Spring 1991), 99.
2. Ibid., 98.
3. Erickson, II-6-12.
4. Capt. Walter Diehl, USN, was BuAer's chief aeronautical engineer. It was his opinion that the helicopter was aerodynamically unable to perform useful flight, and he was respected for his judgment in aerodynamics.
5. Grover Loening, "Helicopters on Freighters Versus Submarines," report to the War Production Board, 14 May 1943 (CG Historian).
6. Joseph F. Farley, "The Coast Guard and the Helicopter," unpublished thirty-four-page version. This is the first draft according to a penciled note, but none is dated. A seventeen-page version of the same title exists at the same archival address. An article, "United States Coast Guard Helicopter Program," appears to be an edited version of the shorter article, published by *American Helicopter,* February 1947, 14 (Entry 279, Records of the United States Coast Guard, Record Group 26, U.S. National Archives and Records Administration, Washington D.C.), 6. Hereafter, all references to Record Group will be RG and the National Archives as NA. Unless otherwise noted, all notes hereafter will refer to the unabridged thirty-four-page version as Farley, "Helicopter."
7. Farley, "Helicopter," 6.

8. Erickson, II-6-13.
9. Ernest J. King, letter from commander in chief, U.S. Fleet, and chief of naval operations, FF1/A16-1, Serial: 0477, 15 February 1943, to chief of Bureau of Aeronautics (CG Historian).
10. British Air Commission, Washington, D.C., to the Admiralty Public Records Office (PRO), Kew, United Kingdom, ADM 1/16464, B.A.D., 8 March 1943.
11. Erickson, II-7-1.
12. Erickson, II-7-2.
13. Ibid.
14. Russell R. Waesche, letter to Kossler, 16 February 1943 (CG Historian).
15. H. F. Johnson, memorandum to Coast Guard chief personnel officer, 16 February 1943 (CG Historian).
16. Kossler, memorandum to commandant, 1 March 1943 (CG Historian).
17. Ibid.
18. Loening, "Helicopters on Freighters," 5.
19. Ibid.
20. Kossler, memorandum to commandant, 1 March 1943 (CG Historian).
21. Waesche, memorandum to chief of the Bureau of Aeronautics, 2 March 1943 (CG Historian).
22. John S. McCain, letter to commandant, 4 March 1943 (CG Historian).
23. Kossler, memorandum to chief, Aviation Engineering Section, 6 March 1943 (CG Historian).
24. Waesche, letter to commanding general, USAAF, 11 March 1943 (CG Historian).
25. Kossler, memorandum to commandant, 12 March 1943 (CG Historian).
26. George D. Synon, letter to Kossler, 18 April 1943 (CG Historian).
27. Ibid.
28. Kossler, memorandum to chief, Aeronautical Engineering Division, 24 April 1943 (CG Historian).
29. Kossler, memorandum to chief, Aeronautical Engineering Division, 27 April 1943, (CG Historian).
30. Loening, "Helicopters on Freighters," 6.
31. R. S. Edwards (writer), letter from commander in chief, United States Fleet, to the chief of the Bureau of Aeronautics, Serial: 01359, 4 May 1943 (CG Historian).
32. Gregory, *Anything*, 175.
33. Erickson, II-7-3.
34. Erickson, letter to Capt. M. G. Shrode, 14 April 1978 (Bohs).
35. Gregory, *Anything*, 176.
36. Ibid.
37. Erickson, II-7-5. Witnesses included Seabury; Grover Loening, War Production Board; Elmer Hutchinson and Dr. P. M. Morse, National Research Council; Capt. L. C. Stevens and Capt. Walter Diehl, Navy Bureau of Aeronautics; Dr. Bowles and Grigs, Office of the Secretary of

War; Col. John Franklin, Army Transportation Corps; Rear Adm. Stanley V. Parker and Capt. Kossler, USCG; Sir Arthur Salter, British Shipping Mission; Air Vice Marshal Mansell, Air Commodore Heslop, and Group Capt. Canning, RAF; Capt. Casper John, RAN; Sir Vivian Gabriel and Dr. J.A.J. Bennett, British Air Mission; Wing Comdr. R.A.C. Brie, RAF; Lt. Comdr. R. P. Garnett and E.G.H. Peat, RAN. Officers of United Aircraft Corporation and Sikorsky were also present.

38. Farley, "Helicopter," 10.
39. Erickson, II-7-5.
40. Loening, "Helicopters on Freighters," 6.
41. Ibid., 7.
42. William R. Kenly, memorandum to engineer-in-chief, 11 May 1943 (CG Historian).
43. Robert L. Scheina, *U.S. Coast Guard Cutters & Craft of World War II* (Annapolis: Naval Institute Press, 1982), 4.
44. Linholm was the Coast Guard aviation personnel officer from headquarters who acted as the Coast Guard's representative to the committee and as recorder.
45. S. C. Linholm, memorandum to engineer-in-chief, 17 May 1943; James L. Bates, director, Technical Division, U.S. Maritime Commission, "Memorandum of Conference of May 17, 1943" (CG Historian).
46. James S. Russell, minutes of "The Combined Board for the Evaluation of the Helicopter in Anti-Submarine Warfare," 18 May 1943 (Bohs).
47. Ibid.
48. Ibid.
49. King, letter to chief of BuAer, 2 August 1943 (Bohs).
50. Russell, ibid.
51. Gregory, memo report from Army Air Forces Materiel Command, 1 June 1943, to: "Asst.C/AS, M.M.&D; Bureau of Aero., Navy Dept., Attn: Comdr. J. S. Russell, U.S.N.; Hdqts. Command, Navy Dept., Attn: Comdr. A. E. Buckley, U.S.N.; Coast Guard Hdqts., Wash., D.C., Attn: Comdr. S. C. Linholm; G.I.N.A., W.F., Attn: Capt. H. E. Ostrander" (CG Historian).
52. Erickson, letter to Combined Board, with proposals for operations for ship-based helicopter, 10 June 1943 (CG Historian).
53. Ibid.
54. Erickson, handwritten note in pencil to Linholm, not dated but probably written about 10 June 1943 at Bridgeport, where Erickson had just begun helicopter training (Bohs). This is transcribed from an obviously quickly scrawled note. It is recorded here in full as an excellent example of Erickson's thinking and methods. It is not censored by the formality of official letters:

Dear Stan,
Enclosed is the letter which I spoke to you about last week. In as much as you are a member of the evaluation board, I routed the letter

direct to Adm. Johnson. Comdr. Russell was up earlier in the week. I showed him a rough draft of the letter. He is anxious to present it to the board, hence am forwarding it via official channels. Frank Gregory will bring the Army YR-4A down about Tuesday (6/15/43). Believe it would be (? best) if the board could have the letter on that date. I am sending a copy of these proposals to Dr. Hayes. Believe it best call him before forwarding letter to make sure it is what he would want. It could probably be arranged for him to see the YR-4A when Gregory brings it down. We started flight training on Wednesday (likely 9 June).

Flying it is most interesting. Expect to solo next week however will require a couple of more weeks to acquire any degree of efficiency. Fisher and the two mechs have entered the new Service Depart. Class. Am sending those letters on a couple of men who are about to be drafted (one was Sergei Sikorsky, Igor's son). Both have been on the Helicopter program from the start and are excellent material (mechanics at the Sikorsky plant). Brooklyn Air Sta. says that no orders have come there on Frauenberger. There must have been a slip up down in the enlisted personnel office.

Best regards,
Swede"

55. Erickson, letter to Combined Board. Erickson, letter to Capt. M. G. Schrode, 14 April 1978 (Bohs).
56. Loening, memorandum to Charles E. Wilson, 18 May 1943, suggesting the proper steps to take in acquiring helicopters over the next year. He would prefer just a few hundred to thousands to allow for developmental advances (CG Historian).

Chapter Three
1. Erickson, III-2-8. Included in the first four military pilots with Erickson were Lt. Comdr. Charles T. Booth, USN, and 2nd Lts. Frank W. Peterson and Harold H. Hermes, USA. Sikorsky's two new test pilots, Dmitry "Jimmy" Viner and C. A. "Connie" Moeller just completed checking out as this project began in the VS-300 with Morris as their instructor.
2. Erickson, II-7-8.
3. Erickson, III-2-9; Erickson, letter to Stella Randolph, 20 January 1970 (Bohs). The British pilots were Lieutenant Commander Brie, Lt. Jeep Cable, and Lieutenant Peat.
4. Erickson, III-2-10.
5. Ibid.
6. Ibid. Erickson, letter to John Redfield, 8 May 1978 (Redfield).
7. Ibid.
8. Erickson, III-2-11; Russell, memorandum for the chief of the Bureau of

Aeronautics, 9 July 1943. Barrett Tillman, *Avenger At War*, (Annapolis: Naval Institute Press, second ed. 1990), 61.

9. Erickson, III-2-12. Twenty-three HNS (R-4B) trainers, 200 horsepower; 100 HOS-1 (R-6), 225 horsepower observation; 50 HO2S (R-5), 450 horsepower observation.

10. Peterson suffered serious injuries and was hospitalized for several months. He eventually recovered and returned to flying. The passenger was only bruised in the crash.

11. Erickson, III-2-13.

12. USCG, *Flight Manual*, 6-3. "Ground resonance is a self-excited vibration that occurs when a coupling interaction occurs between the movement of the blades and the helicopter. For ground resonance to occur, there must be some abnormal lead/lag blade condition which would dynamically unbalance the rotor, and a reaction between the helicopter and ground which could aggravate and further unbalance the rotor. Ground resonance can be caused by a blade being badly out of track, a faulty damper, or a peculiar set of landing conditions. When a wheel reaction occurs, such as a hard one-wheel landing that would cause out-of-phase blades to be aggravated to the point where maximum lead and lag blade displacement is realized, ground resonance may occur."

13. Erickson, "Progress report" for 4 September 1943, Erickson Papers, U.S. Coast Guard Academy, New London (hereafter, Progress Report). Although most reports are from the academy archives, some are from other sources and will be so noted at each entry.

14. Erickson, II-7-12 (early draft, undated) (Bohs).

15. Reginold Brie, letter to Erickson, 15 December 1970. Landings aboard were on 12 and 13 May. His landings were witnessed by Gregory and Comdr. C. H. Able, USCG (Bohs).

16. Erickson, III-2-15.

17. Erickson, Progress Report, 11 September 1943 (USCGA).

18. Erickson, Progress Report, 25 September 1943 (USCGA).

19. The contemporary terms for the flight controls are "Cyclic," the attitude control stick which is normally held in the pilot's right hand, and "Collective," raised and lowered with the pilot's left hand. Sikorsky called them "Azimuth Control Stick" and "Main-Rotor Pitch Control," respectively.

20. Erickson, III-2-16.

21. Letter to author, 2 August 1991, from William J. Kossler Jr., quoting from his father's flight logbook.

22. Erickson, III-2-18; Erickson, Progress Report, 6 November, "Lt. Comdr. Miller, 1st Lt. Edwards, USAAF, and 1st Lt. Barnett, USAAF, soloed during the week. The two Army officers returned to Bridgeport on Friday (5 November) to continue training on Army Aircraft. Ens. Bolton, USCG, reported for flight training" (USCGA).

23. Erickson, Progress Reports, 23 October and 2 November (USCGA).

24. H. C. Hayes, "Submarine Sound Equipment for Helicopters." (Con-

fidential report by Hayes, no date.) A date stamp shows it was received by the Coast Guard on 5 November 1943. It reports results of tests conducted in a cove at Piney Point on 5 August and off Point Lookout on 6 August. It is conjectured this document was composed a short time later because Hayes anticipates installation in helicopters "on or before October 10." A cover letter was not located. Presumably, it was routed through Navy offices, including BuAer.

25. Erickson, III-2-19.
26. Graham, letter to author, 22 November 1994.
27. Erickson, Report to Maj. Gen. Frank E. Lowe, USA, executive for the United States Senate Special Committee Investigating the National Defense Program, 10 April 1946 (Bohs).
28. [Indecipherable] letter to Comdr. C. J. Yelloly, RAN, 28 September 1970. "The very earliest R-4s were known in the RN as GADFLY'S for a short time at least, and in the RAF as HOVERFLYS. The name GADFLY does not appear to have lasted very long and certainly by 1947 and probably 1946 all the R-4s were known in the Royal Navy as HOVERFLYS" (Bohs).
29. Russell, memorandum report of shipboard helicopter trials, 29 November 1943 (Graham).
30. Erickson, III-2-22; Erickson, Progress Report, 25 December 1943 (USCGA).
31. Visitors aboard the SS *Daghestan,* 26 November 1943, included: Brig. Gen. Frank E. Lowe, USA, R. W. Seabury, War Shipping Office, Comdr. G. T. Mundorff, USN, Capt. Casper John, RAN, Comdr. A. E. Buckley, USN, Grp. Capt. J. P. Merer, RAF-BAC, Comdr. William J. Kossler, USCG, Comdr. S. C. Linholm, USCG, Lt. Col. A. P. Tappan, USAAF, Lt. Comdr. J. W. Klopp, USN, Comdr. J. Russell, USN, Lt. Comdr. E. A. Peat, RNVR-FAA, Lt. S. J. Watt, RNVR, Lt. F. G. Tyler, RNVR, J.A.J. Bennett, BAC, Lt. (jg) Stewart R. Graham, USCG, Ens. W. C. Bolton. USCG, Comdr. Richard P. Garnett, RN (Ret.), Lt. A. N. Fisher, USCG, F/O C. H. Loder, RAF, Lt. F. J. Cable, RAF-VR, Maj. W. Greenlee, AAC, ACMM Leo Brzycki, USCG, AMM1c W. J. Woodcock, USCG, J. W. Erickson, chief photographer, USN, Giles Montgomery, Sikorsky Aircraft, AMM1c Carl A. Yanuzzi, USCG, Philip K. Crashaw, Sikorsky Aircraft, E. L. Frohlick, Sikorsky Aircraft, B. L. Whelan, Sikorsky Aircraft, H. F. Kroeger, Sikorsky Aircraft, Wing Commander R.A.C. Brie, RAF, Lt. Comdr. John M. Miller, USN, Lt. S. J. Miller, RNVR, Lt. Comdr. Frank A. Erickson, USCG, B. P. Labensky, Sikorsky Aircraft, Col. H. Frank Gregory, USAAF, Miller E. Wacks, Sikorsky Aircraft, MMC O. F. Berry, USCG, Ens. A. Berta, USN, Lt. Beck, USN, AMM1c G. Jablonski, USCG (USCGA).
32. Erickson, III-2-22; Erickson, Progress Report, 4 December 1943.
33. Erickson, III-2-22; Erickson, Progress Report, 25 December 1943 (USCGA).
34. Erickson, Progress Report, 22 November 1943 (USCGA).

35. Erickson, III-2-20.
36. Erickson, III-2-9; Erickson, Progress Report, 13 December 1943 (USCGA).
37. Graham, letter to author, 8 December 1993.
38. Ibid.
39. Graham, interviews. Some of the helicopters purchased originally for the Army but now operated by the Coast Guard/Navy were khaki colored. The 46445 was painted the dark blue of the Navy aircraft of the period.
40. Erickson, II-8-10.
41. A common term in the early period of the helicopter referring to "Igor" Sikorsky's helicopters.
42. Erickson, III-2-23; Farley, "Helicopter," 22; B. T. Beard, "The First Mission," *Foundations,* vol. 12, no. 1, Spring 1991, 100 (Naval Aviation Museum Foundation, Pensacola).
43. Erickson, II-8-11.
44. Ibid.
45. Erickson, III-2-23; Farley, "Helicopter," 22; B. T. Beard, "The First Mission," 105.

Chapter Four
1. J. W. Klopp and R. P. Garnett, "Ocean Joint Helicopter Trial—Report On," 24 January 1944 (Graham).
2. Graham, "Helicopters and Sonar Detection of Submarines, The Early Years," unpublished manuscript, April 1992 (Graham); Graham, interviews, 1989 through 1995.
3. Graham, letter to author, 9 September 1992.
4. Graham, "A Vision of Ocean Defense" unpublished memoirs, no date (Graham). The United States crew was: Lt. Comdr. James Klopp, USN, BuAer; Lt. Comdr. John Miller, USN, U.S. Navy observer; Lt. (jg) Stewart Graham, USCG, mission helicopter pilot; Mr. Giles N. Montgomery, Sikorsky Company service representative; Berta, Cook, and Baker, official naval photographers. The Great Britain crew was: Comdr. Richard Garnett, mission commander; Lt. Comdr. E.A.H. Peat, RN, mission helicopter pilot; Lt. Charles Loder, RN, mission engineer; Flt. Lt. Jeep Cable, RAF, mission helicopter pilot; Capt. Thomas Waugh, master, the *Daghestan.*
5. Graham, memorandum to author, undated. Graham enlisted in the U.S. Life-Saving Service on 17 March 1939 and was promoted to motor machinist mate second class (MOMM 2/c) in 1937.
6. Graham, interviews.
7. Klopp, "Ocean-Going Helicopter Trial." The helicopter's gross weight during these flights was 2,360 lbs. This total included a crew of one, twenty gallons of fuel, and no radio. The aircraft were fueled by a hose from a five-hundred-gallon gasoline tank located beneath the flight deck.
8. Graham, "A Vision," ibid; Graham, interviews. Graham received the Air Medal for this flight.

9. Graham, interviews.
10. Erickson, II-12-3.
11. Klopp, "Ocean-Going Helicopter Trial."
12. Erickson, III-3-10.
13. Erickson, letter to Capt. A. L. Lonsdale, 26 August 1978 (Bohs).
14. Tillman, *Avengers,* 61.
15. John M. Waters, *Bloody Winter* (Annapolis: Naval Institute Press, 1984 reprinted ed.), ix.

Chapter Five
1. Erickson, Progress Report, 18 January 1944. Lt. W. G. Knapp, USN, Lt. (jg) August Kleisch, USCG, and Lt. (jg) L. V. Perry, USCG, reported for training during the week ending 15 January (USCGA).
2. Dr. Benjamin was the senior medical officer at the Naval Air Station, New York.
3. An early derisive reference to the helicopter.
4. Erickson, Progress Reports, 10 January 1944 (USCGA); 18 December 1943 (Redfield); and 15 January 1944 (USCGA).
5. Sikorsky Aircraft Division of United Aircraft Corporation Bridgeport, Connecticut, "Model Specification, Helicopter, Model R-4B, 8 September 1943, Alternate Loadings," 14 (Redfield).
6. Erickson Progress Reports, 10 and 15 January 1944 (USCGA); Graham, interviews.
7. "Translational lift" is additional lift generated by the entire rotor plane as the helicopter begins forward flight at a low speed—usually above ten knots. It is usually detected by the pilot through a slight roughness followed by a rapid increase of rate climb at a constant power setting. If the helicopter is taking off into the wind at a speed above which translational lift starts, it will be, in effect, at zero ground speed and not as noticeable. A pilot lifting off in a heavy aircraft with no wind under critical conditions—meaning the helicopter must clear obstructions nearby—normally stops breathing and sits lightly until the familiar shudder is felt.
8. "Ground cushion" is not a doughnut of air pressure the helicopter floats on just above the ground, as many believe. For example, an airfoil operating high above the ground, an airplane wing, or a helicopter rotor, develops lift forces perpendicular to the average direction of the airflow over the airfoil. The direction of lift forces is altered to a higher angle away from the vertical rearward toward the trailing edge of the foil as a result of the downwash behind the airfoil. One of two rearward components of this lift force is called the induced drag, or drag induced by the lift. The other drag is friction (which I will not discuss here). If this downwash angle is physically limited by close proximity to the ground, the lift vector is tilted closer to the vertical, shortening the induced drag vector, thus reducing the power required for establishing or maintaining a hover close to the ground. The induced drag is greatest at hover out of "ground effect" or at altitude and decreases as the helicopter closes with

the surface. Since there is no dense pillow of air, it is not possible to slide off of it and lose "ground cushion," as illustrated in this anecdote.

Slight loss of vertical lift when moving into forward flight is due to tilting the rotor plane in the direction of flight, aligning the lift vector forward of vertical to achieve a forward thrust vector. Finally, hovering over tall grass, still water, or in a confined area requires more power because the rotor tip vortex flow is physically amplified by the interference. Since rotor thrust is developed by linear acceleration of an air mass, rather than rotational stirring, induced drag is increased in these conditions requiring additional power. And the HNS did not have the power available, so flying it felt to early pilots just like "falling off a cushion of air."

9. Erickson, III-3-19.
10. Erickson, letter to Laura (last name unknown), probably sister of W. J. Lawerence, 24 June 1968 (Bohs).
11. Donahue was Coast Guard aviator number two, receiving his wings on 13 December 1919. He was a seaplane pilot, as were most early CG aviators.
12. Erickson, letter to Laura; Carl B. Olsen, telephone interview, 19 September 1994. Friends of Erickson referred to him as "Swede," an endearing nickname. Kossler did use "Eric." The "Frankie" quoted here is the only instance where this name came up. Others who worked with Erickson don't remember that name ever being used.
13. Erickson, letter to Laura.
14. Erickson, Progress Reports, 18 and 26 January and 1 February 1944. The unit—Lt. W. G. Knapp, USN, Lt. (jg) August Kleisch, USCG, Lt. (jg) L. V. Perry, USCG—was flying three HNSs: 46445, 46999, and 47000 (USCGA).
15. British Air Commission, Washington, D.C., to the Admiralty, Public Records Office (PRO), Kew, United Kingdom, ADM 1/16464, B.A.D., 23 March 1943; Graham, interviews.
16. Ibid.
17. Ibid.
18. Director of Naval Air Division to the Admiralty, Public Record Office (PRO), Kew, United Kingdom, ADM 1/16464, 2 September 1942.
19. Boyd, endorsing the Admiralty "Minute Sheet No. 3," PRO, Kew, United Kingdom, ADM 1/16464, 29 March 1943.
20. Erickson, letter to Laura.
21. Erickson, Progress Report, 9 February 1944. The committee named for its first chairman (Senator Harry Truman), was chaired by James M. Mead of New York, who replaced Truman when he became vice president. Other members were: Tom Connally, Texas; Mon C. Wallgren, Washington; Carl A. Hatch, New Mexico; Charley M. Kilgore, West Virginia; James M. Tunnell, Delaware; Owen Brewster, Maine; Harold H. Burton, Ohio; Joseph H. Ball, Minnesota; Homer Ferguson, Michigan; Mr. Rudoph Halley, chief counsel, and Mr. Hugh Fulton, consulting counsel. General Lowe was the Committee's executive

(USCGA).

22. Erickson, Progress Report, 1 February 1944 (USCGA).
23. Erickson, 4 July 1972 letter to "Bill," probably William P. Wishar (Redfield).
24. Erickson, report to Frank E. Lowe, 10 April 1946 (Bohs).
25. Farley, "Helicopter," 17.
26. Copies were sent to the commandant, USCG; director of Military Requirements, BuAer; commander, Eastern Sea Frontier; Rotary Wing Design, BuAer; commanding officer, NAS Brooklyn; Coast Guard district commander, Third Naval District; U.S. Navy Bureau of Medicine; Air-Sea Rescue Agency, Washington D.C.; British Admiralty delegation, Washington D.C.; and RAF Delegation, Washington, D.C. (USCGA).
27. Erickson, memorandum to Comdr. Dudley, 7 March 1944 (USCGA).
28. Erickson, Progress Report, 22 March 1944 (USCGA).
29. Erickson, II-8-14.
30. Ibid.
31. Erickson, II-8-15.
32. Erickson, II-8-16.
33. Ibid.
34. Robert M. Browning Jr., "The Eyes and Ears of the Convoy," *Air Power History,* Summer 1993, 34.
35. Erickson, Progress Report, 1 July 1944 (USCGA).
36. Erickson, III-3-7.
37. Ibid.
38. Erickson, III-3-12.
39. Shawn Cafferky, from Ph.D. dissertation and interviews, October 1994, Canadian Ministry of Defense, Ottawa.
40. Erickson, Progress Reports, 1 May, 16 June, and 1 July 1944 (USCGA).
41. Erickson, Progress Report, 1 July 1944 (USCGA).
42. "Foundation," Naval Aviation Museum *Foundations,* vol. 15, no. 2, Fall 1994, 48.
43. Erickson, III-3-14.
44. Erickson, III-3-12.
45. Erickson, II-8-12.
46. Erickson, memorandum to Capt. Ellis Reed-Hill, director of Public Relations, USCG, 24 July 1944 (Graham).
47. Ibid.
48. Erickson, letter to Laura.
49. Lowe, letter to Erickson, 30 August 1944 (USCGA).
50. Graham, interviews.
51. War Production Board, Office of Production Research and Development, Consumer Products Branch: *Program for Regional Development of Industry, July 4, 1944. Excerpts,* Papers of Harry S Truman, senatorial file, box 214, folder, "War Production Board July, 1944." Examples of a few proposed eclectic contracts considered by the committee include: Alcohol from Sweet Potatoes, Pilot Plant for Sacking, Cargo Boat for

Caribbean Trade, Study for Hydroelectric Plant, Prefabricated Steel Farm Buildings, Decorticater for Malva Alba, Carbon Dioxide for Home Refrigerators, Earle Rice Peeler, Avery Helicopter, Mechanical Equipment for Soilless Agriculture, Improved Water Filters from Loofa Sponges, Low Cost Substitutes for Abaca, Cassava Glue, Wind Power Utilization, and Improved Vacuum Maple Sap Evaporator.

52. Erickson, III-3-22.
53. Lowe, transcript of a telephone conversation with Waesche, 1 December 1944 (USCGA).
54. Ibid.
55. Ibid.
56. *The Coast Guard at War,* 72.
57. Erickson, III-3-27.

Chapter Six
1. Farley, "Helicopter," 1.
2. Erickson, Report to General Lowe, 18 April 1946 (USCGA).
3. Graham, interviews.
4. *Flight Training Syllabus,* CG Air Station, Brooklyn, New York, 1944, paragraph, 181 c, Adm. O. R. Smeder papers, (hereafter Smeder).
5. Ibid.
6. Ibid., paragraphs 181–83.
7. Ibid.
8. Erickson, Report to General Lowe.
9. John F. DuFrane, "Movable Landing Light," *American Helicopter,* vol. 3, no. 7, June 1946, 14. The Army Air Forces first helicopter squadron developed a movable landing light mounted on the nose of the R-4. It was controllable by the pilot to light the landing zone. Work on the successful light began in January 1945.
10. S. A. Constantino, "I Learned to Fly the Helicopter," unpublished. At the time this was written, Lieutenant (jg) Constantino, USCG, was student number 52 in the program at New York and in the second class. He completed training on 28 August 1944, and was designated CG helicopter pilot number 30 (Smeder).
11. Army: R-4B, Navy: HNS-1 Pilot's Flight Operating Instructions, 18 (Redfield).
12. Morris, *Pioneering,* 118.
13. Erickson, Report to General Lowe.
14. Erickson, United States Patent 2,581,396, 8 January 1952, Stabilizer for Rotary Wing Aircraft.
15. Dennis L. Noble, *That Others Might Live: The U.S. Life-Saving Service, 1878–1915* (Annapolis: Naval Institute Press, 1994), xi.
16. Ibid.
17. The route to the creation of the modern-day U.S. Coast Guard is complicated. The coastal lifesaving stations started out as isolated volunteer organizations, such as the Massachusetts Humane Society. When the

federal government assumed control, the stations remained basically volunteer until Kimball took over in 1871. The U.S. Revenue Cutter Service
(USRCS) was founded in 1790 to help prevent maritime smuggling. It
had numerous names, but by 1915 it was known as the USRCS. In 1939
the USCG absorbed the U.S. Light House Service and in 1942 the U.S.
Bureau of Marine Inspection and Navigation. For details of the lineage,
see Noble, ibid., 150–55; Dennis R. Means, *"A Heavy Sea Running: The
Formation of the U.S. Life-saving Service, 1846–1878,"* Prologue: Journal
of the National Archives, vol. 19, no. 4 (Winter 1987): 222.

18. Erickson, Report to General Lowe.
19. Erickson, Progress Report, 1 May 1944 (USCGA).
20. Erickson, II-8-16.
21. Ibid.
22. Erickson, III-9-9.
23. Erickson, III-3-20; commandant, Brooklyn Navy Yard, letter to CNO,
    No. S67(M)(40-55-55g), "Subj.: Mark 4, Mark 12, and Mark 22 Fire
    Control Radar Alignment—Use of Helicopters as Target For"
    (USCGA).
24. Erickson, II-8-17.
25. Erickson, Report to General Lowe.
26. Erickson, II-8-18; John Greathouse telephone interview, 14 November
    1994; Graham, interviews.
27. Erickson, III-3-8.
28. Ibid.
29. Ibid.
30. Ibid.
31. Ibid.
32. Graham, interviews.
33. Ibid.
34. Erickson, III-3-10.
35. Ibid.
36. *U.S. Coast Guard Magazine,* April 1945, 28.
37. Erickson, III-3-8.
38. Erickson, III-3-12.
39. Ibid; Sergei Sikorsky interview, 15 July 1994.
40. Redfield, letter to author, 15 August 1989.
41. Graham, telephone interview, 12 November 1994.
42. Erickson, III-3-23.
43. Graham, interviews.
44. Erickson, III-3-14.
45. Erickson, II-8-19.
46. Ibid.
47. Erickson, III-3-12.
48. Ibid.
49. Ibid; Graham, interviews.
50. Erickson, III-3-20.

51. Erickson, letter to chief, BuAer, 13 July 1944 (Graham).
52. Erickson, III-3-24.
53. Ibid.
54. Erickson, Progress Report, 3 December 1944 (USCGA).
55. Erickson, III-3-25.
56. Ibid.
57. Erickson, III-4-1.
58. Ibid.
59. David Gershowitz, interview, 31 March 1989.
60. Erickson, II-8-20; Gershowitz, interview; Joseph S. Yuill, project outline, "The possible uses of the helicopter in malaria control, suggestions for testing," 12 October 1944 (USCGA).
61. Erickson, Progress Report, 22 December 1944. "HNS-1 helicopters, Bureau No. 39040 and 39043 returned from CNAPT, NAS, Glenview Illinois, upon completion of assignment at the Navy's Sixth War Loan Exhibition in Chicago. Going to and from Chicago, the aircraft cruised at 65 to 70 miles per hour." Total time for the trip and exhibition for both aircraft was 90.5 hours. They flew 31.1 hours during the demonstrations (USCGA).
62. Erickson, III-4-1.
63. Graham, interviews.

Chapter Seven

1. *The Coast Guard at War,* U.S. Coast Guard, Washington, D.C., 1945, 26, 30 (CG Historian); Arthur Hesford, telephone interviews, 6 and 7 October and 26 November 1994. Hesford returned to the United States in the winter of 1944 following a year's exchange service with the British Rescue Service. He flew the "Hudson" bomber on search-and-rescue patrols as a part of that service.
2. *The Coast Guard at War,* ibid., 26.
3. Erickson, letter to J. J. Coop, 8 September 1969 (Bohs).
4. Erickson, letter to Bill (possibly William Wisher), 4 July 1972 (Graham).
5. *U.S. Coast Guard Magazine,* June 1946, 42.
6. The "Provisional bomb" was a standard water-filled practice bomb converted to drop provisions to survivors in the water. It was loaded with about twenty pounds of supplies in a watertight container and dropped from an aircraft flying at about a hundred feet. A plane normally carried two "bombs." This was a variation on an earlier scheme of Erickson's. He wrote about it in an article titled "Aviation and Safety," which was published in *The U.S. Coast Guard Magazine,* circa 1940, 6 (Graham). See also *The Coast Guard at War,* 34. Other emergency equipment optionally carried was: dinghy gear, life rings and jackets with buoyant lines, message blocks, or cans, and "exposure suits."
7. *The Coast Guard at War,* 28.
8. William Coffee, telephone interview, 19 December 1994.
9. Ibid.

10. Erickson, Progress Report, 7 March 1945 (Graham).
11. Hesford, telephone interviews, 6 and 7 October and 26 November 1994.
12. Hesford, telephone interview, 31 July 1994.
13. Graham, interviews.
14. Hesford, telephone interviews.
15. Erickson, letter to Walter S. Anderson, 4 March 1969 (Bohs). Probably Carl B. Olsen—at the time he was head of the Office of Aviation in Coast Guard Headquarters. Admiral Olsen says he did not make a statement like this, however (telephone interview, January 1994).
16. Graham, interview, 10 July 1994.
17. Erickson, letter to Roy Rather, 22 August 1969 (Bohs).
18. Betty Erickson, interview; Kossler papers held by William J. Kossler Jr., Alexandria, Va. (hereafter Kossler). Kossler died in St. Elizabeth's Hospital in Washington, D.C., on 16 November 1945 at the age of forty-nine. His career spanned twenty-five years, ten of which were in aviation assignments (Kossler).
19. Erickson, letter to Rear Adm. C. R. Bender, 21 March 1967 (Bohs).
20. Erickson, II-8-22.
21. Kossler, letter to the commandant, 26 January 1945 (Graham).
22. Ibid.
23. Lowe, letter to Erickson, 30 January 1945 (USCGA).
24. Merlin O'Neill, address presenting "Kossler Award" in 1952. "I think it most appropriate that the name of the late Captain William J. Kossler, United States Coast Guard, should be associated with this award given each year by the American Helicopter Society. Not only did Captain Kossler foresee the value of rotary wing aircraft, but, of equal importance, he won the support of the armed services and civil aviation authorities both in this country and Great Britain. The Award commemorates the work of Captain Kossler, who pioneered in the use of helicopters by the Coast Guard. The spirit of cooperation between the manufacturers, the armed services, and civil aviation authorities has been a large factor in the development of the rotary wing aircraft" (Kossler).
25. *Pterogram*, "Sitrep 1-95," March 1995, "ATC Aviation Hall of Fame Revisited," 2. Honorees included in the Hall of Fame are: Comdr. Elmer Stone, Capt. Donald B. MacDiarmid, Lt. Jack Rittichier, Radm. B. M. Chiswell, and Capt. Carl C. Von Paulsen. Comdr. Stewart Graham was installed in August 1995.
26. Erickson, letter to Bill (Graham).
27. Graham, interviews.

Chapter Eight
1. Erickson, III-4-4.
2. Memo from COMINCH for Vice CNO dated 12 January 1945 FF1/S68 Serial: 0102 (USCGA).
3. Ibid.

4. Erickson, II-8-20.
5. Graham, unpublished manuscript; Graham, interviews (Graham).
6. Erickson, II-8-23.
7. P. V. Engineering Forum changed to Piasecki Aircraft Corporation following the success of the XHRP-1. Later the name changed to Vertol Aircraft Corporation and eventually to Boeing-Vertol.
8. Erickson, III-4-5.
9. Ibid.
10. Ibid.
11. Graham, unpublished manuscript; Graham, interviews (Graham).
12. Erickson, II-8-25.
13. Erickson, Progress Report, 7 March 1945 (USCGA).
14. K. M. Molson and & H. A. Taylor, *Canadian Aircraft since 1909* (London: Putnam & Co., Ltd., 1982), 396. The C-64 Norseman is a single-engine high-wing airplane built for the northern bush country; it usually mounts floats or skis. It was designed in 1934 by R.B.C. Noorduyn and was built subsequently by the Noorduyn Aviation Company of Montreal, Canada. The USAAF purchased either six or seven, according to separate accounts, with more than six hundred on order (later canceled), designating the Noorduyn Norseman VI the C-64A in 1941 for use in retrieving downed flyers along the ferry routes to Europe. It was a Norseman that disappeared over the English Channel on 15 December 1944 with bandleader Glenn Miller aboard. Three were transferred from the USAAF to the Navy and designated JA-1s. The USAAF purchased seven YC-64s in 1942, with 746 on order.
15. August Kleisch, "Labrador Rescue," article in uncited publication (Graham).
16. *Air Sea Rescue Bulletin,* Number 11, May 1945, NAVCG 128, 4; Kleisch, "Labrador Rescue."
17. Robert L. Scheina, "The Helicopter's First Arctic Rescue," Naval Aviation Museum *Foundations,* vol. 2, no. 1 (March 1981), 60.
18. Kleisch, "Labrador Rescue."
19. Ibid.
20. Erickson, III-4-7; Scheina, "The Helicopter's First Arctic Rescue," 60.
21. The Army later adopted a form of landing skids which are still a standard configuration on most Army helicopters a half century later.
22. Erickson, III-4-8.
23. Erickson, III-4-10.
24. Sergei Sikorsky, interviews.
25. Erickson, III-4-13.
26. Ibid.
27. Ibid.
28. Robert M. Browning Jr., "The Eyes and Ears of the Convoy: The Development of the Helicopter as an Antisubmarine Weapon," *Air Power History,* Summer 1993, 37.
29. Erickson, III-4-14.

30. Ibid.
31. Erickson, II-8-26.
32. Graham, letter to author, 9 September 1992.
33. Ibid. Ranges up to four thousand yards were achieved.
34. Ibid.
35. Erickson, II-8-26.
36. Graham, unpublished manuscript; Graham, interviews (Graham).
37. Erickson, III-4-16; William Coffee, telephone interview, 28 December 1994.
38. Erickson, III-8-6; Graham, unpublished manuscript; Graham, interviews (Graham).
39. John M. Waters, "Little Ships with Long Arms," U.S. Naval Institute *Proceedings,* 91 (August 1965): 75.
40. Erickson, III-4-17.
41. Erickson, III-4-19.
42. Erickson, III-4-18.
43. Erickson, III-5-1.
44. Erickson, letter to Laura, 24 June 1968, (Bohs).

Chapter Nine

1. Ken Bilderback, "Cigars and Rough Water," *Naval Aviation News,* November–December 1994, 18.
2. Waters, "Finally the Twain Did Meet," 93.
3. Donald B. MacDiarmid, memorandum to Comdr. S. F. Gray, 4 January 1946 (USCGA); MacDiarmid, "Biography of Capt. D. B. MacDiarmid for SAE," n. d. (USCGA).
4. Arthur Hesford, telephone interviews, May and June 1995. MacDiarmid might have nearly been dropped from flight training the second time except for the intervention of Hesford, then the Coast Guard's liaison officer at Pensacola.
5. Shrode, interview.
6. Coast Guard and National Search and Rescue Manual CG16000.4.
7. Fahey, James C., *Ships and Aircraft,* War edition (Annapolis: Naval Institute Press, eighth printing, 1994), 58.
8. Arthur Pearcy, *A History of U.S. Coast Guard Aviation* (Annapolis: Naval Institute Press, 1989), 45.
9. Erickson, "The Flying Life Boats," draft for a chapter, incomplete and undated (Bohs).
10. Pearcy, *Coast Guard Aviation,* 18.
11. Fahey, ibid., 58.
12. Kossler, W. J., "Helicopter," *Coast Guard Magazine,* February 1943, 14.
13. Ibid.
14. Ibid.
15. René J. Francillon, *Grumman Aircraft since 1929* (Annapolis: Naval Institute Press, 1989), 98.

16. Erickson, II-8-4. Erickson recounted that "Hank Kurt, the Military Sales Representative at Grumman Aircraft, told me that it gave LeRoy Grumman greater pleasure to learn of the Widgeon's successful attack on the German sub than in the accomplishments of any of his combat planes" (Fahey, *Ships and Aircraft*, 58).

17. Erickson, II-8-7.

18. Waters, "Finally the Twain Did Meet," 92.

19. Erickson, "A Brief History of Coast Guard Aviation," U.S. Coast Guard Alumni Association *Bulletin*, November–December, 1966, 424.

20. MacDiarmid, memorandum to W. L. Sinton, 14 January 1946 (USCGA).

21. Chief of Naval Operations, letter, serial #132920 (USCGA).

22. MacDiarmid, memorandum to Sinton.

23. Marion G. Shrode, telephone interview, 28 May 1995.

24. Ken Bilderback, "Cigars and Rough Water," *Naval Aviation News,* November–December 1994, 18.

25. MacDiarmid memorandum to Gray; MacDiarmid letter to commandant, 29 June 1959 (USCGA). In this letter MacDiarmid seeks an award because his flight crew was recognized, but he was not. "Subj: Award, earned beyond question; request for 1. Reference (a) formally recognized an individual for flying as co-pilot of a Coast Guard PBM-3 through a difficult and dangerous flight. Captain D. B. MacDiarmid, then a Commander, was the pilot in command on that flight, made the take-off, the sea landing, the maneuver to recover 8 survivors and a dog from dinghies on the sea, the open sea take-off, sweated the long ride home almost out of fuel, made the landing in San Diego harbor and maneuvered to the buoy. This rescue was widely recognized by the press and wire services. John Vukic richly earned the ribbon he received. MacDiarmid, the command pilot who flew the mission, certainly earned it as well."

2. This issue was not raised previously by the writer for fear it would jeopardize and prejudice chances of recognition of officers and men subsequently serving under the then Commander, later Captain MacDiarmid. Among the more than 370 assistance sorties the writer has personally flown, there were many more difficult and dangerous day flights and night flights in rain and fog and snow, searches in mountains when all other aircraft were grounded, landings in seas so rough the captain of the ship present refused to lower a boat, taxiing into a 13-foot surf, night sea operations, landing on a tiny mountain mesa where one mistake was death, flights in foul weather to the very limit of fuel, a helicopter landing and take-off in winds gusting to over 50 knots with the only possible touch-down crosswind, rescues and rescue attempts from beaches, mountain dry lakes, etc., etc. This incident is cited because it has been investigated and recognized.

3. The writer believes he was ignored in this rescue deliberately as a matter of palace politics. He is retiring in a few days. NO mediocre officer

need fear his reputation now. D. B. MacDiarmid."

26. MacDiarmid, "The Seaplane in the U.S. Coast Guard," paper presented at the SAE National Aeronautic Meeting, New York City, 16 April 1951 (USCGA).

27. Francillon, *Grumman Aircraft*, 294.

28. MacDiarmid, letter to John Bate and Carl F. Reupsch, 26 June 1953 (USCGA).

29. MacDiarmid, letter from commanding officer, CGAS Elizabeth City, in which MacDiarmid designates himself qualified in the "HO5S type helicopter" (USCGA).

30. Waters, letter to MacDiarmid, undated (circa 1953) (USCGA).

31. Erickson, letter to "Harold" (Erickson's brother), 25 November 1969.

Chapter Ten

1. Graham, interviews. This name is recorded in Graham's logbook and was changed to "Helicopter Test and Development Unit" on 9 July 1946; Erickson, II-9-12; *Tandemeer,* Piasecki Helicopter Corporation newspaper, vol. 4, no. 2, February 10, 1950, 7. With Erickson was Lt. Stewart R. Graham as the only other officer. The first crew consisted of: ADC Oliver Berry, ADC Leo Brzycki, AMC Edmond E. Hainstock, AD1 Merwin E. Westerberg, and E. E. Challberg. By 1948 the following were in the crew: AMC James E. Reeves, ADC (AP) John P. Greathouse, SK1 Marion L. Adrain, AT1 Louis H. Barchard, AD2 Colon E. Best, AD2 Robert E. Feiok, AD2 Preston J. Garrish, SN Raymond T. Hite, AM1 Hugh J. Junor, AM1 Joseph B. Riffle, AD2 Carl F. Ringwold, and SN Charles H. Studstill.

2. Erickson, III-5-10.

3. MacDiarmid, letter to Macon Reed Jr., 14 October 1954 (USCGA); Fahey, *Ships and Aircraft,* Victory edition, 52.

4. MacDiarmid, letter to Macon Reed Jr.

5. A common term meaning flying without accomplishing anything.

6. Informal list of helicopter SAR cases dating from Erickson's first case in New York "1/13/44" (actual date was 3 January 1944) to "11/28/48" (n.a.); Graham, interviews. Many more cases were not recorded on this list; therefore, its accuracy is suspect. Newspaper accounts in author's files tell of rescues not appearing on the list.

7. Erickson, III-5-3.

8. Erickson, III-5-4.

9. Erickson, III-5-2; Graham, unpublished memoirs (Graham).

10. Erickson, I-6-6.

11. Farley, "The Coast Guard and the Helicopter," unpublished version, 16 (n.a.).

12. Erickson, III-5-20.

13. Ibid.

14. Ibid.

15. Erickson, I-6-5.

16. Ibid; Erickson, incomplete chapter thirteen of a partial manuscript

attached to undated enclosure to his daughter, Kay, enclosed in a letter to his wife, Betty, dated 20 October 1969. (Bohs).

17. Erickson, III-11-8.
18. R. L. Burke, letter to Erickson, 30 December 1955 (Bohs).
19. Erickson, III-11-12.
20. Erickson, memorandum to chief, Aviation Division, 12 December 1951 (CG Historian).
21. Erickson, memorandum to chief, Aviation Division.
22. Erickson, III-6-6.
23. Erickson, II-9-16.
24. Erickson, I-6-17.
25. Ibid.
26. Sergei Sikorsky, "Early Helicopter Rescues," unpublished personal account, Sergei Sikorsky.
27. W. B. Crosby, T. Wright, "Helicopters Cop Collier's Trophy," *Colliers,* 22 December 1951, 30; Erickson, II-9-20.
28. Erickson, letter to R. E. Hammond, 31 December 1970 (Bohs).
29. Erickson, letter to Capt. R. E. Larson, 6 May 1978 (Bohs).
30. Erickson, letter to Gus Shrode, 14 April 1978 (Bohs).
31. Erickson, letter to Walter S. Anderson, 4 March 1969 (Bohs).
32. Erickson, letter to John Waters, 20 September 1969 (Bohs).

Chapter Eleven
1. Erickson, III-5-6; Gershowitz, interviews.
2. Gershowitz, "Antarctic Adventure," *American Helicopter,* September 1947, 14; Gershowitz, interviews.
3. Ibid.
4. Erickson, III-5-7.
5. Erickson, letter to J. Rankine Strang, 8 December 1970 (Bohs); Graham, interviews.
6. Robert Erwin Johnson, *Guardians of the Sea* (Annapolis: Naval Institute Press, 1987), 328.
7. Ibid., 329.
8. John S. McDonald, letter to author, 3 January 1995; USCGC Polar Sea message, 260255Z AUG 94 (ATC Mobile).
9. Erickson, III-9-15.
10. Ibid.
11. Jack (probably John P. Lattimer), letter to Erickson dated 5 December 1969 (Bohs).
12. Johnson, *Guardians,* 354.
13. Jack, letter to Erickson, 5 December 1969.
14. Ibid.
15. Ibid.
16. John Redfield, interviews, 1991 through 1995.
17. John Redfield, letter to Erickson, date unknown (possibly 1970 [Graham]).

18. The "G" in the designation meant "Rescue" in the former system of air-craft designations. In September 1962 the Department of Defense established a uniform system for designating all military aircraft. Nor-mally, one or two letters are used, which are followed by the aircraft design number and a series symbol. The first letter alone or the first of a pair indicates the mission of the aircraft. Some examples: A, attack; E, electronic surveillance; F, fighter; H, search and rescue; K, tanker; Q, drone; R, reconnaissance; S, antisubmarine. The second letter or the sole letter stands for the type of service the aircraft was designed for, such as C for cargo, H for helicopter, T for trainer. An HC-130H is Rescue, Cargo, 130 design number in a series of cargo aircraft, and the eighth, or H, model in a design series by the manufacturer. An AC-130B would be a C-130 used as an attack aircraft. A C-5A is a cargo aircraft. A TA-4C would be an attack aircraft, number four in a series of attack aircraft, third version by the manufacturer, used as a training airplane. An HH-60J is Rescue, Helicopter, 60 in a series of helicopters and the tenth, or J, model of this aircraft in the series by Sikorsky. A SH-60B would be a similar helicopter used for antisubmarine warfare.
19. Howard B. Thorsen, letter to author, 22 May 1995.
20. Redfield, report on helicopter/ship towing experiment, St. Petersburg, Florida, 1958 (Redfield).
21. Frank L. Shelley, letter to author, 4 February 1995.
22. Erickson, III-10-18.
23. Redfield, interviews; Shelley, letter.
24. Shelley, letter; Charles Tighe, telephone interview, 2 May 1995.

Chapter Twelve
1. Bill Gunston, *Military Helicopters* (New York: Arco, 1981), 142. A jet-powered turbine Kaman K-225 helicopter flew successfully in December 1951. Sikorsky built an experimental helicopter specifically designed for a turbine power plant, the XH-39. This helicopter set a world's speed record of 156.005 MPH on 26 August 1954. A few days later, it set a new helicopter altitude record of 24,500 feet. It was three years later, however, before the military services purchased jet-powered helicopters. The Navy awarded the Kaman Aircraft Corporation a production con-tract for its first turbine-powered helicopter, the sixth-place HU2K-1. Late in 1957 the Army sponsored a program carried out by Vertol in which two General Electric T-58 gas turbines were tested for the first time in one H-21 and two Lycoming T-53 gas turbines in a second. The project was abandoned. The Army then awarded Bell Aircraft a contract for the X-40, the forerunner of the now classic "Huey" family of heli-copters. It first flew on 20 October 1956. The British, however, were the first to produce turbine-powered helicopters. They built the Sikorsky S-58, originally designed for the 1,525 horsepower Wright 1820-84 nine-cylinder radial engine, under license and installed a 1,450 horsepower Rolls-Royce (Napier) Gazelle 161 free-turbine turboshaft.

It flew its test flight 17 May 1957 and was delivered to the British Fleet
in April 1960.

2. Shelley, letter.
3. Ibid.
4. Erickson, untitled, undated manuscript (Bohs).
5. USCG Flight Manual, Model HH-52A helicopters (Washington, DC:
Coast Guard, 1972).
6. The helicopter is referred to by a number of shortened and sometimes
derogatory terms. Many appellations are quoted in this text. I use only the
terms "helicopter," "aircraft," and "machine" in my narrative, however.
The term "helicopter" frequently is shortened to "helo" or "chopper."
The term "machine" is frequently used by its operators. This expression
perhaps best describes the complexities of engineering genius, exposed
in a mechanical form, that lifts itself into the air. It is not flight but a
mechanical thrashing that keeps this un-birdlike object airborne. Hence,
"machine" is perhaps a term of respect or of awe by those closest to it.
7. Waters, *Rescue at Sea,* 151.
8. Ibid.
9. Ibid.
10. Shelley, letter. One proposed name did not make it out of the office.
Shelly and Penn located one base between the towns of Barnstable and
Sandwich. Their tongue-in-cheek proposal ended up as CGAS Cape
Cod.
11. Waters, *Rescue at Sea,* 154.
12. I. James Leskinovitch, interviews in 1995.
13. "Coast Guard Anniversary, Fifty Years of Aviation," *Sikorsky News,*
August 1966, 5.
14. Redfield, interviews in 1994 and 1995.
15. Erickson, III-16-31.
16. Anonymous.
17. E. D. Fales, "The Ocean Express Disaster—A Hard Lesson At Sea,"
Popular Mechanics, December 1980.
18. John Lewis, telephone interviews in 1995; Fales, ibid.
19. Ibid.
20. Lewis, telephone interviews.
21. Ibid; Fales, ibid; Howard B. Thorsen, telephone interview, 18 May
1995.
22. Lewis, telephone interviews.
23. Ibid.
24. Ibid.
25. Ibid.
26. Thorsen, telephone interview.
27. Thomas's heart attack was a mild one; he recovered.
28. Commandant, USCG, memorandum to inspector general, U.S.
Department of Transportation, December 1983, attachment (2) to enclosure (1) (author's files). This was an average for 1980 through 1982.

29. Richard Appelbaum, comments at dedication of an HH-52A to Chicago's Museum of Science and Industry.
30. *Foundations*, Spring, 1991, 107; accident report, HH-52A CGNR 1420 (CG Historian).
31. MacDiarmid, Appendix E, "Minority Report by Captain Donald B. MacDiarmid" (circa 1955), (USCGA).
32. Ray Miller, interviews in 1995.
33. AVTRACEN Mobile information bulletin (circa 1975), (author's files).
34. Erickson, III-11-16.
35. Gunston, *Military Helicopters*, 119; Erickson, III-10-16.
36. *Vertiflight*, March 1968, 24.
37. William P. Wishar, letter to Warren Roberts, 3 December 1968 (USCGA); Erickson, I-2-16.
38. Roger Ray, telephone interview in 1995.
39. Bruce E. Melnick, telephone interview, 31 May 1995; R. M. Wright, "Leading the Way: Fifty Years of U.S. Coast Guard Helicopter Aviation, 1943–1993," *Rotor Review*, Winter 1993, 26.
40. Capt. Terry Sinclair, personal account of *Prinsendam*, no date, unpublished; "Citation to Accompany The Award of The Coast Guard Medal to Lieutenant (Junior Grade) Terry William Sinclair, United States Coast Guard" (CG Headquarters).
41. Co-pilot Lt. (jg) Bob Abair, and AE1 Dave Seavey.
42. John P. Currier, telephone interviews, May 1995. Apparently, through administrative error, Currier was never notified of this award until his parents, while visiting the Smithsonian Air and Space Museum six years later, saw his name engraved on the trophy. It still took four more years of action by headquarters and the Ancient Order of The Pterodactyl (an association of Coast Guard aviators and supporters of Coast Guard Aviation) before Currier received his award from the vice president.
43. News Release, cover sheet, Harmon International Trophies, New York, N.Y.
44. Don Estes, remarks as commanding officer, CGAS Clearwater, during HH-3F retirement ceremony, 6 May 1994 (CGAS Clearwater).
45. Robert L. Scheina, "A History of Coast Guard Aviation," *Commandant's Bulletin*, 21-86, October 1986, 12.
46. Acquisition paper for a short-range recovery (SRR) system, Coast Guard, May 1977, I-5 (author's files).
47. Howard B. Thorsen and James F. Butler, interviews, September 1994.
48. Source Evaluation Board (SEB) Final Report, U.S. Coast Guard Short Range Recovery (SRR) Helicopter, 11 June 1979, USCG (author's files).
49. Thorsen, letter to author, 22 May 1995.
50. Ibid; Thorsen interviews; David Poulsen, "HH-65A Dolphin," *Naval Aviation News*, November–December 1994, 17.
51. Samantha Coit and Greg Walsh, "Rescue Swimmers," *Ocean Navigator*, May/June 1995, 71.
52. Farmer and his son, Brian, are both Coast Guard rescue swimmers.

53. R. M. Wright, "Leading the Way," *Rotor Review,* Winter 1993, 26.
54. E. K. DeLong Jr. and B. A. Pimental, "Astoria Crew Rescues Pilot in Heavy Seas," *Commandant's Bulletin,* February 1989, 18; John C. Nordquist, "Rescue! Northwest," *The Sunday Oregonian Magazine,* 5 June 1988.
55. Ibid.
56. Edward J. Gibbons, telephone interview, 23 May 1995.
57. Ibid.
58. Gibbons, telephone interview; COMCOGARDGRU ASTORIA, message 051000Z April 93; CGAS Astoria Press Release, 4 April 93.
59. As of this writing, twenty-six women have served as Coast Guard aviators with about half a dozen more currently in flight training. The Coast Guard hopes to increase the number of women qualified to fly aircraft. They fly the same missions, standing the same duty and handling the same responsibilities as their male counterpart.
60. CGAS Port Angeles, Public Affairs News Release No: 94-008, 10 November 1994. "Citation to Accompany the Award of the Coast Guard Medal to Lieutenant Alda L. Siebrands, United States Coast Guard. Citation to Accompany the Award of the Air Medal to Kevin T. Parkinson, Avionics Technician Third Class, United States Coast Guard. Citation to Accompany the Award of the Air Medal to Lieutenant (junior grade) Erik C. Langenbacher, United States Coast Guard"; author interviews with Lieutenants Siebrands and Langenbacher, 1995.
61. Ibid.
62. Erickson, III-16-9.
63. CGAS Elizabeth City, "Summary of action for HH-60J CG 6008 in response to S/V Malachite," 13 December 1993 (CGAS Elizabeth City).
64. Ibid.
65. Crew on the 6008: Lt. Bruce Jones, pilot; Lt.(jg) Randy Watson, copilot; AD2 Dave Barber, flight mechanic/hoist operator; ASM2 Dave Yoder, rescue swimmer.
66. CGAS Elizabeth City, "Summary," ibid.

Chapter Thirteen

1. 1968: Lonnie L. Mixon, Lance Eagan, Jack C. Rittichier; 1969: James M. Loomis, Richard Butchka, Robert T. Ritchie; 1971: Joseph L. Crowe Jr., Rodrick Martin III; 1972: Jack K. Stice, Robert E. Long.
2. C. Douglas Kroll, "To Fight to Save, or Fight and Die," *On Scene,* USCG publication P16100.4, 19.
3. Lonnie L. Mixon, letter to commandant, undated (CG Historian).
4. U.S. Coast Guard Public Information Office, "Biographical Sketch of Lieutenant Jack C. Rittichier, USCG," *On Scene,* USCG publication P16100.4, 18.
5. Lance A. Eagan, "Statement Concerning the Conspicuous Gallantry of A1C Joel E. Talley, USAF, in North Vietnam on 2 July 1968," undated (CG Historian); Erickson, III-15-3; J. W. Moreau, "The Coast Guard in the Central and Western Pacific," unpublished draft, 1973, 57 (author's files).

6. Joseph L. Crowe, interviews in 1994 and 1995. The same two pilots were picked up again by Crowe two weeks later after being shot down once more.
7. Crowe, letter to J. W. Moreau, 27 April 1973, J. L. Crowe, Port Angeles, Wash.
8. Ibid.
9. Erickson, III-16-24.
10. U.S. Coast Guard Air Interdiction Program, 6 July 1987, (CG Historian), 4.
11. Chief, Office of Operations, CG Headquarters, memorandum, "Air Interdiction C3I Center Implementation," 13 May 1987, to Chief of Staff, CG Headquarters, (CG Historian).
12. CGAS Clearwater, "OPBAT Slide Show Narrative," 9 August 1994, (CGAS Clearwater)."
13. Mark Feldman, letter to author, 17 November 1994.
14. Ibid.
15. Ibid.
16. Ibid.
17. CGAS Clearwater, "OPBAT," ibid.
18. Another resource in the Coast Guard's law enforcement effort in the Caribbean is a stealth spotter aircraft, RG-8 also flown by the Coast Guard. This propeller driven sailplane can patrol nearly unobserved and unheard with its quiet, muffled gasoline piston engine (soon modified to be a twin engine airplane) watching for suspected illicit shipping. The airframe supports the latest in sensing and surveillance equipment.
19. Alexander Larzelere, "Coast Guard: New and Broadened Roles Make It Difficult to Maintain Traditional Flexibility," *The Almanac of Seapower,* January 1990, 24.
20. "U.S. Coast Guard Drug Interdiction Operations," no date, (CGAS Clearwater).
21. Feldman, letter, ibid.

Chapter Fourteen
1. Michael Odom, telephone interview, recorded with his permission, 2 March 1995.
2. Message 272139Z, CGAS Elizabeth City, January 1995.
3. Thomas Steier, telephone interview, recorded with his permission, 27 February 1995; and Mark A. Cole, telephone interview, recorded with his permission, 24 February 1995.
4. Cole, interview, ibid.
5. Steier, interview, ibid.
6. Crew on board CGNR-6019: Lt. Jay Balda, Lt. (jg) Guy Pearce, AD3 Mark Bafetti, ASM1 Michael Odom, ASM3 Mario Vittone.
7. CG Air Station Elizabeth City, video tape recording from camera mounted in CGNR 6019 taken at the scene, 26 January 1995.
8. Message 241530Z, CGAS Elizabeth City, January 1995.
9. Odom, interview; Message 272139Z; Cole, interview.
10. Cole, interview; Odom, interview.

11. Steier, interview; Odom, interview.
12. Ibid.
13. Odom, interview.
14. Ibid.
15. Steier was observing Vittone.
16. Cole, interview.
17. Crew on board CGNR 1502: Lt. Matt Reid, Lt. Mark Russell, AD1 Berry Freeman, AT1 David Ebert, AT3 Steve Rost, AM2 James Washington, AD2 Keith Browne.
18. Odom, interview.
19. Crew on board CGNR-1504: Lt. Comdr. Dan Osborn, Lt. (jg) Dan Rocco, AE2 Matt Elliot, AT3 Kent Hammack, AT3 Ron Mitchell, AD3 Mike Gardner, AM3 Cory Gibbons, AM3 James Josey, AD3 Damien Hopkins; crew on board CGNR-1714: Lt. Comdr. Larry Cheek, Lt. Comdr. Norville Wicker, AE1 Frank Saprito, AT3 John Browning, AT2 Stephen Twardy, AM3 Jerrod Bowden, AD3 Jon Johnson; crew on board CGNR-6034: Lt. Comdr. Bruce Jones, Lt. (jg) Dan Molthen, AD3 Chris Shawl, ASM3 Jim Peterson, AM3 Warren Bernard.
20. Odom, interview; Message 272139Z.
21. Odom, interview.
22. Cole, interview.

Epilogue
1. Floyd D. Kennedy Jr., "U.S. Naval Aircraft and Weapon Development in Review," U.S. Naval Institute *Proceedings,* May 1995, 157.
2. Erickson, *Fishers of Men,* ii.

SELECT BIBLIOGRAPHY

Articles

"Above and Beyond," Naval Aviation Museum *Foundations,* 12 (Spring 1991): 30.

"C3I East," *Commandant's Bulletin,* May 1989, 1–3.

"Captain Kossler Was Pioneer with Helicopters," *U.S. Coast Guard Magazine,* 19 (January 1946): 49.

"Carolina Jayhawk Stretches Sea Legs to Bermuda," *Sikorsky Lifeline,* Spring/Summer 1994, 7.

"Coast Guard Aviation," *Naval Aviation News,* May–June 1983, 1.

"Coast Guard Pilots Do Rescue Service, Patrol Harbors Approaches, and Escort Coastal and Transocean Convoys," *Flying,* XXV (October 1944).

"Destroyer Sinks in Bay, 163 Men Saved, 50 Hurt; Another Is U-Boat Victim," *New York Times,* 4 January 1944, 1.

"Elizabeth City USCG in Action," *Wings of Gold,* 19 (Winter 1994): 25.

"An Exclusive Club Made Up of Pilots Who Flew Helicopters Prior to V.J. Day," *Rotor & Wing,* February 1969, 27–29.

"Farewell to an Ancient Mariner: Albatross," *Naval Aviation News,* May–June 1983, 49.

"Foundation," Naval Aviation Museum *Foundations,* vol. 15, no. 2 (Fall 1994): 48.

"Helicopter to the Rescue," *New York Times,* 5 January 1944.

"Helicopters Critical to Hurricane Andrew Relief," *Sikorsky Lifeline,* April 1993, 6.

"How the Coast Guard Solved the Helicopter Lifting Problem," *U.S. Coast Guard Magazine,* April 1945, 28.

"Interview: Admiral Owen W. Siler," *Wings of Gold,* II (Winter 1977): 4–5.

"Interview: Vice Admiral D. C. Thompson," U.S. Naval Institute *Proceedings,* 112 (October 1986): 167–74.

"Jayhawk Crew Feted for Heroism," *Sikorsky Lifeline,* September 1992, 1.

"Jayhawk Stretches Sea Legs in Joint Coast Guard–Navy Rescue," *Sikorsky Lifeline,* November 1993, 3.

"'Just Say It Was the Comancheros.'" *Newsweek,* 15 March 1971, 39.

"Labrador Rescue with Helicopter," *Air-Sea Rescue Bulletin,* 11 (May 1945): 2–10.

"Manufacturers of Helicopter: Ten of Plane's Abilities and Limitations," *U.S. Coast Guard Magazine,* February 1946, 26–27.

"In Memory of Captain William J. Kossler ('21)," U.S. Coast Guard Academy Alumni Association *Bulletin,* 7 (January 1946): 330–31.

"Miami Missions—Coast Guard Air," *Wings of Gold,* 18 (Fall 1993): 18–21.

"New Jinx for Axis Subs!" *U.S. Coast Guard Magazine,* July 1943.

"Progress Keynotes Coast Guard's 175th Anniversary," Merchant Marine Council *Proceedings,* 22 (August 1965): 171–74.

"Proud Past . . . Naval Helicopter Aviation: The Men, The Machines, The Missions," 1993 Naval Helicopter Association *Symposium,* 9 March 1993, Jacksonville, Florida.

"RG-8 . . . Coast Guard Goes Stealth," *Naval Aviation News,* November–December 1994, 17.

"Son Receives Citation for Father," *U.S. Coast Guard Magazine,* 19 (September 1946): 14–15.

"Tigers in the Caribbean," *Wings of Gold,* 19 (Winter 1994): 28–29.

"The U.S. Coast Guard," *Military Aviation Review,* II (May 1977): 14–15.

"The USCG Pterodactyls," *Naval Aviation News,* May–June 1983, 39.

"USCG Rotary Wing Development Unit Has to Its Credit Numerous Important Achievements," Piasecke Helicopter Corporation *Tandemeer,* 4 (10 February 1950): 1, 6.

"Windmills to the Rescue," *All Hands,* May 1944, 5.

Andrews, Hal. "HOS-1," *Naval Aviation News,* November–December 1994, 22–23.

Bandos, Doug. "The USCG's Last NAP," *Naval Aviation News,* May–June 1983, 40–41.

Barrow, Jess C. "VP Coast Guard Style," *Naval Aviation News,* May–June 1983, 32–35.

Beard, Barrett Thomas. "Coast Guard Rescue Swimmer: Filling the Void," Naval Institute *Proceedings,* 117 (January 1991): 106–7.

———"The Deception: Helicopter ASW," Naval Aviation Museum *Foundation,* 15 (Spring 1994): 82–87.

———"The First Mission," Naval Aviation Museum *Foundation,* 12 (Spring 1991): 100–105.

———"USCG puts new jet aircraft to work on fisheries patrols," *National Fisherman,* 64 (August 1984): 92–93.

Bilderback, Ken. "Cigars and Rough Water," *Naval Aviation News,* November–December 1994, 18–19.

Bradbury, Richard. "The RAF'S Helicopters," *American Helicopter,* April 1946, 30–33.

Browning, Robert M. Jr. "The Eyes and Ears of the Convoy: Development of the Helicopter as an Anti-submarine Weapon," *Commandant's Bulletin,* September 1993, insert. *N.B.* A similar version was published by the Air Force Historical Foundation in *Air Power History,* Summer 1993.

Bruce, Jack D. "The Enigma of Battleship *Nevada.*" U.S. Naval Institute *Naval History,* 5 (Winter 1991): 52–54.

Butler, John R. "Coast Guard Choppers to the Rescue," *Boating,* 12 (August 1968).

Christmann, Timothy J. "Naval Air Tags Smugglers," *Naval Aviation News,* May–June 1983, 46–49.

Cochrane, Dorothy, Von Hardesty, and Russell Lee. "Pioneer of Flight: Igor Sikorsky," *American History Illustrated,* XXV (May/June 1990): 40–49.

Coletti, Phil. "HU-25 Falcon," *Naval Aviation News,* November–December 1994, 16.

Colt, Samantha, and Greg Walsh. "Rescue Swimmers," *Ocean Navigator,* 68 (May–June 1995): 71–74.

Crosby, W. B. and T. Wright. "Helicopters Cop Collier's Trophy," *Colliers,* 22 December 1951: 30.

DeLong, E. K. Jr., and B. A. Pimental. "Astoria Crew Rescues Pilot in Heavy Seas," *Commandant's Bulletin,* February 1989, 18–19.

Dombeck, Deborah A. "Lifesaving the Hard Way," *Naval Aviation News,* May–June 1983, 20–21.

Duca, Stephan G. "The Ad Hoc Drug War," U.S. Naval Institute *Proceedings,* 113 (December 1987): 85–91.

Erickson, Frank A. "Aviation and Safety," *U.S. Coast Guard Magazine* (circa 1940): 6, 38–40.

———"A Brief History of Coast Guard Aviation," U.S. Coast Guard Alumni Association *Bulletin,* XXVII (November–December 1966): 418–27.

———"Coast Guard Cutter-Helicopter Team," Paper presented to the Operations Session of the Philadelphia Forum of the American Helicopter Society, 23 April 1948.

———"The First Coast Guard Helicopters," U.S. Naval Institute *Proceedings,* 107 (July 1981): 62–66.

———"The First Transatlantic Flight," U.S. Coast Guard Academy Alumni Association *Bulletin,* 39 (May–June 1977): 18–23.

———"Helicopter Air-Sea Rescue Developments," *Sperryscope,* X (January 1945): 3–6.

Fales, E. D. "The Ocean Express Disaster—A Hard Lesson At Sea," *Popular Mechanics,* December 1980.

Farley, Joseph F. "United States Coast Guard Helicopter Program," *American Helicopter,* February 1947.

Gallagher, Paul A. "MSC Ships Deliver Vital Supplies to Men on 'Ice'—Coast Guard Cuts Pain for Ships," *Sealift,* March 1971, 7–9.

Graham, Stewart R. "Helicopters and Sonar Detection of Submarines: The Early Years," Silver Eagles Association *The Scuttlebutt*, 24 (July 1992): 20–26.

———"Stewart Ross Graham," Silver Eagles Association *The Scuttlebutt*, 24 (July 1992): 18–19.

Hayenga, Ralph, Frank Williams, Richard Wilcox, Howard Howes, Elias Schutman, and Arland Christ-Jance. "By the crew of a B-29: Lifeboat from the Sky," *U.S. Coast Guard Magazine*, June 1946, 42–44.

Hickey, Doyle O. "The Helicopter's Role in the Armed Forces," *American Helicopter*, January 1949, 13–23.

Hockman, Lee J. "Coast Guard Air Search and Rescue," *Profile*, 25 (April 1982): 12–15.

Hodges, William R. Jr. "From Aztec Shore to Arctic Zone," *Wings of Gold*, II (Winter 1977): 18–21.

Jenkins, William A. "A New Dimension of Coast Guard Aviation," *Naval Aviation News*, May–June 1983, 6–7.

Johnson, Harvey F. "Development of Ice-Breaking Vessels for the U.S. Coast Guard," Society of Naval Architects and Marine Engineers *Transactions*, 54 (1947): 1–33.

Kaplan, H. R. "Airborne Computer for C.G. Helicopters," Supplement No. 10, *Commandant's Bulletin*, No. 50-69 (1969).

Knott, Dick. "Workaday SAR: Coast Guard Miami," *Naval Aviation News*, April 1981, 18–23.

Kossler, William J. "The Helicopter," *U.S. Coast Guard Magazine*, February 1943, 12–15.

Krietemeyer, George E. "Coast Guard Aviation Exhibit in the Museum of Naval Aviation," U.S. Coast Guard Academy Alumni Association *Bulletin*, 52 (February–March 1990): 18–20.

Kroll, Douglas C. "To Fight to Save, or Fight and Die," COMDTPUB P16100.4 *On Scene*, March 1991, 18–20.

———"Jack C. Rittichier: Coast Guard Aviation Hero," *Naval Aviation News*, November–December 1991, 26–27.

Laning, Caleb B. "Why Don't We Do This More Often?" U.S. Naval Institute *Naval History*, 5 (Winter 1991): 55–60.

Larzelere, Alex. "Coast Guard: New and Broadened Roles Make It Difficult to Maintain Traditional Flexibility," *The Almanac of Seapower*, 33 (January 1990): 24–28.

Lee, Christopher L. "Guardians on Station," *Naval Aviation News*, May–June 1983, 24–27.

Logan, Doug. "One Mayday," *Sailing World*, August 1994, 50–53.

Long, Henry A. Jr. "Tactical Exercises Ended," U.S. Naval Institute *Naval History*, 5 (Winter 1991): 41–45.

Marini, Mario. "Taking the Plunge," *Commandant's Bulletin*, March 1993, 28–29.

McGuffin, G. R. "The Future of Coast Guard Aviation," *Naval Aviation News*, November–December 1994, 10–11.

McNatt, Herman S. "The USCG VTOL Inventory—Now and Tomorrow," *Vertiflite*, March 1968, 23–24.

Morgan, Gary T. "Pilot Training," *Wings of Gold*, II (Winter 1977): 32–35.

Neilsen, Richard. "World Icebreaker Fleets and Post-War Icebreaker Construction," Coast Guard *Engineer's Digest*, April–June 1968, 64–70.

Newark, Steve. "A Swimmer's Struggle," *Ocean Navigator*, 68 (May–June 1995): 75–83.

Noble, Dennis L. "Southwest Pacific," *Commandant's Bulletin* (May 1989), insert.

———and T. Michael O'Brien. "'That Others Might Live': The Saga of the U.S. Coast Guard," *American History Illustrated*, 12 (June 1977).

———and Truman R. Strobridge. "Polar Icebreakers of the United States Coast Guard," *Polar Record: Journal of the Scott Polar Research Institute*, 18 (January 1977): 351–60.

Nordquist, John C. "Rescue," The Sunday Oregonian Magazine *Northwest*, 5 June 1988: 8–12.

O'Brian, T. Michael, and Robert L. Scheina. "Coast Guard—In at the Beginning," *Wings of Gold*, II (Winter 1977), 8–13.

O'Dell, Jack. "Jayhawk!" *Commandant's Bulletin*, May 1989, 23.

O'Loughlin, Jim. "HC-130H Hercules," *Naval Aviation News*, November–December 1994, 14.

Ogden, Jeff. "OIS . . . The Way of the Future?" *Naval Aviation News*, November–December 1994, 20–21.

Poulsen, David. "HH-65A Dolphin," *Naval Aviation News*, November-December 1994, 15.

Price, Scott. "Rescue at Sea," *Commandant's Bulletin*, December 1993, 26–29.

Raithel, Albert L. Jr. "Patrol Aviation in the Atlantic in World War II," *Naval Aviation News*, November–December 1994, 28–33.

Ramsey, Mary Ann. "Only Yesterday," U.S. Naval Institute *Naval History*, 5 (Winter 1991): 23–27.

Reisinger, Harold C. "Coast Guard Ambulance Flights," U.S. Naval Institute *Proceedings*, 62 (January 1936): 57–72.

———"The Flying Lifeboat of the Coast Guard," U.S. Naval Institute *Proceedings*, 59 (January 1933): 81–88.

Russell, Sandy. "Doctors on the Wing," *Naval Aviation News*, May–June 1983, 22–23.

Salmon, Theodore R. "U.S. Coast Guard Polar Operations: The Untold Story," Mobile, Alabama: Coast Guard AVTRACEN, n.d.

Scheina, Robert L. "The Early Years: Coast Guard Aviation," *Naval Aviation News*, May–June 1983, 8–11.

———"The Helicopter's First Arctic Rescue," Naval Aviation Museum *Foundation*, II (March 1981): 60–65.

———"The Marriage of Fixed-Winged Aviation and the Cutter," *Naval Aviation News*, May–June 1983, 12–15.

———"Patron of the Helicopter during World War II," *Wings of Gold*, II (Winter 1977): 26–29.

Scotti, Paul C. "Coast Guard Air in the Northwest," *Naval Aviation News*, June 1979, 8–15.

Sikorsky, Igor I. "Direct Lift Aircraft," *U.S. Coast Guard Magazine*, January 1945, 56.

Sims, Don. "USCG Aviation," *Air Classics Quarterly Review*, 2 (Summer 1976).

Smeder, O. R. "Coast Guard Helicopter Program," *American Helicopter*, 3 (June 1946): 10–11.

Sparks, Tom. "HH-60J Jayhawk," *Naval Aviation News*, November–December 1994, 16.

Sturm, Ted R. "Miracle Mission," Official Magazine of the U.S. Air Force *Airman*, XVII (August 1973): 43–47.

Stuyvesant, William B. "Helo Heritage," *Wings of Gold*, 18 (Fall 1993): 35.

Thomason, Tommy H. "Carrier-Based Helicopter ASW," *The Hook*, Fall 1985, 16–25.

Thorsen, Howard B. "The Dolphin that Flies!" U.S. Naval Institute *Proceedings*, 106 (October 1980): 148–50.

Tilford, Earl H. "The Development of Search and Rescue: World War II to 1961," *Aerospace Historian*, 24 (December 1977): 228–39.

Townson, George. "The Otis Elevator Co. Helicopter Simulator," *Rotor & Wing International*, December 1991. N.B. "Otis" is incorrect; the company building the simulator was in was the Atlantic Elevator Company.

Trimble, Robert L. "The Flying Mule," *Air Classics Quarterly Review*, Summer 1979, 14–18.

———"Silver Wings for the Coast Guard," *Air Progress Aviation Review*, Winter 1979, 18–25.

Turk, D. L. "Changing the Guard," *Commandant's Bulletin*, 17 July 1986, 30–32.

Vennel, Woodrow W. "The Helicopter in Rescue," National Safety Council *Proceedings*, 48th Annual Congress (1960): 24–28.

Waldron, Bob. "Helpful Helicopters: Great Lakes Boating Made Safer by Coast Guard's Watchful Eyes," *The Columbus Dispatch Magazine*, 12 July 1970, 8–11.

Wallace, W. J. "Coast Guard Aviation: A Way of Life . . . Not Merely a Job," *Wings of Gold*, Spring 1985, 3.

Waters, John M. "Finally the Twain Did Meet," Naval Aviation Museum *Foundation*, 12 (Spring 1991): 92–99.

———"Little Ships with Long Arms," U.S. Naval Institute *Proceedings*, 91 (August 1965): 74–81.

———"Search and Rescue Problem Areas," Merchant Marine Council *Proceedings*, 22 (August 1965): 175–78.

Wendt, Pat. "Icebreaker Flying," *Naval Aviation News*, May–June 1983, 16–18.

———"Up Over and Down Under," *Naval Aviation News*, May–June 1983, 19.

White, James R. "On the Step," *Naval Aviation News*, May–June 1983, 42–45.

Wilkinson, Stephen. "Flying with the Coasties," *Oceans* 20 (November–December 1987): 12–19.

Wright, R. M. "Leading the Way: Fifty Years of U.S. Coast Guard Helicopter Aviation, 1943–1993," *Rotor Review,* Winter 1993, 24–27.

Yonce, Kathy. "Former Enlisted CG Aviator Recalls 28 Years of Service," *Commandant's Bulletin,* October 1992, 19–21.

Books

Bloomfield, Howard E. *Compact History of the U.S. Coast Guard.* New York: Hawthorn Books, 1966.

Chinnery, Philip D. *Vietnam: The Helicopter War.* Annapolis: Naval Institute Press, 1991.

Cochrane, Dorothy, Von Hardesty, and Russell Lee. *The Aviation Career of Igor Sikorsky.* Seattle: University of Washington Press, 1989.

Delear, Frank J. *The Miracle of the Helicopter.* Stratford, Connecticut: Sikorsky Division of United Aircraft Corporation, 1961. Revised 1963 and 1968.

Dorr, Robert. *US Coast Guard Aviation.* Osceola, Wisconsin: Motorbooks International, 1992.

Fahey, James C. *The Ships and Aircraft of the United States Fleet.* 1939, War, Two-Ocean Fleet, and Victory editions; sixth, seventh, and eighth editions. Annapolis: Naval Institute Press.

Francillon, René J. *Grumman Aircraft since 1929.* Annapolis: Naval Institute Press, 1989.

————*The Naval Institute Guide to World Military Aviation 1995.* Annapolis: Naval Institute Press, 1995.

Gregory, H. F. *Anything A Horse Can Do: The Story of the Helicopter.* New York: Reynal & Hitchcock, 1944.

Gunston, Bill. *An Illustrated Guide to Military Helicopters.* New York: Arco Publishing Co., 1981.

Higham, Robin, and Donald J. Mrozek. *A Guide to the Sources of United States Military History: Supplement III.* Hamdon, Connecticut: Archon Book, 1993.

Johnson, Robert Erwin. *Guardians of the Sea.* Annapolis: Naval Institute Press, 1987.

Kime, J. W. *1994 U.S. Coast Guard Overview.* Washington: U.S. Coast Guard, 1994.

King, Ernest J. *The United States Navy at War, 1941–1945: Official Reports to the Secretary of the Navy.* Washington: Government Printing Office, 1946.

————and Walter M. Whitehill. *Fleet Admiral King: A Naval Record.* New York: Norton, 1952.

Lamirande, Richard. *US Coast Guard Air Station Brooklyn: Fifty Years' Service.* New York: CGAS Brooklyn, n.d.

Larkin, William T. *U.S. Navy Aircraft, 1921–1941; U.S. Marine Corps Aircraft, 1914–1959.* New York: Orion Books, 1988.

Morris, Charles, Lester. *Pioneering the Helicopter.* New York: McGraw-Hill Book Co., Inc., 1945.

Munson, Kenneth. *Helicopters and Other Rotorcraft Since 1907.* New York: The Macmillan Company, 1968.

Nalty, Benard C., Dennis L. Noble, and Truman R. Strobridge. *Wrecks, Rescues, & Investigations: Selected Documents of the U.S. Coast Guard and Its Predecessors.* Wilmington, Delaware: Scholarly Resources, 1978.

Noble, Dennis L. *A Legacy: The U.S. Life-Saving Service.* Washington: Public Affairs Division, U.S. Coast Guard, 1987.

———*That Others Might Live: The U.S. Life-Saving Service, 1878–1915.* Annapolis: Naval Institute Press, 1994.

Pearcy, Arthur. *Flying the Frontiers: NACA and NASA Experimental Aircraft.* Annapolis: Naval Institute Press 1993.

———*A History of U.S. Coast Guard Aviation.* Annapolis: Naval Institute Press, 1989.

Scheina, Robert L. *A History of Coast Guard Aviation.* Washington: U.S. Coast Guard, 1986.

———*U.S. Coast Guard Cutters & Craft of World War II.* Annapolis: Naval Institute Press, 1982.

Shea, John M. "Adventure Under the Wings of the United States Coast Guard," Othello, Washington: published by the author, n.d.

———"History of the United States Coast Guard Catalina Flying Boat PBY-5A V-189 1941–1945," Othello, Washington: published by the author, n.d.

Smeder, O. R. *Flight Training Syllabus* (HNS). Miami: Smeder Papers, 1944.

Swanborough, Gordon, and Peter M. Bowers. *United States Navy Aircraft Since 1911.* New York: Funk & Wagnalls, 1968.

Taylor, Michael J. H., and John W. R. Taylor. *Jane's Pocket Book of Helicopters.* New York: Collier Books, 1978.

Tillman, Barrett. *Avenger at War,* 2nd ed. Annapolis: Naval Institute Press, 1990.

U.S. Coast Guard. *Air Search and Rescue: 63 Years of Aerial Lifesaving.* Washington: Government Printing Office, 1978.

———C.G.T.O. 1H-52A-1 *Flight Manual Model HH 52A Helicopters.* Washington: U.S. Coast Guard, 1972.

———*The Coast Guard at War: Aviation XXI.* Washington: U.S. Coast Guard, 1945.

———*Pilots Flight Operating Instructions for Army: YR-4A Helicopters Navy HNS-1 Helicopters.* Washington: U.S. Government Document, 1944.

———*Records of Movements, Vessels of the United States Coast Guard, 1790–December 31, 1933.* 2 vols. Washington: U.S. Coast Guard, Office of Assistant Commandant (circa 1935).

———*United States Coast Guard Ships, Planes, and Stations.* Washington: Government Printing Office, 1955.

U.S. Government. *Handbook of Erection and Maintenance Instructions for Army Model YR-4A and YR-4B Helicopters.* Washington: U.S. Government Document, 1944.

Waters, John M. *Bloody Winter.* Reprinted ed. Annapolis: Naval Institute Press, 1984.

———*Rescue at Sea.* 2nd ed. Annapolis: Naval Institute Press, 1989.

Private Collections

Bentley, John. *Yearly Count of New Types of Aircraft Owned or Used by the Coast Guard Since Flying Became an Integral Part of Its Duties: 1915–1971* (1983).

Erickson, Frank A. *The Coast Guard's Flying Life Boats: A History of Coast Guard Aviation,* n.d., Erickson papers.

———*The Development of Seagoing Helicopters,* or a nearly identical manuscript, *Fishers of Men,* n.d., Erickson papers.

———*Papers.* Edmonds, Washington, and Gaithersburg, Maryland. Privately held by family, Betty Erickson Bohs and Kay Erickson McGoff.

———*A Proposed History of U.S. Coast Guard Aviation,* or a nearly identical manuscript, *The Coast Guard's Flying Life Boats: Fifty-Five Years of Coast Guard Aviation,* n.d., Erickson papers.

———and A. L. Lonsdale. "The Birth of the Sea-Going Helicopter," n.d., Erickson papers.

———and George Spratt. "A New Approach to Helicopter Stability," n.d., Erickson papers.

Graham, Stewart R. *Papers.* Naples, Maine. Privately held.

MacDiarmid, Donald B. *Coast Guard Air Station Port Angeles War Diary,* 29 December 1941 to 19 June 1943, Port Angeles, Washington: CGAS Port Angeles.

Redfield, John C. *Papers.* Pensacola, Florida: National Museum of Naval Aviation.

INDEX

Note: Until the end of World War II, helicopters had two designations: one for the Army Air Forces and the other for the Navy. Thus, the R-4 (R-4B, XR4, XR-4C, YR-4A, and YR-4B) is the same aircraft as the Navy's HNS-1, though there might have been slight modifications between aircraft. With the R-5, Sikorsky began applying a company identification number and a civil aviation code, while the Army and Navy each applied their own designation to the same aircraft series. So, a Sikorsky VS-327 was the civil aircraft S-51. The Army identified it variously as an H-5 or R-5, wih X and Y prefixes and suffixes through the letter H for the different models. The Navy designated the same aircraft the HO2S-1 (the Army YR-5A transferred to the Navy), HO3S-1, XHO3S-2, and XHOS-3. The British called the same aircraft a "Dragonfly." Later, when the Defense Department unified all aircraft designations, only one U.S. military identification existed for each aircraft. Sikorsky, however, still maintained a production identification and, in many cases, a civil designation.

For usage in the text, where an aircraft is introduced, more than one identification may be used, separated with a slash (/). Therefore, an R-4A/HNS-1 is the same aircraft. An S-62 (civil)/HU2S-1G (Navy)/HH-52A (later, unified military) is the same aircraft. Normally, a single designation follows in the text as it is referred to by the users under discussion.

In addition to the letter/number designation, an aircraft will also carry a name. This name may change between users and countries. So, a single aircraft (in different configurations and missions) such as Sikorsky's commercial S-61/HSS-2/HH-3E/HH-3F/CH-124 will carry the names Sea King, Jolly Green Giant, Pelican, and Commando.

233

ABOUT THE AUTHOR

Barrett Thomas "Tom" Beard entered the Navy as an enlisted man in 1953 and completed flight training as a Navcad in 1955. With a commission in the U.S. Naval Reserve, he flew operational missions—including carrier landings—in A-1 Skyraiders and E-1 Tracers. He qualified in more than a dozen other types of Navy aircraft, including F-9 Cougars. He served two tours as flight instructor in his ten years with the Navy.

In 1965, following his return from a Vietnam tour at Yankee Station, Mr. Beard entered the Coast Guard. He flew in SAR operations in the HU-16E Albatross, the C-130 Hercules, and the HH-52A Seaguard. He qualified as a seaplane pilot, a shipboard helicopters pilot, and a Coast Guard standardization pilot, accumulating more than 6,000 military flight hours during his career. Mr. Beard holds an FAA airline transport pilot rating and a commercial helicopter rating, plus a Coast Guard master's license for inspected vessels.

After retiring in 1975, Mr. Beard returned to college, earning a master's degree in history from Western Washington University in Bellingham. Following employment as a museum director, he turned back to the sea, in sailboats. Over the past twenty years, he and his wife, Carolyn, have sailed nearly 150,000 miles and visited about fifty countries as they've circled the world one and a half times. Mr. Beard takes vacations from these voyages to return home to research and write articles in his field of maritime history.